The Manageri

The Managerial Mystique

Restoring Leadership in Business

Abraham Zaleznik

1817

An Edward Burlingame Book

HARPER & ROW, PUBLISHERS, New York
Cambridge, Grand Rapids, Philadelphia, St. Louis,
San Francisco, London, Singapore, Sydney, Tokyo

FIRST EDITION

Designed by Karen Savary

Library of Congress Cataloging-in-Publication Data

Zaleznik, Abraham, 1924–
    The managerial mystique: restoring leadership in business/Abraham Zaleznik.
        p.   cm.
    Includes index
    "An Edward Burlingame book."
    ISBN 0-06-016105-1
    1. Management.   2. Leadership.   3. Executive ability.   I. Title.
HD38.Z315   1989   658.4'09—dc19   88-39086

89 90 91 92 93 DT/RRD 10 9 8 7 6 5 4 3 2 1

Dedicated to
George Pierce Baker
Dean of the Harvard Business School from 1962 to 1969
and James J. Hill Professor of Transportation (Emeritus)
with gratitude and respect

Contents

Acknowledgments

While it is difficult to date the precise moment when I began to write *The Managerial Mystique,* surely one beginning was the *Time* conference on Leadership in Washington, D.C., in 1977. My paper for this conference generated a lively controversy. Subsequently revised, it appeared in the *Harvard Business Review* as "Managers and Leaders: Are They Different?". I am grateful to the editors and staff of both *Time* and the *Harvard Business Review* for their encouragement and comments.

I thank Maurice Segall, chairman and chief executive of Zayre Corporation, who read an early draft, offered extensive comments, and urged me on the path of revision. Professor Edmund P. Learned's remarkable reading of an early draft of the manuscript enabled me to examine it with fresh eyes and a clearer image of my audience. Professor C. Roland Christensen, my friend and colleague of many years, a man with whom I have toiled in the vineyards of research and teaching at the Harvard Business School for more than forty years, set me straight when I wandered from my way of writing. In his comments on an early draft, he reminded me that writing in the first person is an art I have not mastered and that a certain anonymity helps me write what I want to write more clearly.

Audrey Whitfield edited an early draft. When Audrey moved to California to pursue a new career, Tom Cameron took over the editing job and provided expert help in improving the successive drafts of the manuscript. Audrey and Tom, along with Judy Kahn, a copy editor who free-lances for Harper & Row, have my admiration and respect for their help in improving the book. I also thank Elizabeth Altman and Sharon Kleefield for help in research. Dr. Altman, a scholar in the history of ideas, taught me much about modernization. I appreciated her companionship while we investigated the structure of ideas and sentiments underlying corporate management.

My heartfelt thanks go to Susan McWade, Linda Bowers, and Elaine Journey. They labored hard and long in entering revisions on the word processor. I am especially grateful to Elaine, who refused to believe the book was finished until she saw the galleys.

Harriet Rubin, a former editor at Harper & Row who is now with Doubleday, contracted for this book and helped in offering advice on revising early drafts. I am proud to have this book appear under Edward Burlingame's imprint at Harper & Row. He is a keen editor and a forthright man.

To Bibs, Dori, Ira, Janet, and now Daniel, I offer my love and appreciation. When Daniel is old enough to read this book, I hope he realizes how much a family depends on everyone pulling an oar.

In dedicating this book to George Pierce Baker, I acknowledge my indebtedness not only to him, but also to the institution he loves and served so well as Dean. The Harvard Business School is a complex place, difficult at times to fathom, but singular in its dedication. I hope the present Dean, John H. McArthur, and my colleagues recognize that the best way to serve an institution is to achieve objectivity and to learn to criticize. Both of these qualities are difficult to nourish, particularly when an institution occupies a special position in the minds and hearts of its devoted members.

Abraham Zaleznik
Palm Beach, Florida
December 9, 1988

The Managerial Mystique

Introduction

The Managerial Mystique

*O*nce upon a time, smart businesspeople were healthy skeptics. They took new ideas with a grain of salt and, generally, avoided theoretical discourse. When confronted with theory, the business-person asked, "What use does it have?" Theory for the sake of theory evoked only a bored look.

While generally optimistic and sympathetic to positive think-ing, successful businessmen and -women cast a suspicious eye on advocates of utopias. They did not expect perfection (at least in this world), although they believed in visions of a future worthy of today's commitment and hard work. Based on the hard-earned lessons of experience, these executives eschewed the quick cure and believed that visions become reality through perseverance: Chip away at problems, take a day at a time, and hope for the best while expecting the worst. It was probably such an executive who invented Murphy's Law—whatever can go wrong will—not out of fatalism, but as a reminder that life is unpredictable. The uto-pian, therefore, seldom expected to make a convert of the savvy business executive. But times have changed.

It is cause for wonder to observe today's corporation. At least once each year, if not more, executives participate in a "retreat," a workshop, a management conference, and other assemblies (call them what you will) for indoctrination into the managerial mys-tique. The rate at which spin-offs of the managerial mystique are conjured up to cure whatever ails business is astonishing.

These business executives, who used to think of themselves

1

as leaders, potential if not actual, became professional managers and absorbed the managerial mystique. While walking blindly along the path of the corporate career, they fell into the trap that Sigmund Freud first identified as "suggestibility," one of the mental states in which thinking and feeling separate and hence widen the rift between the mind and the heart and between logic and common sense.

The managerial mystique is only tenuously tied to reality. As it evolved in practice, the mystique required managers to dedicate themselves to process, structures, roles, and indirect forms of communication and to ignore ideas, people, emotions, and direct talk. It deflected attention from the realities of business, while it reassured and rewarded those who believed in the mystique.

The extent to which reality becomes distorted in the workings of the managerial mystique is illustrated in a case involving General Motors. A man who had bought a GM luxury car complained to his dealer that the transmission was not working properly. He was told that the problem would clear up after a suitable break-in period. The problem did not clear up, and, moreover, the irate customer discovered that he had to replace the transmission at his expense, because the warranty period had expired while he awaited the spontaneous cure promised by the dealer. The mechanic who examined the car pointed out that he could replace the transmission, but that it would not last six months because the transmission specified for this large car belonged to a small car. Evidently, people at General Motors had neglected product quality and customer satisfaction, probably to get around their own mistakes in scheduling or to cut additional expenses. The man initiated a class action suit, and in February 1987 General Motors agreed to settle for $19.2 million.

Within a few days after General Motors settled the suit, the corporation declared its intention to repurchase up to 20 percent of its common stock at a cost estimated at over $5 billion. The purpose of the stock buy-back was plain: to increase the price of the stock by dividing the existing earnings among fewer shares. In the meantime General Motors had lost market share not only to foreign competition, but also to Ford and Chrysler. Instead of presenting a program of improved product design, quality, and value to overcome its competitive weakness, GM chose a financial solution to refurbish its image to the investment community. This solution typifies the thinking inherent in the managerial mystique: Act on form and hope substantive solutions will follow.

The malaise of the managerial mystique has infected almost every sector of society. Evidence from the investigation of the 1986 Challenger crash indicates not only that American ingenuity through technological advance and rising productivity has fallen by the wayside, but, perhaps more importantly, that managers don't care. Morton Thiokol engineers claimed that they could not penetrate the hierarchy of managers to present their expert knowledge on the effects of low temperatures on the rocket fuel seals. Instead of accepting responsibility, managers evade it, and not only at the lower levels of organizations. The heads of organizations, including the president of the United States, claim ignorance of what is going on when incompetence, disastrous policies, shoddy work, unethical and illegal behavior, depletion of the productivity base, and loss of competitive advantage infect large organizations like a virus in the bloodstream.

The Tower Commission, which studied the National Security Council's involvement in the Iran-contra arms sales, concluded that the "style" of management was at issue in this debacle.[1] The commission raised questions about so-called hands-on and hands-off management styles and their consequences for subordinates' activities and responsibilities. Style is a superficial issue and has little to do with the fundamental questions raised by the Iran-contra affair or, for that matter, by the diminished performance of business leadership today. More significant issues are how people define themselves while holding and using power and whether the intent in these definitions is to maintain and defend a world view or to alter and enlarge purposes.

Yet executives today have little awareness of the deeply personal side of power. Without this awareness, power goes awry while power holders disclaim responsibility. Executives, intent on adapting to the world around them and to making their way up the career ladder, actively seek to be indoctrinated into modern management. They relinquish their ability to think. They adopt slogans and formulas instead of developing the arts of self-examination that stimulate the imagination as well as toughen analytical thinking.

Writing in the 1950s, David Reisman described "other-directedness" and William H. Whyte the "organization man."[2] They saw a fundamental shift in the American psyche. There is a dramatic difference between Ralph Waldo Emerson's celebration of individualism and the modern idealization of "teamwork" personified by such beloved figures as President, and General of the Army, Dwight David Eisenhower and the American astronauts. Although these figures were in the public arena and had no formal association with business, they represented the new consciousness of business, which had evolved from the corporate approach of Alfred Sloan during the 1920s and became the dogma of business practice following World War II. This era saw unprecedented prosperity and at the same time the weakening of business's capacity to produce and compete in the long term.

The growing impact of business schools, which in the 1960s began mass-producing MBAs, drove dissenters from the managerial mystique underground. It was not until Watergate revealed the critical distortions of the narrowly focused idea of management that dissent from the new orthodoxy could be heard. For example, in response to Watergate, *Time* published a special section on leadership.[3] According to *Time,* "the turmoil of the 1960s and early 70s left a corrosive residue of apathy and skepticism that has eaten away at all major institutions."[4] Survey results showed that confidence in Congress, the Supreme Court, business, and university presidents had dropped sharply from the mid-1960s and early 1970s.[5]

In following up its special report, in September 1976, *Time* conducted a conference on leadership in Washington, D.C. *Time* invited 200 young leaders to consider "that illusive, indefinable, yet recognizable quality"[6] called leadership, which it had become apparent now existed in such a diminished state. *Time* also invited four professors to present their analyses on what had gone wrong with leadership in the United States. The working paper, which subsequently appeared in the *Harvard Business Review* as "Managers and Leaders: Are They Different?,"[7] argued that managers and leaders are different. They differ in what they attend to and in how they think, work, and interact. Above all, managers and leaders have different personalities and experience different developmental paths from childhood to adulthood.

One of the ideas generating the most controversy as well as interest at the *Time* conference was that leaders grow through mastering painful conflict during their developmental years, while managers confront few of the experiences that generally cause people to turn inward. Managers perceive life as a steady progression of positive events, resulting in security at home, in school, in the community, and at work. Leaders are "twice born" individuals who endure major events that lead to a sense of separateness, or perhaps estrangement, from their environments.[8] As a result, they turn inward in order to reemerge with a created rather than an inherited sense of identity. That sense of separateness may be a necessary condition for the ability to lead.

One of the groups discussing this idea at the *Time* conference decided, at Gloria Steinem's urging, to test it by examining their own experiences. Almost every member of the group could report personal upheavals that had led them into a struggle for a sense of identity unique to themselves. A fight with a father that led to a rupture in the relationship, the early death of a loved parent, an illness, or some other psychic event resulted in the feeling of separateness.

Senator Bill Bradley described the phenomenon this way:

> I came from a small town in Missouri of 3,000 people. My father was the local banker. So I do not qualify for the Abe Lincoln syndrome. Do I feel separate? Yes. I did not identify with any of the institutions or with any of the groups I was placed in as a child.[9]

The then governor of South Dakota, Richard Kneip, described his experience:

> I would count myself separate from my family. I was one of nine children. My father started out as a shoemaker. He was a very hard man. It was not a very loving kind of relationship then, but in the past ten years I could not have been closer to anyone than I was to my father. In his later years he mellowed. Earlier he was very anti-education. He threw me down the stairs of his office when I told him that I wanted to go to college. He thought it was a waste of time, unless you wanted to be a doctor or a lawyer.[10]

It is easy to confuse the idea of separateness with narcissism. Narcissism is a pathology in which the individual unconsciously tries to overcome a fragmented ego by overvaluing personal fantasy and undervaluing the real world, including people. The historian Christopher Lasch, among other thinkers, claims that a whole generation can be infected with the pathology of narcissism and asserts that young people reflect this pathology in valuing their own pleasures at the expense of obligation to others.[11]

The feeling of being separate, which is characteristic of leaders, is different from narcissism. The leader is aware of boundaries and distinguishes the inner and outer worlds, fantasy and reality, self and other people. Career-oriented managers are more likely to exhibit the effects of narcissism than leaders. While busily adapting to their environment, managers are narrowly engaged in maintaining their identity and self-esteem through others, whereas leaders have self-confidence growing out of the awareness of who they are and the visions that drive them to achieve.

Upon reflection, it is striking to note how rarely leadership is associated with business. Businesspeople were underrepresented at the *Time* conference, a paradoxical situation given the fact that America is a business society. The fact that recently business books have become popular—Lee Iacocca's biography sold well over a million copies—does not contradict the assertion that leadership and business do not go together in popular image or conventional wisdom. Iacocca had a great human interest story to tell. Laced with gossip about Henry Ford and his drinking habits, Iacocca's book is about an Italian immigrant's son who finally makes it to the top. He overcomes obstacles, especially the envy of his boss, and proves his ability by taking a down-and-out company and bringing it back to life.[12] His book was so appealing as a modern Horatio Alger drama that rumors began to float of presidential possibilities. If a movie actor can run the country, why not an automaker?

That business and leadership are not popularly associated is a result of the anonymity that is cherished in the managerial mystique. It is an antihero ethos that places a premium on the team over the individual. And in its team orientation, the managerial mystique views cooperation as a technical device, along with a host of others, that helps secure goals while enhancing one's professional image. The tail has come to wag the dog. In our obsession with teamwork, collectively we have failed to recognize that individuals are the only source of ideas and energy.

This book is a critical assessment of the managerial mystique as it is currently practiced in business and taught in our business schools. It is also a call to rediscover leadership, which may be tantamount to restoring the individual to his or her proper place as the source of vision and drive that can make an organization unique. This book seeks to bring the human character back to center stage in the drama of business. The image of leadership projected is one of substance, humanity, and morality. We are painfully short of all three qualities in our collective lives.

Part I

The Argument

Chapter 1

The Leadership Gap

*B*usiness in America has lost its way, adrift in a sea of managerial mediocrity, desperately needing leadership to face worldwide economic competition. Once the dominant innovator in technology, marketing, and manufacturing, American business has lost ground to foreign competition. Our smokestack industries such as steel have been decimated. The machine tool industry, crucial to increased productivity, has fallen behind Japanese and European competition. The automobile industry has relinquished a third of its market share to imports. Consumer electronics producers have lost the race for dominance.

The dimensions of the decline are staggering. In his report "U.S. Competitiveness in the World Economy,"[1] Bruce Scott of the Harvard Business School evaluates the decline in terms of market share, productivity, and real income. Throughout the 1970s the United States lost world trade market share measured in dollar value. Since 1980 the loss in market share has continued, measured both in physical volume of product and in dollar value. In terms of productivity gain the United States ranks last, particularly in the manufacturing sector. Finally, Scott points out that real hourly wages for workers in the United States are at approximately the same level as in 1973; in Japan real wages have almost doubled.

The causes of this decline in competitiveness are complex, but at the forefront is the attitude of American management. After World War II the United States focused primarily on maintaining and exploiting technological developments in the mature industries, such as steelmaking and metal fabrication and machine tool and electric appliance manufacturing, instead of fostering innovation. In the 1960s and 1970s managers deemphasized manufacturing and focused instead on superficial product changes and finance, which led to lower quality products. Essentially, business in America lost its competitive advantage by focusing on profits and stock prices instead of fostering innovation and long-term goals.

Perhaps worst of all, the United States is now a debtor nation and, as any other debtor nation, must deal with the serious consequences of that condition. Soon we will rudely awaken to realize that we must tighten our belts, save instead of spend, and invest instead of consume. In addition, we must revitalize our exports to overcome the large merchandise trade deficit, which will be $130 billion in 1988, down only 17.6% compared with the deficit of $170 billion in 1987.

The tendency is to look to Washington for leadership in times of economic crises. Executive and congressional leadership, however, will react slowly and keep the nation asleep until the crisis is full blown. Until that time business itself will have to assume responsibility for the deterioration in America's competitive position. After all, someone was in charge of the United States Steel Corporation when it failed to renew itself technologically and to make productivity its main goal after the fat years of post–World War II. Someone was in charge of General Motors and other automobile producers when they gave up market share to the Japanese companies. Someone was in charge of the conglomerates that alternated between binges of acquisition and sober divestment of companies that did not fit their strategic plans.

An argument can be made that the problems of American industry derive from political rather than managerial causes. Labor relations in the United States, for instance in the automobile industry, always have been adversarial. During the prosperous post–World War II years labor leaders exercised enormous political clout and extracted rich wage-and-benefits concessions. These agreements, in addition, limited managements' ability to control work assignments. The net effect was excessive labor costs compared with competitors in Asia and countries such as West Germany. As less developed countries such as Japan, South Korea, and Malaysia leapfrogged the steps toward modernization, they took advantage of low labor rates to achieve competitive advantage in industries such as shipbuilding, steel, and electronics.

A second political argument that seeks to absolve management from responsibility in the decline in competitiveness lays the blame on the foreign policy of the United States during the post–World War II era. Because of the cold war a large proportion of resources were spent on the military, in both preparedness and actual warfare. Foreign policy supported the rise of West German and Japanese industrial power, showing a willingness to overlook protectionist policies to support the development of these economies—to the detriment of the domestic economy. Managers of advanced technology companies, such as semiconductor manufacturing, have shown and continue to show no reluctance to press the government for reprisal measures despite traditional principles of free trade.

Although these political arguments contain grains of truth, they overlook the broader aims of society. To maintain the U.S. economy by keeping other economies weak would have been shortsighted and destined to repeat the mistakes of World War I. The response of business leadership should have been a determined drive to increase productivity through research and development in new products and manufacturing processes. With the exception of the high-technology sectors, the response was just the opposite. Steelmakers, automakers, and other top managers in the traditional industry sectors treated their companies as "cash cows" and left innovation to others.

As for labor relations, scarcely any serious efforts were taken to alter the adversarial relationship between organized labor and management. The shortsightedness of labor representatives was more than equaled by the absence of a long-range perspective by management. Making concessions was easy because increased costs could simply be passed along to consumers who, with ample credit, had become extravagant in their buying habits.

If leadership in different times and circumstances has a common thread, it is to face situations actively rather than passively, to overcome and transform conditions, not simply to react and adapt to them. The failures of business in the 1980s reflect a lack of this kind of effective leadership and an overconcentration on the false virtues of the managerial mystique.

Business executives erroneously believe that management and leadership are synonymous, that to manage according to the principles of its mystique is to lead. For the last forty years managers in business have put their faith in numbers, managed by process, and formed elaborate structures to get people to do the predictable thing. The truth is that managing and leading are vastly different activities and that, as a result of confusing the two, corporate enterprise has lost its way.

Managers no longer distinguish between form and creativity. Leadership moves beyond the accepted body of knowledge of how to manage a process. The creative executive strikes out in unexplored directions, perhaps extrapolating from management theory but unencumbered by it. Leadership may manifest itself through an idea so compelling that it forces the formal structure to change either permanently or until the idea has been pursued to its conclusion. Leaders are not bound by a process. Indeed, they overcome it, to establish creative programs, ideas, and actions.

Unfortunately, the managerial mystique seduces business executives and even potential leaders into a false sense of security—believing that running a business is not unlike tending a plant nursery, where one prepares the soil, plants the seeds, applies fertilizer and water, and watches as Mother Nature works her magic with the flora. The mistake in the analogy is that in corporate business caretakers, even if they are kindly and diligent, work with no superior entity—no Mother Nature—on hand to ensure survival and to make creative changes during both stable and unpredictable conditions. As the utopian yet fallacious managerial mystique continues to be followed, executive performance and business strategies will continue to stagnate and diminish. A rebirth, indeed a resurgence of creative leadership, is essential to overcome the diminished capacity of executive management in American enterprise.

Harold Geneen, the former chief executive officer of ITT, epitomizes the managerial mystique. He believes that if you can manage one business, you can manage any business.[2] Geneen's belief reflects the arrogant confidence in the mystique that has overpowered the mentality of corporate chief executives. If these executives possessed a modicum of sensitivity, they would soon become aware of the cynicism that their confidence engenders in subordinates who actually run the business. It is doubtful that Mr. Geneen knew that many ITT people derisively called their employer "International This and That," expressing the confusion generated as the company acted out the tenets of the managerial mystique practiced by its chief executive.

No institution has been spared the atrophy in the quality of leadership. President Jimmy Carter in 1979 declared that this nation suffered from the effects of a "crisis in leadership." Even though his declaration was foremost a criticism of himself (after all, he was in charge), he made all heads of organizations responsible for the loss of confidence in authority. He placed the blame on the men and women who were running business, government, and education, rather than on impersonal social, political, and economic forces.

Examine, for instance, the highest office in the nation. A generation of Americans knows little about the presidency of the United States except adventurism, incompetence, diffuseness, slickness, stubbornness, and even lawlessness, along with an obsession with image and public opinion. The recent case of President Reagan's debacle in the Iran-contra affair is a dreary repetition of the incompetence in the White House that has plagued our nation for the last quarter of a century or more.

General Edward C. Meyer, former chief of staff of the Army, pointed to the decline of the leadership ideal in the military as it moved away from command and toward bureaucratic politics.[3] He claimed that currently there were two careers in the military, the field and Washington. In General Meyer's view, careerism has turned the officer corps away from the field with its commitment of responsibility to subordinates and superiors toward Washington where self-interest and political adeptness merge.[4]

Look at education at all its levels. From the elementary school to the university, it encourages mediocrity because educators rely on programs and procedures rather than developing personal leadership to maintain vitality in purpose and action. Education has become a dismal exercise in maintaining control instead of creative activity to foster curiosity, exploration, and learning.[5]

Leadership is based on a compact that binds those who lead and those who follow into the same moral, intellectual, and emotional commitment. There were times when this compact existed widely, and it probably still exists in certain places. But, by and large, the tie that binds men and women in organizations today, particularly at the professional and managerial levels, is narrow self-interest, rather than a sense of mutual obligations and responsibilities.

The leadership compact demands commitment to the organization. In the past this commitment was embodied in strong leaders such as Andrew Carnegie, Henry Ford, Pierre du Pont, Thomas Watson. In more recent times people such as Edwin Land, Walter Wriston, Kenneth Olsen, Ross Perot, An Wang and Steven Jobs represented it.

Sam Walton, the founder of the Wal-Mart retail chain, exemplifies the leadership compact. His personal attention to merchandising and customer service expresses what he expects from subordinates in the conduct of this business. Failure to maintain these standards is both a personal defeat as well as a shortfall in mutual obligation.

The legitimacy of the leadership compact arises either from tradition or from the personal qualities of the leader. Tradition operates in monarchies, the military, and religion. It is not as much a factor in purely secular and modern organizations. For a leader to secure commitment from subordinates in business and political organizations, he or she has to demonstrate extraordinary competence or other qualities that subordinates admire. If the leader fails to demonstrate these personal qualities and is not maintained in his or her role by tradition, the leadership compact begins to disintegrate.

Ronald Reagan's presidency provides an illuminating case. As the report of the Tower Commission demonstrated, he had little grasp of the issues involved in the Iran-contra affair almost from its inception. Instead, the basis for his action was sentiment: the desire to bring home the hostages regardless of the immediate costs and the expediencies involved. His repeated conversion of complex issues into apocryphal anecdotes reflected his desire to avoid material issues while fostering management by sentiment. Garry Wills described Reagan's approach to the presidency as a form of making movies, attempting to reduce the complexities of policy to the elements of a script with a happy ending.[6] Reagan's style is reminiscent of managers who are long on exhortation to "do your best" and short on helping to solve problems. Under such laissez-faire management, subordinates will either act chaotically or will abandon serious effort to get a job done.

An executive vice president of a manufacturing company complained bitterly about the failure of the chief executive officer to heed warnings about the inadequacy of the company's data processing methods. The executive vice president tried every device at his command to show what the inadequacies would mean in terms of delayed shipments, poor production scheduling, and imbalanced as well as bloated inventories. The CEO refused to act, urging all his subordinates to make do with what they had available. When the dire predictions became reality, the CEO had already lost the respect of his key subordinates, and they left him to solve the problems without their active support and intervention. In a sense, his incompetence freed them from their obligations and commitment in the leadership compact.

The claim of the leadership compact is that superiors and subordinates should do their utmost to help the organization succeed. Specifically, everyone should help to make authority effective. This principle lies in back of the Tower Commission's analysis of the Iran-contra affair, which implies that it is a responsibility of subordinates to adapt their behavior to the style of the person in charge. The Tower Commission states, "President Reagan's personal management style places an especially heavy responsibility on his key advisors. Knowing his style, they should have been particularly mindful of the needs for special attention to the manner in which this arms sale initiative developed and proceeded."[7] The Tower Commission was not expressing a new principle governing the relationship between superior and subordinate in the leadership compact. They found a current case to support a traditional view of authority relationships.

In a lecture to the students of the Harvard Business School in 1909, Frederick Winslow Taylor, "the father of scientific management," expressed in hyperbole the claim embedded in the leadership compact. He told the students that their job in business was to find out what their boss wanted and give it to him exactly as he wanted it. In giving an example of how his attempts at initiative to surpass the boss came to grief, Taylor implied not that initiative is wrong, but that an attitude of competitiveness toward an authority figure is damaging.[8] Quaint as it sounds today, the idea in the leadership compact is to support superiors, to try to see the world through their eyes, to do everything in one's power to help them do their job, and to make up for their shortcomings by diligently overcompensating for their weaknesses.

This principle tells us that we are all in the enterprise together and we must cooperate with our superiors for the success of it. Therefore, under the leadership compact the central question for each generation to solve is not what is leadership, or where do we find leaders for today and tomorrow, or how are they to be made fit for the responsibility, but how to follow. Followership requires a particular mind set into which the younger generation is indoctrinated.

Felix Rohatyn, the investment banker of the house of Lazard Frères, expressed the emotions that cement the relationship between leader and follower in his eulogy of André Meyer. Meyer was Rohatyn's mentor, teacher, leader, and possibly father figure. At a memorial service for Meyer in New York on October 12, 1979, Rohatyn said in a voice that cracked with his grief that he still instinctively reached for the phone to speak to Meyer: "Sometimes I imagine what the conversations would be like, what he would say, but I can't be sure—it's left a terrible void. . . . " Rohatyn concluded, " . . . He was an Olympian figure: Zeus hurling thunderbolts. Then he was my teacher. He taught me not only to achieve perfection, but to do it in style."[9]

With the leadership compact in place, leadership is a straightforward task. Leadership progresses from followership. It is legitimate for an individual selected for formal leadership to expect dedication, support, hard work, and loyalty from subordinates, so that he or she is not ordinarily confronting subordinates as rivals and enemies, but is working in concert with them to further the goals of the organization.

This concept of leadership changes the idea that "it is lonely at the top" to the idea that the position "at the top" involves shared purposes, mutual trust, and implicit support. But the critical factor in the leadership compact is the willingness of people in elevated positions to use their power in the best interests of their subordinates and of their organization. In this sense, a leader is simultaneously a follower in that he or she serves the interests of multiple groups such as shareholders in a business, subordinates in the organization, and customers in the marketplace.

The image of management today falls far short of dedicated, sometimes selfless, devotion associated with leadership. Instead of compact, the word is contract, so that managers prosper whether the enterprise succeeds or fails. This is the era of "golden parachutes," stock options almost guaranteed against market declines, and near obscene levels of cash compensation at the top.

The leadership compact in business, government, the military, and education today is more a relic than a vital idea. Anyone ascending to a position of power has little basis to believe that his or her job will be simplified because everyone is committed to supporting authority. In business, for example, every newly appointed chief executive officer can expect to find people within the organization who believe that they should have been named to the job instead and that they would have performed more ably. Instead of finding people who are at least willing to suspend judgment, if not grant enthusiastic acceptance, new chief executives find critical observers who too often are glad to see them blunder. As one newly appointed CEO put it, "I didn't necessarily expect to find friends among my vice presidents, but I surely didn't plan on living in a hostile world where key people see my missteps as a chance to add to their power."

At the same time executives who ascend to positions of power all too often have risen in their careers without the experience of the leadership compact. They were never really followers during all the years of their movement upward. As a result, they come ill equipped to build mutual responsibility and trust as a cornerstone of morale. Dr. An Wang, founder of the computer company bearing his name, underscored the importance of morale while succinctly delineating the difference between chief executive officers who understand the leadership compact and those who live in the detached world of the managerial mystique. "A management structure or theory is an abstraction, while a company is made up of people. When morale is good, an employee will often perform beyond expectations; when morale is bad, even the most brilliant organization will not be productive." [10]

Admittedly, the leadership compact worked at its best in a simpler time, when organizations could easily define their competition, when the rate of change was much slower than it is today, when family and community stability provided a buttress of support for authority, and when people's conduct and performance on the job was governed by a work ethic. But it is because of the complexity of the times that business and other organizations need leaders who can revive the leadership compact and make it work for the benefit of everyone.

Instead of being leaders, people who rise to the top of organizations are more often than not managers. To make matters worse, they identify themselves as managers and make what they do and how they think synonymous with leadership. The crucial difference between managers and leaders is in their respective commitments. A manager is concerned with how decisions get made and how communication flows; a leader is concerned with what decisions get made and what he or she communicates. In short, for the manager it is style over substance and process over reality.

One of the reasons for the demise of the leadership compact is the failure of authority figures to do their job. Although the traditional view is that a subordinate should support authority figures and the values represented in the idea of authority, it has become exceedingly difficult to maintain this position. Too many examples of incompetence and selfishness appear at the top to sustain the attachment to authority that is necessary in the leadership compact.

An engineer in RCA expressed the disillusionment with authority he and other middle managers felt after the company's merger with General Electric. Whether true or not, he believed the sale to GE came about because top executives in RCA wanted to cash in their golden parachutes. The view from below contrasted the riches enjoyed at the top with the insecurity and dislocation experienced in the middle and lower ranks.

Fundamental questions persist: Why believe in authority? Why support your boss? Those who aspire to lead must provide answers to these questions. The answers depend on the rediscovery of the principle that people who run organizations should contribute substance to their jobs and add value beyond superficial symbols and sentiment. Authority is under scrutiny. A demand for accountability is being reviewed. And, above all, there is an urgent need to make business work again.

Chapter 2

Management and Leadership

*T*o some, the notion that a manager and a leader are different seems wrong, if not offensive. For example, in a letter written to the editors of the *Harvard Business Review* about the article "Managers and Leaders: Are They Different?" Fred Bucy, then president of Texas Instruments Inc., said: "I disagree completely with the premise that distinguishes the manager from the leader and says, in effect, that an individual cannot fulfill both roles. This is nonsense." [1]

Yet, Mr. Bucy went on to say that there is a distinction to be drawn between the bureaucrat and the innovator. Bucy said that problems with mature industries in the United States arise when bureaucrats are put in charge as a result of their ability to move up the organization, implying that they have few other abilities. Bucy continued, "However, in high-technology industries, the bureaucratic manager will not succeed. The competition and technology move too fast. A combination of strong leadership and excellent managerial capability is required for success." [2]

Although Fred Bucy and other business executives are correct to believe that management is necessary to the orderly guidance of activity in enterprises, they do not understand that it is not sufficient to maintain the vitality of a business.

The Evans Products Company, with headquarters in Portland, Oregon, was a large conglomerate operating in the housing, rail car, forest products, retail home center, and industrial products businesses. Its organization structure was a model of decentralization, with clearly delineated profit centers coordinated by a strong staff sitting in corporate headquarters reporting to Monford Orloff, the chief executive officer. A McKinsey executive compensation plan assured that bonuses were a direct correlate of earnings so that financial incentives were directed toward meeting goals. Sophisticated budgets provided the tools for measuring performance even within the divisions of the major groups. From top to bottom the credo governing Evans was order, control, and coordination. Yet the company sought protection under Chapter 11 of the Federal Bankruptcy Code in 1985 and was substantially liquidated in 1987.

Evans failed not because of lack of management, but despite its remarkably efficient management outlook and operation or, perhaps, because of it. The housing and rail car businesses were in a cyclical downturn common to these industries, particularly in response to rising interest rates. Not willing to let sales and profits decline as a result of scaling down operations in response to the business cycle, Mr. Orloff and two of his group presidents decided to continue operations and encourage sales by providing liberal financing for customers. The company put rail cars out on lease and sold houses to consumers so that sales and profit reports continued to look rosy, while increased borrowings buttressed a negative cash flow for the corporation as a whole. The company continued to borrow short and lend long until it ran out of cash and its ability to borrow.

Evans's troubles, along with those of other well-managed companies, began and ended with bad substantive decisions. The delusion of the managerial mystique is that solid methods will produce good results. Management's overriding fantasy is that an array of organizational devices and techniques of control will overcome all human frailties. Managers find it difficult to believe the reality that good and bad substantive decisions are directly related to the strengths and weaknesses of the individuals involved. Their fantasy neglects the fact that their devices and techniques have little effect on the decision makers at the top of the organizational pyramid.

The emphasis on smooth process may even cloud judgment and contribute to distorted thinking. Managers become so attached to their orderly structures and procedures that they erroneously assume wise decisions automatically follow. This confidence in process commits the error that the philosopher

Alfred North Whitehead called "misplaced concreteness," in which process is made real and substance is ignored.[3]

Whereas managers focus on process, leaders focus on imaginative ideas. Leaders not only dream up ideas, but stimulate and drive other people to work hard and create reality out of ideas. One such leader had the opportunity to sell a revolutionary product he had invented to a large, established company. Instead of selling to this formidable competitor, the entrepreneur decided to ignore the advice of business consultants and continue with his own company. The consultants believed that instituting management processes would be too costly, time-consuming, and difficult for the entrepreneur. They advised, "Why not sell out? Take a large amount of money now. Avoid the risks of a competitive battle with a world-class corporation that has an infrastructure in place and is ready to do battle rather than give up market share to a newcomer." The consultants overstated the importance of process and underestimated the effects of the driving vision of the leader on key subordinates. The company remained independent and produced enormous wealth for the entrepreneur, his associates, and investors.

In comparison to visionary leaders such as Edwin Land, An Wang, and Sam Walton, managers are practical people. Typically, they are hard working, intelligent, analytical, and tolerant of others. Because they hold few convictions with passion, except perhaps for the need to extract order out of potential chaos, they exhibit a high degree of fair-mindedness in dealing with people.

Leaders are more dramatic in style and unpredictable in behavior. They seem to overcome the conflict between order and chaos with an authority legitimized by personal magnetism and a commitment to their own undertakings and destinies.

André Meyer was the great charismatic figure in the banking house of Lazard Frères, New York. His clients, subordinates, and friends were in awe of him. Foremost among the characteristics that elicited awe was his genius in putting together deals that satisfied diverse needs that the people involved often could not articulate or did not even sense. He was quoted as saying that investment banking was 10 percent arithmetic and 90 percent psychoanalysis.[4] He could interpret clients by keeping them off balance while drawing from them a multitude of facts that he used in shaping deals. Although less than admirable in his frequent abuses of partners, there was no doubt his imagination, self-confidence, and financial ability created a presence worthy of respect. These qualities appeared not in pedestrian reasoning, but in leaps of insight and imagination, characteristics that leaders value and that managers often fail to understand.

Managerial goals are passive, deeply embedded in the structure of the organization, in contrast to entrepreneurial or individual leadership goals that actively shape ideas and tastes. Instead of boldly adopting technical innovation or taking risks to test new ideas, managers survey constituents' needs and build their actions on anticipated responses. They avoid direct confrontation and solutions that could stir up strong feelings of support or opposition. The ideal of managers is to make decisions that fall inside what Chester Barnard, the organization theorist, called the "zone of indifference," the range of subjects which people feel personally unaffected by or are not actively concerned about. [5] To tighten their control, managers aim to widen their constituents' zone of indifference, hoping to stop just short of the point at which people lose all interest and also motivation.

When conflicts arise, managers attempt to reconcile them by compromises that give something to the contenders so that there are no losers. Good compromises occur, managers believe, by focusing on process and procedure, not on substance and individuals. If people feel a decision has gone against their interests, they are supposed to overcome their disappointment by realizing that the procedure, not individuals, led to the decision. If they maintain belief in process, they live with the hope that another encounter with the same process will result in a decision more in their favor. This faith in process transcends the immediate reactions to winning and losing.

Communication is important to both managers and leaders, but the modes differ. Managers communicate in signals, whereas leaders prefer clearly stated messages. For example, executives who fall out of favor with their bosses in managerially driven companies learn of their decline indirectly. In Lee Iacocca's unhappy experience in the Ford Motor Company, invitations to meetings were withheld, key decisions were made without his participation, and other "signals" told him it was time to look elsewhere.

Secretary of State George Shultz experienced the tactic of indirect communication when an underling in the White House, undoubtedly following directions from above, refused to schedule an airplane to fly to an important meeting. This gesture was the White House staff's way of getting even for Shultz's refusal to accept the Iran initiative.

In one company a senior executive learned he would not be named chief executive officer when a principal shareholder outside the executive ranks dropped a hint at a cocktail party. The excuse used to justify withholding this vital information was that the head of the company was concerned that direct confrontation would so damage the candidate's self-esteem that it would be better to break the news indirectly and slowly. A more probable explanation is that indirect communication reflected the head of the company's guilt feelings, and the expression of concern for the executive's self-esteem was a rationalization after the fact.

The penchant for indirect and ambiguous communications, as described in recent books about business, such as Michael McCaskey's *The Executive Challenge: Managing Change and Ambiguity,* [6] arises out of the fear of aggression. Managers tend to fear aggression as a force leading to chaos. Yet, many psychological theories hold that aggression plays a constructive part in work and, indeed, that there can be no useful work without its release. At the same time the inhibition of aggression can lead to depressive reactions and diminish productivity. What leaders do for followers is show them how to release aggression in constructive ways and toward desirable ends.

The head of a *Fortune* 500 corporation vigorously attacked a study on financing new ventures. He focused not on how the task force carried out its study (the process), but on the analysis and recommendations (the substance). He presented new perspectives on the problem and pointed to other ways of approaching it. The task force examined his suggestions and arrived at a new plan that incorporated some of the CEO's ideas and also some innovations of its own. Not reluctant to risk bruising egos, this CEO made it a point to direct his aggression toward ideas, expecting those who had developed them to stand up to the challenge of detaching themselves from their immediate product long enough to look at it critically.

This scenario is hardly as crude as the actions of the first Henry Ford, who expressed his ire over attempts to change the Model T by literally tearing apart the mock-up. Most leaders are careful to deal directly with subordinates when expressing displeasure over performance.

Leaders comfortable with aggression often create a climate of ferment that intensifies individual motivation. The ferment is a risk because it is uncertain whether this intensity will produce innovation and high performance or, as managers fear, wasted energy and futile conflict. To stimulate thinking, however, the risk is worth taking.

Managers have a strong sense of belonging, of being a part of a group or organization. Perpetuating and strengthening existing institutions enhances the manager's self-esteem; he or she is performing in a role that harmonizes with the goals of prediction and control. Leaders' sense of separateness can support a powerful appreciation for individuals. It is this sense of a separate self that makes leaders powerful forces of change, whether technological, political, or ideological.

Individuals identified as potential managers or leaders in the product development department of a large capital goods producer were given the psychological test known as the Thematic Apperception Test (TAT).[7] Subjects construct stories about ambiguous pictures, and the tester interprets the stories as clues to the subjects' fantasy or inner world. The procedure is commonly used in psychological research and in clinical assessments. Included in the test was a picture of a young boy looking at a violin on a table in front of him. Two typical stories significantly illustrate how managers and leaders differ.

A manager wrote:

> Mom and Dad insisted that junior take music lessons so that someday he could become a concert musician. His instrument was ordered and had just arrived. Junior is weighing the alternative of playing football with the other kids or playing with the squeak box. He can't understand how his parents could think a violin is better than a touchdown.
>
> After four months of practicing the violin, junior has had more than enough. Daddy is going out of his mind, and Mommy is willing to give in reluctantly to the men's wishes. Football season is now over, but a good third baseman will take the field next spring.[8]

This story illustrates two tendencies that express managerial attitudes toward human relations and conflict. The first is to seek out activity with other people (the football team) and the second is to maintain a low level of emotional involvement in these relationships. Low emotional involvement appears in the writer's use of conventional metaphors, even clichés, and in the depiction of the ready shift from issues threatening to evoke conflict into harmonious decisions in which everyone wins. In this case junior, Mommy, and Daddy agree to give up the violin for manly sports.

These two themes may seem paradoxical, but their coexistence supports what a manager does: reconcile differences, seek compromises, and establish a balance of power. Another idea demonstrated by the manager's story is that managers may lack empathy, or the capacity to sense the thoughts and feelings of others. To illustrate the attempt to be empathetic, here is a story written in response to the same stimulus picture by someone considered by his peers to be a leader:

> This little boy has the appearance of being a sincere artist, one who is deeply affected by the violin, and has an intense desire to master the instrument.
>
> He seems to have just completed his normal practice session and appears to be somewhat crestfallen at his inability to produce the sounds which he is sure lie within the violin.
>
> He appears to be in the process of making a vow to himself to expend the necessary time and effort to play this instrument until he satisfies himself that he is able to bring forth the qualities of music which he feels within himself.
>
> With this type of determination and carry through, this boy became one of the great violinists of his day. [9]

Empathy is not simply a matter of paying attention to other people; it is the capacity to take in emotional signals and to make them mean something in a relationship with an individual. People who describe another person as "deeply affected," with "intense desire," as capable of feeling "crestfallen," and as one who can "vow to himself" would seem to have perceptiveness that they can use in their relationship with others.

Managers relate to people according to the role the people play in a sequence of events or in a process. Leaders, who are concerned with ideas, relate in more intuitive and empathetic ways. The managers' way of viewing people deflects their attention away from the substance of the people's concerns and toward their role in a process. Managers pay attention to how things get done, and leaders pay attention to what things mean to people.[10]

Leaders, like artists, are inconsistent in their ability to function well. They are vulnerable to mood swings and experience periods of elation as well as depression, depending on how events affect their self-esteem. Managers, on the other hand, operate within a narrow range of emotions. This emotional blandness, when combined with the preoccupation with process, leads to the impression that managers are inscrutable, detached, and even manipulative.

Indeed, one writer on management acknowledges that management is manipulation carried to the point that subordinates are not supposed to be aware of the fact that they are being manipulated. Professor H. Edward Wrapp of the University of Chicago Business School states, "[A manager's methods] border on manipulation, and the stigma associated with manipulation can be fatal. If the organization ever identifies him as a manipulator, his job becomes more difficult. No one willingly submits to manipulation, and those around him organize to protect themselves."[11] Those around the manipulator, however, are rarely unaware that they are being manipulated. They recognize it and plan their counter-manipulations, also trying to conceal the manipulative motive behind their moves. The game of politics takes root in organizations run by managers rather than leaders.

A classic example of manipulation was orchestrated in 1923 by Alfred P. Sloan when he ran General Motors. Sloan was the management genius responsible for developing a program of balanced centralization and decentralization in General Motors. This organizational innovation became a model for organizing and managing large corporations that remains in place to this day. Sloan faced a problem in the conflict between his manufacturing people and GM's inventor, Charles Kettering. The manufacturing people wanted to standardize design so they could mass produce automobiles efficiently. Kettering proposed an innovation in engine cooling called the copper-cooled engine. This engine still had bugs, whereas the water-cooled engine operated well. The issue was whether the company should move for a better product in the longer run or settle for a good workable product immediately? Sloan sided with the manufacturing people, but did not let his views be known. He did not want to oppose Kettering, who had the support and admiration of Pierre du Pont, who represented a major block of stock in General Motors.

The managerial solution that Sloan devised appeared to be a compromise. Instead of exercising his authority to make the practical decision in favor of the manufacturing heads, Sloan maneuvered his way through the problem by creating a new structure, an organization for the copper-cooled engine company, with Kettering in charge. Sloan knew that Kettering was an inventor and not an executive and that the copper-cooled engine probably would not materialize as a practical product because of Kettering's lack of interest in running an organization. His maneuver was superficially brilliant because it ostensibly gave both sides what they wanted. It seemed to be an ideal situation in which everyone won and, presumably, had increased confidence in the process. Years later Sloan wrote: "The copper-cooled car never came up again in a big way. It just died out, I don't know why." [12]

It is true that General Motors under Sloan's direction developed a reputation for order, system, and control that was new to the automobile industry, especially in comparison with the Ford Motor Company. But it is also true that as a consequence of the managerial ethos, the company became conservative in product design and technological innovation. While rationalizing its behavior by claiming that it was giving the customers what they wanted (supposedly, big cars loaded with accessories), the company, for all practical purposes, lost the spirit of technological innovation that was so dear to Charles Kettering.

Tactical manipulations appear useful to managers, particularly to those who do not know how to confront conflicts that might generate aggression. The stultifying effect on innovation, as in the case of GM, is one consequence. Another danger in such manipulations is the politicization of organizations and human relationships. As the French sociologist Michel Crozier pointed out in his study of bureaucracy, what starts as logical and objective organizational practices changes into interest politics, and self and group interests now take precedence over purpose and work. [13] The tendency to encourage the politicization of relationships, although not intentional on the managers' part, results from the way managers use power and their lack of attachment to the substance of the business.

Politicization occurs in business when substance takes a back seat to process—when people become preoccupied with power as an end in itself rather than with what the power is supposed to accomplish. Perhaps, without realizing what they are doing, managers shift from working on tasks to working on other people. Under the real conditions of inequality of power, which is characteristic of organizations, this shift tyrannizes subordinates and elicits defensive behavior.

In business, politics is a game of defense. But what people are defending against is seldom revealed in the superficial effort to adhere to an ideology of cooperation and teamwork. Politicization is not a malaise of mature industries only. The high-technology industries are also vulnerable, especially when goals are unclear.

A senior vice president for manufacturing of a major computer firm, for example, was a product of the dominance of politics over purpose. In a decision concerning plant expansion his major preoccupation was tactics and timing in presenting the proposal to the chief executive and ultimately to the board of directors. As a result, he appeared confused and even uninformed about the merits of the decision, which undoubtedly began with initiatives from his subordinates. When discussing the use of consultants in this major proposal, the issue for him was the personal style of the consultants rather than their ability to contribute to the substance of the recommendation.

The structure of American business lends itself to strong leadership. The benign authority figure who holds no strong opinions but views the job of running an organization as facilitating instead of directing and as managing instead of leading misunderstands and ultimately misuses the instrument of business. The purpose of business is to create products for customers, work for employees, and profit for shareholders. It takes talent to run a business, and the talent must focus on the content of business. Organizational adroitness is secondary to the talents of figuring out what people want and creating the products that will succeed in the marketplace.

Organizations are costly to maintain. Every activity that supports organization structure and procedure potentially draws energy from the fundamentals of substance into the intricacies of power relations. Although these intricate relationships exist, they should not be viewed either as intrinsic to or necessary in business. Politics in business diminishes the capacity of people to work and solve problems.

In early 1988 IBM announced a major change in its organization. It created broad product groups and eliminated central staffs. IBM's top management intended with this change to push decision making down the hierarchy and flatten the organization. But the beneficial effect of this decision was the reduction of politics by lessening the power of central staffs and strengthening that of line management. IBM's moves came on the heels of less than satisfactory results in the personal computer field, flat performance in other sectors of its business, and a general perception that it was being outfought by smaller and more resourceful competitors.

The relative simplicity and unity of authority are why business lends itself to strong leadership. Most theories of authority, and for that matter leadership, come from political and social scientists who know more about government than they do about business. Government, with its paradox of election politics and bureaucratic continuity, differs from business in how people get and maintain power. Because of these differences, government encourages duplicity, whereas business encourages forthrightness. Often government works toward unclear goals that are subject to conflicting forces within the apparatus and are obscured by the need for contending groups to preserve their power base. The rise to chief executive of a business should not be an exercise in running for office. Many people view it as election politics, misunderstanding both the purpose of business and the flow of authority from top to bottom.

How many executives would agree that the following description of the job of president of the United States should be taken as an accurate portrayal of a chief executive's job in American business?

In form all presidents are leaders nowadays. In fact this guarantees no more than that they will be clerks. Everybody now expects the man inside the White House to do something about everything. Laws and customs now reflect acceptance of him as the Great Initiator, and acceptance quite as widespread at the Capitol as at his end of Pennsylvania Avenue. But such acceptance does not signify that all the rest of government is at his feet. It merely signifies that other men have found it practically impossible to do their jobs without assurance of initiatives from him. Service for themselves, not power for the President, has brought them to accept his leadership in form. They find his actions useful in their business. The transformation of his routine obligations testifies to their dependence on an active White House. A President, these days, is an invaluable clerk. His influence, however, is a very different matter. Laws and customs tell us little about leadership in fact.[14]

The idea that a chief executive officer is a clerk and that his power stands in proportion to the need other people have of him for their goals may reflect the realities of election politics and bureaucratic continuity, but it is bizarre if applied to business. A chief executive officer in a modern corporation has enormous clout. This job, unlike that of the president of the United States, is less a problem of persuasion than of deciding what is the right thing to do. Once a course of action has been formed, it is relatively easy to persuade subordinates to work hard to get the job done and easy to appeal to reason, but it is difficult to determine what is rational in a public policy decision.

Political scientist Morton Halperin, in his book *Bureaucratic Politics and Foreign Policy*,[15] makes this point in describing the way the Johnson administration grappled with the decision whether to deploy an antiballistic missile system (ABM). According to Halperin, that President Johnson was uncommitted allowed various federal agencies to compete in determining national policy. This resulted in a host of absurdities, including asking the Congress for funds but promising not to use them for the purpose voted. The ostensible reason for this contradictory behavior was to establish a new premise in bargaining with the Russians. But whether the decision made any difference to the Russians could never be determined. What could be determined, however, was the cost to the American taxpayers of contradiction and power rivalries generated by the president's uncommitted position.

If chief executives in business follow government and political officeholders using indirectness and ambiguity to exercise power, one thing is sure: They will generate mischief and encourage political infighting and backbiting. Why create aberrations in business by distorting the essence of authority relations? Business thrives on the principle of unity of command. To give up this principle destroys the ability of business to perform.

If not the originator, NASA was probably the most ardent advocate of matrix management. An organizational matrix locates management and technical employees in a cell derived from two axes in an organization. The first axis is a program and the second is a functional specialty. A materials engineer is simultaneously a member of a project group and the materials department. He or she is on assignment to the project, but is a permanent member of the engineering department. The matrix structure is not unlike the homeroom system in secondary schools. While assigned to a particular section for each subject studied, the pupil always lands back at homeroom.

Matrix management enjoyed some popularity in the 1970s and early 1980s, but has become discredited because of an excessive preoccupation with dual membership and the attendant problems of coordination when an employee has more than one boss. It can be relatively simple to assign an employee to one boss who can then name the projects on which that employee will work. Project heads direct work without altering the sole reporting relationship. The elaboration of the matrix concept, with the intention of making ambiguous who reports to whom, invites political activity instead of substantive work.

The rationale for the uncommitted position in politics is that the chief executive can maintain control over all the options until it is timely to reach a decision. If the chief executive commits too early, before all the agencies are persuaded, the decision may be undermined by opponents within the government apparatus who know too well how to use their independent power bases to fight for their position. But, even in government, a chief executive who remains uncommitted too long soon discovers that desirable policies may be buried among the ruins of the power conflicts that ensue.

David Stockman, President Reagan's controversial director of the Office of Management and Budget, described the successive "battles of the budget" in which he was pitted against Caspar Weinberger, the secretary of defense. Stockman fought for spending cuts to balance a budget based on drastic cuts in taxes. The defense department had proposed an unprecedented peacetime budget of $1.46 trillion and adamantly refused to reduce the level of expenditures. Stockman tried desperately to get President Reagan's attention in the belief that the president, whose position in the early winter of 1982 was not known, would decide to avoid the risk of huge deficits and order the department to lower its request. Whether by intent, inertia, or being maneuvered by Weinberger, Reagan allowed the defense department to go forward. In Stockman's view the situation "was ironic in the extreme: the Secretary of Defense of the most tight-fisted and anti-bureaucratic administration of this century had produced a $1.46 trillion budget by delegating the job to the world's largest bureaucracy. Cap the Knife had become Cap the Shovel." [16]

That there are no power bases independent of the chief executive officer is the reality of power in corporate business. Authority flows from the shareholder to the board of directors to the chief executive officer and from there to other executives. Any subordinate who seeks to create a power base independent of the chief executive, who so to speak creates a barony within a princely state, can do so only because the chief executive officer is weak or misunderstands authority and executive responsibility.

Some types of businesses do breed politics, family business being a notorious example. These situations, in which people tend to spend excessive time building and maintaining coalitions, resemble elective politics. Control of the organization depends on the ability to create alignments of power. The net result, however, is to arrive at innocuous decisions that create the least divisiveness within the ruling alliance. Divisive decisions put the alliance at risk. One of the reasons for the high mortality rate of family businesses is that coalition politics allows incompetence to gain the upper hand. The exception, of course, is where one family member dominates through either ownership or force of personality. During the time of that person's dominance the situation returns to one of command, but if later succession to power results in fostering alliances and coalition politics, the business will be in danger. One way to address the problem is to institute integrity of command and marry competence with power.

Sidney Rabb, the late chairman and chief executive officer of the Stop & Shop companies, was the undisputed head of this public company that remained under family control from its inception before World War I until 1988 when Kohlberg Kravis executed a leveraged buy-out. The first-born in his family, Rabb early on gained the respect of his siblings as the family leader. They deferred to him not only because of the force of his personality, but also because the business prospered, enabling the family to accumulate wealth. His outstanding reputation as a community leader augmented his personal power in the family and the corporation, enabling him to direct the company in its diversification from food retailing to discount merchandising. While the corporation and the family were not free from political sensitivities, Rabb managed to attract his siblings' and professional managers' desires and ambitions so that he in turn controlled how power was distributed in the business.

Some will argue that as a business grows larger and becomes organizationally complex, it inevitably becomes political because of the increased possibility of independent power bases and the differences in perceptions that arise from different positions. Thus, someone from a marketing group will see the problems of the business differently from someone in a manufacturing group; a division head will see problems differently from someone in the headquarters. Each operates under different constraints and the imperatives create unique perceptions and judgments.

Although it is true that these differences do arise, they can be exacerbated or minimized by leadership. It is precisely the job of leadership to create commitments that override the immediacy of personal interests. Perceptions based on position can affect thinking, but perceptions can be focused and challenged by desire, reason, and necessity. If a forewoman, for example, sees her responsibility as meeting production deadlines, efficiency will be more important to her than quality. But if she views the enterprise as a whole, she will recognize the value of extra time for quality control. Executives who leave perceptions of position unchallenged permit them to develop into the politics of self-interest and ultimately into organizational paralysis. Although such phenomena may be inherent in elective politics, in business, where logic necessitates unity of command, they are distortions. One of the goals of leadership is to keep politics out of human relationships.

In business organizations as in the family, politics flourishes in the absence of content and expression of talents. Cooperation for self-protection, although an understandable tendency, is not true cooperation. One of the critical jobs of leadership is to overcome these political inclinations and to encourage the expression of talent and the performance of useful work. True cooperation then follows because people are working for a dynamic organization that has direction. Leadership also amplifies the motivation to work because people experience the fusion of rationality with talent.

Content in organizations is precisely what business is about:

making and selling products and services. It has to do with markets, technology, finance, manufacturing, and competition. What academics see when they look superficially at business is the crassness of commercial affairs: people vying with each other to get customers to buy what they do not need. Once beyond this superficiality, the academic is likely to see those things closest to his or her experience. Universities are notorious for their abhorrence of executive functions and responsibility. The appointment of presidents and deans involves search committees and complicated procedures. Instead of encouraging strong appointments, the governance procedure attracts compromise candidates noted for their ability to avoid controversy. The appointments generate managers and not leaders.

Even after a president or a dean is appointed, power considerations bear strongly on setting goals and determining activities. Faculty members tend to protect their autonomy and their turf. The ideal is to be a self-supporting baron who controls resources. The barons form coalitions and limit the executive's capacities to influence activity.

To complicate matters, academics fear a lack of control over their abilities. They cannot predict the effectiveness of their performance in writing or teaching. Self-esteem is constantly at risk and one means for protection, if not self-fulfillment, is to become political—to take the organization as an object of desire and control.

There is no narrower group than professors engaged in power relations. Ostensibly, what drives these power relations is the effort to gain a fair or proportionate share of the scarce resources such as time, money, and prestige. The rules of collegiality mean that these decisions are delegated to a corporate body rather than to an executive. Faculties as a body, therefore, learn to bargain and accrue credits to be used in other exchanges. Even if deans are given some executive responsibility, they easily develop insecurities because in reality their initiatives come to fruition only if they are able to raise money to support new programs. To exercise influence, deans often become duplicitous, a situation matched by faculty rivalries and collusions. Executive frustration in academia is notorious. A president of a university allegedly expressed the irony of his job this way: "I'm supposed to provide money for the faculty, sex for the students, and football for the alumni."

This type of atmosphere is bound to warp the views of its participants, particularly when it comes time to study business organizations and to generalize about how they operate. The professors studying business either become absorbed by superficial or obscure details or project a view of organizations most familiar to them: a world tenuous in substance, fragile in human relationships, and inundated with political intrigue.

Students of business can avoid the traps of trivia on the one hand and politics on the other. The ones most likely to avoid these traps are those professors who concentrate on studying the substance of business and the people most closely engaged in its activity. The least likely sources of information and enlightenment are organizational behaviorists. They know little about the substance of business and, more importantly, they act as though the substance is unimportant. What they try to generalize is the process of organizations, and in this effort they manage to ignore the character and especially the interests of people.

What interests people in business is substance. When they lose sight of their work, when they become insecure as a result of poor leadership, or when they are asked to do what they are not capable of doing and therefore must endure the humiliations of poor performance, they turn to process, which becomes equivalent to politics. As a result of these distortions, the lesson people learn is how to be devious. Whether it is in the form of nondirective counseling, management-by-objective, participation, or quality circles, the end result is the same: detaching work from authority relations and the consequent encouragement of irrationality.

One of the jobs of business leaders is to keep politics out and substance in. The managerial orientation, with its emphasis on form over substance, on structure over people, and on power relationships over work, is at the heart of the disability of modern business in the United States and probably in other countries as well. What started out as a rational attempt to organize, motivate, and control the actions of large numbers of people in business organizations has been transformed into a managerial mystique that subordinates the work of organizations to the forms in which people relate to each other. These forms, in turn, are dominated by conceptions of authority that discourage assertiveness, individual responsibility, and creativity.

While attending an advanced management course, a group of

senior executives holding responsible jobs in marketing in a number of *Fortune* 500 corporations met with a group of business professors to discuss new trends and problems in marketing. It was surprising that the executives had little to say about the substance of marketing and what lay ahead in this field. Instead, they spoke about organizations and politics, claiming that one cannot separate the substance of marketing from process in large organizations. They appeared to have given up their attachment to the concepts and techniques involved in moving products from the designer's workbench and the factory floor to customers. After the meeting the academics met to review the material presented and to speculate on possible interpretations.

Were these executives confirming a view that business school academics frequently espouse, the view that the substance of large-scale business *is* the process of getting things done in organizations? Or, was this meeting an example of how insecure people may try to protect themselves by deflecting from substance to process? Or, was this meeting an example of the executives' technique of telling others what they think the others want to hear? With any of these explanations, the meeting reflected the pathology of organizations in which the medium has become the message and people give little thought to what they are supposed to be doing.

Whatever the true explanation, the material revealed at the meeting suggests a fundamental weakness in making decisions in organizations. When senior executives feel disengaged from the content of their work and instead focus exclusively on process, they cannot lead in their organizations. They are reduced to being conveners and leaving to others, usually subordinates, the important work of generating ideas. The results are several: The rational uses of power become obscure and reduce the confidence people feel in their leaders; a model of style over knowledge is established for those who aspire to leadership; and communication goes out of focus so that people try to concentrate on the hidden instead of the manifest messages. The net effect is that people feel as though they are dealing with a monumental structure, immovable and insensitive to the pressure of reality. Or, as expressed by a consultant describing what it's like trying to get things done in a large organization: The work is like trying to push around a two-hundred foot sponge—you lean into it and it swallows you!

The managerial mystique is inherently optimistic but also

misguided. It believes in progress through the perfection of structures in order to control behavior. It believes in process as the performance of roles assigned to people in the various structures. It believes in politics, the art of manipulating people to get things done. Finally, it believes in personal advancement through single-mindedly holding and practicing these beliefs.

The managerial mystique has dominated the consciousness of American business executives for the past twenty-five years. But as with any set of ideas, it has a history. Starting at the end of the nineteenth century and continuing through World War II, a change occurred in authority relations. The heroic, often autocratic personalities at the head of corporations became dinosaurs, doomed to extinction. Henry Ford's surrender of his power over the Ford Motor Company sounded the death knell for personal leadership. In its place came the dispassionate and coldly clinical professionals.

These professionals imposed the managerial order on corporations. They brought what they learned from the business schools, namely, principles of bargaining, emotional control, human relations skills, and the technology of quantitative control. They left behind commitment, creativity, concern for others, and experimentation. They had learned to be managers instead of leaders. In exercising their craft, the professional managers revealed no less a penchant for power than the autocrats whom they succeeded. But the achievement of power shifted from control through ownership to control through manipulation in the guise of eliciting participation and cooperation.

American business lost its way while the professional manager ascended the corporate hierarchy, empowered with the tools of organizational control and the mystique of a new elite. Professional management was born out of necessity. The newly emerging corporation could not sustain the irrationality of autocratic leaders. But the antidote of the managerial mystique overlooked the need for personal influence as the driving force for economic growth and human satisfaction.

Part II

Analysis

Chapter 3

How Managers Think

*I*n *My Years with General Motors*, Alfred Sloan tells of a meeting in the spring of 1916 with William C. Durant, the founder of General Motors. Durant made Sloan an offer to buy the Hyatt Roller Bearing Company. Sloan not only ran Hyatt, he was also a major shareholder. Sloan describes his reaction to the proposition: "After all those years of building up the Hyatt business, the idea of selling it was a shock to me, but it opened up a new vista in my thinking and caused me to analyze the situation at Hyatt."[1]

What ensued was a clear example of how managers think. After the initial shock, three thoughts came to Sloan. First, Hyatt was vulnerable in the marketplace because of its excessive reliance on one customer, Ford Motor Company. Second, Hyatt products could be made obsolete by technological development, which neither he nor others could reasonably foresee: "I have always been interested in improving a product; but this was a special-product business and the *choice* was whether to proceed independently or within an integrated enterprise."[2] Third, "I had spent my working life—I was forty years old then—developing a property and I had a large plant with a great deal of responsibility, but I never got much yield out of it in dividends. Mr. Durant's offer presented an opportunity to convert Hyatt's profits into readily salable assets."[3]

Alfred Sloan is properly credited with bringing the art of management to its present state of sophistication. His account of how he reacted to Durant's offer demonstrates three key elements in how managers think: objectivity, analysis, and evaluation. These elements can be enhanced by using formal techniques, such as decision theory and linear programming. Whether formal or informal approaches are used, making decisions requires the ability to be dispassionate in the face of a problem, the skill to analyze facts, and the willingness to evaluate costs and benefits.

These qualities of the managerial mind are indisputably assets. They are also generally accepted as objective and value-neutral. When authors such as Peters and Waterman[4] and Pascale and Athos[5] attack them, they are appealing to sentiment without confronting the fundamental defects in management thinking. What is wrong with objectivity, analysis, and the weighing of costs and benefits? These qualities of mind are timeless and universally applicable. To denigrate them is to appeal to impulsive behavior and even to encourage irrationality.

To comprehend the weaknesses of managerial thinking requires analysis not only of its elements, but also of its underlying motives. The urge to control, to defend against the fear of chaos, to maintain distance in human involvement, and to separate thinking and feeling ultimately distort the forms as well as the validity of rational behavior.

The Evans Products Company bankruptcy is an example of the repetition of foolish risk taking. The recession of 1974 almost resulted in bankruptcy because the company borrowed short and loaned long to sustain sales in its housing group. Despite the close encounter with Chapter 11 in 1974, Monford Orloff, the chief executive officer, encouraged the same practice in the company five years later. Aided by bankers eager to grant loans, Evans pursued aggressive financing not only in the housing group, but also in the cyclical rail car group. With interest rates skyrocketing in the early 1980s, the company could not maneuver past the period of high fixed charges and reduced income.

While hindsight reveals the error in Evans's tactics to overcome cyclicality, on the surface executives appeared to be acting rationally. The rational consideration at the time was the risk-reward ratio. They were making a high-risk decision in anticipation of a proportionately high return. From the narrow perspective of risk analysis, there is a hypothetical return that is high enough to justify an "all or nothing" gamble. But to engage in such a calculation misses the point. What return would be proportional to the risk of insolvency? Why would anyone risk an entire enterprise for even astronomical short-term gains? The answer goes beyond the logic of decision making and risk analysis. We enter the realm of unconscious motivation, and, perhaps more than other human beings, managers have a capacity to rationalize behavior and, consequently, misunderstand underlying motives.

Managers have in common a deep conviction that thought and action should be logical and objective. People of similar convictions can cooperate because they believe they can resolve differences by reaching a compromise through logic. When the time came for Alfred Sloan to consummate the sale of Hyatt to Mr. Durant, Sloan wanted half the proceeds in cash and the other half in stock. His partners wanted all their proceeds in cash. In the compromise Sloan took a greater share of stock to allow his conservative partners to take out more cash.[6]

Managers apply their logic to a wide range of problems, not just problems of investment. Questions of people and organization, of product policy and economics of scale in manufacturing are subject to the same methods—logical analysis and objective appraisal. What are the goals to be achieved, the costs to be endured, and the yields of the alternatives available? Indisputable logic applied to a wide range of problems distinguishes the modern manager from the seat-of-the-pants operator who has no control over events.

Managers impose a hard discipline on themselves and other people. There is no room for emotion in the calculation that controls their thought. But beneath this layer of professionalism, objectivity, and cool-headed rationality is a substructure of nonlogical belief that supports managers' thinking.

Managers dread chaos and revere order. Some observers have sought a psychological explanation for these characteristics. Some statistical studies seem to suggest that many managers are the first-born child or the eldest male child in the family.[7] The first born often mediates between siblings and parents, and from the point of view of the mediator, emotions and needs often appear fraught with danger, that is, likely to cause parents to lose their temper, and conflicting demands involving emotions are not easily resolved. In short, the family experience produces the dread of chaos and the urgent need to bring order into human affairs.

This dread of chaos, whatever its source, is an overreaction, since most human interchange involves far less danger than most managers fear. The reaction to dread is overkill. Managers rely to an excessive degree on structure, process, and control as a means of assuring order in the organization.

Managers pride themselves on their ability to orchestrate events in organizations. To bring about change in accordance with a plan is one of their most satisfying experiences. As a result, managers spend a great deal of time in creating scenarios. They envision a process involving many actors who perform according to the script, that is, who can be persuaded to alter their perceptions and abandon self or group interests for the benefit of the enterprise as a whole.

When, for example, Prime Computer convinced the directors of Computervision to approve a tender offer, Joe Henson, Prime's president and chief executive officer, already had in place a process for integrating the two companies. According to the scenario, a high-level task force of key executives from both companies would appoint groups to work on particular projects such as joint selling, purchasing, product development, marketing, and manufacturing. Each group would have representation from Prime and Computervision. The goal was the total integration of Computervision into Prime's CAD-CAM marketing, production, and sales organizations.

Within a month of the takeover, Robert Gable, Computervision's chief executive, announced his resignation, stating publicly that having once run a business, he would not be satisfied in a subordinate role in the now expanded Prime Computer.

Whether fully aware of its implication or not, the basic decision Henson supported soon after Computervision agreed to a takeover was to fuse Computervision's market expertise in computer-aided design products into Prime's CAD-CAM group. The focus on process, with its elaborate apparatus of task force and multiple work groups, was of secondary importance to the substantive decision to integrate.

Process in management can be tool-oriented or organization-oriented. Henry Ford II introduced tool-oriented process to his company when he brought in executives who practiced coordination and control through advanced accounting techniques. General Motors under Alfred Sloan developed an organization-oriented process through the systematic use of committees, ranging from the executive committee to the general technical and purchasing committee. These activities cut across autonomous divisions and consequently provided opportunities for savings through collaborative efforts. At Ford the tool-oriented process became an issue in a power struggle between product and financial people. At General Motors Sloan introduced the committee system to overcome conflicts that had erupted between Kettering's engineering group and operations people concerned with maintaining their autonomy while maximizing profits. In this case, though, organization-oriented process subordinated substance to methods of coordination in the higher echelons of General Motors.

Someday economists will be able to estimate the costs involved in maintaining organizational process. They are approaching this estimate in recent developments in agency theory, which considers top managers as agents of shareholders who pay an agency fee for services rendered.[8] Agency fees differ from ordinary compensation such as salary and bonus. When senior executives act to further stockholders' interests, as when they secure the best price during a takeover battle, they expect compensation that reflects their position as agents. Indeed, special bonuses, golden parachutes, and contracts with liberal termination clauses provide compensation. Managers are supposed to act in ways contrary to their best interests to maximize value for the shareholders. Agency fees are the costs of motivating managers to subordinate their interests in favor of the shareholders' interests.

Whether agency theory can be extended to the relationship between superior and subordinate in higher management remains to be seen. But it is clear that costs are incurred in organizations to achieve order and avoid chaos. The problem of decentralization is a good example. Advocates of decentralization point to the virtues of driving decision making down to the lowest possible level in an organization. But once they implement this policy, despite their stated belief in the beneficial effects of autonomy on motivation, the advocates' anxiety about coordination takes over. Tool- and organization-oriented process appears as reports, analyses, committees, and, of course, staff. Advocates of decentralization seem to talk out of two sides of their mouths at once. They preach local autonomy and at the same time institute massive procedures to make sure that order reigns and chaos is avoided.

The costs of process are clear, although difficult to quantify, in venture companies that get past the early rounds of financing and start to grow. The typical response of venture capitalists is to encourage the entrepreneur to bring in a professional manager to act as chief operating officer, relieving the chief executive of responsibility for day-to-day management. This move often makes sense, because many entrepreneurs dislike running things; they even appear to relish chaos and to despise order.

All too often the first thing these professional managers do is institute tool- and organization-oriented process. They immediately and automatically repeat what they have done in other companies, instead of taking time to learn what is going on, to develop relationships with people who may find the new manager's entrance disturbing, and to develop a good working rapport with the boss. The process enmeshes high-level and middle-level executives in activity that is new, in their eyes unnecessary, and often calling for skills unfamiliar to them.

The professional managers are highly articulate and can gain the advantage in any argument about process. They argue most logically and vehemently when they are apprehensive and feel the need to make an impact in a new job. In turn, subordinates respond to process initiatives defensively, stop thinking clearly, and lose sight of priorities. They lose the ability to solve problems, which is one of the most precious abilities in any business, large or small. The net result is an increase in anger with little outlet for constructive expression of it. An air of resignation and despair soon permeates the business and all too often downward momentum accelerates. The only difference between venture businesses and large corporations is how long it takes to notice downward momentum.

Engineers in a venture company, for example, spent increasing amounts of time in formal meetings with a new president and chief operating officer. They were used to attending meetings, whether formal or informal, that were called to solve design and manufacturing problems. Under the new regime meetings were held to consider methods of organizing and coordinating efforts. These engineers felt irritated over the time away from their work and also inadequate because of the unfamiliar subject and procedure for the meetings. As new problems appeared, particularly in defective production, it became obvious that coordinating meetings were not going to provide solutions. Morale declined throughout the organization, and the company finally went out of business.

Managers hate surprises. Like security analysts and professional investors, managers believe in realizable expectations as the currency of credibility and esteem. Ask a manager to choose between creativity and reliability in subordinates and without hesitation the answer is reliability. A divisional president of a large corporation lost his job because the corporate chief executive was constantly on edge about his division's ability to meet projections. In truth, the divisional president was not indifferent to results. He always tried to beat projections by taking risks in product mix and market forecasts. For a number of years, he won his bets steadily, but he did lose sometimes. The organization could not tolerate his unpredictable approach. A professional manager, whether chief executive or subordinate, is measured by the same yardstick. Expectation and realization must match. The reward is a reputation for reliability. A manager may be moving in the wrong direction, but this fact is often obscured by the aura of reliability that surrounds a steady performer.

To meet expectations, managers depend on controlling the behavior of subordinates. There is no apparent tyranny in management. The behavioral control arises from benign structures embedded in process. Managers do not threaten or browbeat, but depend on subtlety. If subordinates believe that it is in their best interest to do what is expected, the result is what Elton Mayo called "spontaneous cooperation." It is more rewarding to do what is expected than to deviate from standards of behavior. People also cooperate because they have no alternatives readily at hand. The end result may be cooperation, but not commitment.

From the lessons of behavioral psychology, managers have learned that freedom is the result of a calculation, an equation comparing the cost of certain behavior with the reward. If the reward for behaving in an expected way exceeds the cost, the individual acts in that way to forward self-interest. The behavior is considered volitional and the person is considered free. If the balance of rewards and costs is unsatisfactory, the individual may then look for alternatives.

Organizations in the United States tend not to be totalitarian. During the reign of the first Henry Ford, the Ford Motor Company resembled a dictatorship. It pried into the lives of its workers and staff and through its sociology department attempted to control their habits and ways of thinking.[9] One of the first acts of Henry Ford II after succeeding his grandfather was to fire Harry Bennett, who exercised power through intimidation.

While business organizations are not totalitarian, neither do they provide communal feeling. The sense of membership in organizations diminished as businesses blurred their identity and institutional character during the era of corporate diversification and conglomeration. As this trend increased in the 1960s through the 1980s, managers placed greater stress on behavioral control through tool- and organization-oriented process. To work effectively in such an environment requires a cool head and considerable facility in the mathematics of costs and benefits.

One of the unforeseen effects of the decline in the sense of membership in corporations was the compartmentalization of work, home, and community. This division of activities into separate compartments increases privacy, but it also isolates employees and requires precision in corporate process. When individuals feel integrated in all aspects of their lives, any one of their memberships presents fewer problems in coordination and control. When the control of behavior is supported across a wide range of institutions, it is easy to reach a meeting of the minds.

Japanese society illustrates this degree of integration and accounts, in part, for the ability of Japanese managers to increase productivity. Japanese managers and institutions accept dependency without question and also expect compliance. Their goals are driven by the perception that for Japan to survive as a society, it must grow economically through export. The Japanese readily accept the idea that what is good for Toyota is good for Japan. When Charles E. Wilson suggested that what was good for General Motors was good for the United States, he sounded alien, as though he neither knew about nor understood the separation among the institutions of this country.

Process becomes precise when participants are trained in the calculation of interests. Managers assume calculation will occur and count on it as a means of controlling behavior. They also rely on the theory of indifference. It is impossible for people to become emotionally involved in all aspects of organizational life. Selectivity is the key to rational behavior. Every individual has a structure of motives, with a different value attached to each one. Some motives are closely tied to an individual's sense of self-worth and consequently weigh heavily in personal calculations. Other motives relate to needs that can be satisfied by a variety of means. If there are many ways to satisfy a need, the need itself becomes less important in the scale of motives. A worker who receives recognition on the job, in the community, and in the family is less concerned about his status than a worker whose recognition comes only from within his family. Motives that involve these less important needs exist in the individual's zone of indifference.

Managers act on the theory of indifference by using persuasion. There are at least two ways to persuade people. One is to convince them that a certain action will serve their interests well. The individual is easily persuaded to follow a course of action best suited to the manager's interest, with the expectation that the action will also satisfy self-interest. This type of persuasion addresses the reward side of the calculation. Another way to persuade is to change the way people value their motives. If a woman can be convinced that what she wants is less important than she had thought, she will be inclined to accept a proposed course of action that does not seem to satisfy her wants. In attaching less importance to those wants, she will have broadened her zone of indifference. If she becomes convinced that there are a variety of ways to realize her goal, then the value attached to the goal diminishes. Once again, her zone of indifference has broadened. Together, self-interest and indifference are the foundations of a psychology of power and control that dominate modern corporations. They create the politics of compliance, the heart of the managerial culture.

It is true that managers acknowledge the humanistic psychologies. When the psychologist Abraham Maslow presented his needs hierarchy theory of motivation, it met with great approval, at least initially.[10] Maslow suggested that individual needs are arranged in a pyramid ranging from safety at the base to self-actualization at the apex. Once one level of needs is satisfied and secure, then a higher level of needs becomes dominant. Maslow argued that the job of managing workers is to activate higher level needs and to show the means by which they can be satisfied. If successful, the manager would assure the commitment of individuals to the purpose and activities of an organization. But as managers know from experience and intuition, there are dangers inherent in Maslow's ideas. The main danger arises from the familiar problem of the discontent of rising expectations.

One of the few certain findings available in the study of organizations concerns the problem of satisfaction. An individual's satisfaction varies directly with the amount of reward received and inversely with the amount of reward expected. Assuming a constant expectation, the more one gets, the higher the satisfaction.

Assuming a constant reward, the more one expects, the higher the dissatisfaction. This formula of satisfaction works in a variety of organizations. It proved true in studies conducted in factories during the 1950s,[11] and it proved true in studies conducted in the military during World War II, as reported in the famous series called *The American Soldier.*[12]

Studies of factory workers found that if individuals carried symbols that identified them with the dominant group culture and they expected to be rewarded by group membership, they were satisfied if they were accepted by the group and were drawn into the activities membership promised. If individuals carried no symbols of group identity and were not rewarded by the group, their satisfaction level was just as high. Since they did not expect to be included, the lack of reward (in the form of group membership) was fully offset by their lack of expectation.

In the studies of morale described in *The American Soldier*, investigators noted that rates of promotion for officers varied considerably among branches of service. The rate of promotion in the Air Corps, for example, was high compared to that in the Military Police. Yet satisfaction with promotion was higher in the Military Police than in the Air Corps, because the level of expectation was much lower in the Military Police than in the Air Corps.

The same principle of satisfaction applies to the national situation. When authority figures arouse the expectation of followers and are unable to deliver commensurate rewards, the frustration level of followers is bound to increase and lead to dissatisfaction and violence. President John F. Kennedy masterfully aroused the expectations of the masses, particularly the disadvantaged sectors. Despite his efforts or intention to improve conditions, unrest and violence increased during his tenure and during the tenure of his successor, Lyndon B. Johnson, who was as committed to the New Frontier as Kennedy. The rising expectations stirred violence because conditions could not change as rapidly as rising expectations required.

During the earlier years of President Reagan's tenure the level of discontent seemed to diminish, despite a substantial rise in unemployment. The perceived level of deprivation depends upon a comparison of actual deprivation and expectations, and reduced expectations led to a reduction in overt discontent in Reagan's administration.

Management is a conservative activity and managers are cautious in the risks they undertake. They dislike impulsiveness and favor self-discipline—the ability to function within a cost-and-benefit calculation. Managers act in their own interests and expect others to do the same. There are two consequences of this managerial world view: a high degree of objectivity and a finely honed sense of organizational politics. Managers idealize objectivity. They admire the capacity to deal with conflicting points of view without becoming themselves emotionally aroused or involved in the joys and pains of other people's experiences.

Managers, like doctors, are not supposed to get angry at the maladies other people present to them. There are symptoms and causes, and the job at hand is to distinguish between them and to discover and present the applicable remedy. In fact, managers expect that their objectivity and coolness will become a standard for others to emulate. Once subordinates adopt the manager's objectivity, or coolness, then the manager can persuade them to change expectations and consequently widen their zone of indifference.

Whether consciously or not, managers manipulate subordinates in order to meet their own ends. All that prevents them from total manipulation is the fact that they work with other managers, who have an identical ego-ideal. All managers at all levels of an organization value the same things. They derive self-esteem from prediction and control; they want to be seen as reliable; they want to control their emotions. The individual with the most authority (in the case of business organizations, the chief executive officer) does not necessarily hold psychological advantage over his or her subordinates. True, CEOs have more power, but they share with other managers a strategy of career and ideology of profession. CEOs, in spite of their clout, face formidable competition. In an atmosphere of managerial politics all are silently scrutinizing their own and others' performance. Everyone is a player.

The politics of management is the game of playing with other minds. In theory, this guarantees prediction and control, since the psychological game manipulates others to accept the managers' goals as their own. In fact, though, this collective work easily becomes an end in itself and the condition in which the politics of the organization overwhelms its purposes.

Moreover, managers are extremely sensitive to power and consequently feel insecure about their power base. This insecurity is exacerbated when professional managers own few shares in the business they manage and have only modest personal wealth. They become dependent on their income, which provides an excellent standard of living, but the dependence makes them vulnerable. Managers, therefore, calculate their relative advantage. They become precise in thinking about their job and discipline themselves to do what is necessary to secure favorable judgments from the constituencies that count. The main objective of the manager is to control his boss and the staff executives who assist in evaluating performance. Obviously, the operating executives often feel vulnerable to staff who achieve power through information. To secure a power base requires the ability to lessen vulnerabilities and to reverse the normal dependency flow.

One group president working in a highly diversified conglomerate mastered the art of marshaling power in the interest of his autonomy. He understood the CEO's strategy of sheltering earnings and recognized that the corporation depended upon his group's earnings and cash flow to make the strategy work. During corporate presentations he emphasized his group's performance, stressing through charts and graphs the proportion of annual cash flow it contributed to the corporation. Simultaneously, he stressed the openness of his group to corporate scrutiny. For example, he issued invitations to corporate staff to visit his group and study its operations. During directors' meetings he humorously, but pointedly, urged the chairman and CEO to convene the board at his group's headquarters. Yet, he also made clear that he would brook no interference in managing his business. Through his staff's voluminous reports, he rebuffed attempts to create centralized purchasing. To have promoted this initiative in the face of the group's complex internal study would have more than absorbed the corporate staff's time for a year or more. The chairman-CEO soon got the message that they were engaged in the classic trade-off: the group's performance in exchange for a hands-off policy. The corporation as a whole in turn lost the value of exchanging ideas and the potential benefit of enriched thinking at both the group and the corporate levels.

In the typical dependency flow executives with less power are dependent on those who have more. Power holders control the resources necessary to get a job done. To maneuver the flow of resources, the less powerful individual must know what the power figures need and then bargain with the promise to meet their needs in exchange for the necessary resources. Once a manager knows what the powerful constituents need and gets them to commit resources, the dependency flow will reverse. As soon as the manager delivers what has been promised, the manager's power base is strengthened and can be used in the future to persuade and control.

Ideally, a professional manager would like to enter a business at a time of crisis when there is a reasonable opportunity to resolve it. To outsiders, this task seems formidable, but in fact it is not, provided the manager approaches the job with the utmost clear-sightedness. It is a cardinal rule not to take jobs that are "no-win" situations. The best jobs are those that allow a variety of ways to win, for example, being able to sell a losing subsidiary if profitability cannot be restored through cost reduction or sales promotion.

Smart managers know that they do not have to invent the programs that will be credited to them and that, especially in times of crisis, there are people who have a plan to correct problem conditions. The so-called turnaround situation often results from plans already in existence and seldom from programs that have to be invented or brought in from the outside.

Ron Dolbin, the newly appointed CEO of Rockford Savings and Loan, accepted the job out of a sense of community obligation. Dolbin, a successful manufacturer, knew nothing about banking. He met with the bank's officers and discovered that the controller had a clear picture of what was wrong and how to solve the problem. The chief loan officer had managed to infect the bank's loan committee with his enthusiasm for speculative loans, which subsequently turned sour. By simply taking deposits and investing cash in highly liquid, safe securities, the bank would have made profits through the small spread between interest paid and earned. The controller presented a simple plan for liquidating the bad loans over a reasonable period of time. He outlined a role for the new CEO—bringing in fresh deposits through his prestige and standing in the community. Dolbin appointed his controller to the job of chief operating officer, followed the plan outlined, and enjoyed enhanced prestige as the person responsible for the turnaround.

When executives are strong on process and weak on substance, they rely on knowledgeable insiders to design a particular course of action. Once managers determine which insiders have a workable program, they can support their solution and form a coalition with them. Since the managers are the means by which the insiders' ideas can be actualized, reciprocity is established: In exchange for the insiders' loyalty, the managers endorse their programs. In the course of this endorsement, the programs become the managers'. If they are successful, the managers are given sole credit. To build coalitions, managers must amply reward other people and make them visible to outside constituents. Managers know they will enhance their power base if they distribute reward widely among members of their inside coalition.

While managers expose their coalition to outside constituents, such as the board of directors, they make certain that there are no attempts to form alliances between board members and inside management. The most important preventive is the willingness of the managers to terminate either executives or directors who try to build these alliances. Managers do not equivocate in fear that those alliances would threaten their power base. If the managers have succeeded in reversing the normal dependency, so that constituents need the managers to secure what they want, then the managers have the power to threaten and carry out termination.

The way managers think is close to the principles that Niccolò Machiavelli outlined in *The Prince.*[13] Machiavelli formulated his rules for acquiring, securing, and using power in the context of the fragility of power in sixteenth-century Europe, where there were many weak domains and rapidly shifting alliances. A prince had a constant need to protect the little power available to him. Duplicity was less a result of marred character than a necessity for survival. Machiavelli argued that for a prince to be "good" among people who were willing to lie, cheat, and be disloyal if it served their interests was to be naive and to assure a temporary reign. The important talent was to be able to don the mask that suited the situation. Machiavelli was unique in his ability to display the nature of contextual thinking.

In contextual thinking the more assumptions one makes, the greater the risks of complicating matters and obscuring the essential with the trivial. The fewer the assumptions, the greater the ability to grasp the necessities of the situation. The most harmful assumptions managers make are ideologies and idealizations, especially about character. Whether people are good or bad, trustworthy or untrustworthy, is usually beside the point. Some people are clearheaded and capable of calculating interest, and it pays to distinguish the clearheaded from the muddleheaded, since it is possible to negotiate and reach conclusions with the former. With the latter managers fear endless and fruitless discussions, which only make the proponents feel morally secure, even if they are practically ungrounded.

As contextual thinkers, managers are sparing in their relationships. They make few attachments, and above all, they keep their emotions to themselves. Emotional attachments create obligations or a feeling of entitlement that managers are not prepared to accept. Once managers feel that other individuals have a legitimate claim on them for a benefit or reward, the managers' freedom of action is limited by the weight of guilt. Managers, therefore, are willing to accept people for the role they play, but not for expectations beyond the confines of the role.

Working with managers is, in a peculiar way, a liberating experience. Managers do not ask for the heart and mind of their subordinates, but only their performance. It is interesting to examine executives who have become a part of the managerial culture for the first time in their lives, perhaps as newly graduated MBAs or as experienced businesspeople who have sold their firm to a publicly held company. The most revealing moment for these newcomers is often witnessing a leave-taking, as an individual exits a corporation, usually having been fired. Once a person loses his or her position in an executive group that person becomes a blank actor, a player without a role. The loss of role is a loss of identity and it requires that the person exit rapidly to avoid embarrassment to himself and other people. Newcomers to the managerial culture are often horrified when they observe the effects of loss of role. To them, it is as though an individual suddenly becomes a nonperson. They interpret the loss of identity as a result of suddenly released sadistic impulses. Nothing could be further from reality. There is no malevolence intended in this loss of identity. It is simply a result of the fact that organizations operate through roles. Feelings have to be kept out to avoid confounding the parts that people have to play. When organizations operate in a managerial culture, the only claim for attention is the value of the role one performs: Absent the role, gone the identity.

Individuals who lose their identity this way are susceptible to the emotional reactions associated with deprivations. But even then, they are expected to act appropriately in their new, if short-lived, role of leave-taker and to keep feelings under control. Managers make sure that during a leave-taking enough time and compensation are placed on the table to enable the individual to make plans and find suitable employment. Besides matters of equity there is the encouragement, unstated but nevertheless real, to maintain a constant focus on one's own best interests. This focus begins with the need to control emotional reactions. To someone unschooled in the language of emotional control and rational calculation of self-interest, this detachment seems almost unhuman. Again, this perception is only partially correct. It is not less than human, but only a different mind set than one may encounter outside formal organizations.

Human relations on the whole are built on the risk of exploitation. But relationships in managerial organizations would collapse if they were governed by rules of unlimited trust and the willingness to risk exploitation. The safe, and indeed sane, strategy is to calculate interests, define roles, and engage in reciprocities in which people allow others to use their power in the service of shared objectives.

In sum, the organizations run by managers function well and herein lies their main problem. People are not inclined to look for trouble or to solve problems that are not seriously affecting them at the moment. In the words of President Carter's trusted advisor Bert Lance, "If it ain't broke, don't fix it." Because the troubles generated in managerially run companies are incipient and not likely to appear during the incumbency of those most responsible, the maladies act like time bombs that will explode long after the perpetrators are gone from the scene. Did the problems facing the Continental Illinois bank arise during the short-term activity of the people who authorized the oil loans that went sour and led to the $2 billion of nonperforming loans? A cancerous condition that has metastasized travels a long way from its source to the destination that finally causes death.

Managers can unconsciously hide problems from themselves and from other people. This disguise is neither intentional nor malicious. It results from a way of thinking and acting that is simplistic, attempts to take up problems one at a time as they are presented, builds on the psychology of calculation and compliance, and above all uses politics. It presses people to measure short-term costs and returns, including, especially, the transactions of power.

The question that begs for an answer is whether the managerial point of view is an outcome of the way organizations are or whether it comes from the kinds of people who seek and gain power as managers. Machiavelli recognized the possibility that people make their own universe and reality. In considering the effects of fortune in a prince's success, Machiavelli believed that people act according to their nature. Some are bold and some are timid. According to Machiavelli, if times favor timidity, the timid individual will be judged a success. If times change, then the disruptions and even failures will seem a result of bad luck. In fact, the turn of fortune is really the individual's inability to adapt to changing circumstances because of a fixed character. In Machiavelli's words:

> . . . for, if a man governs himself with caution and patience, and the times and circumstances are in accord so that his course of procedure is good, he will go along prospering; but, if times and circumstances change, he is ruined, because he does not change his course of action. Nor does one find a man wise enough to know how to adapt himself to this; not only because he cannot deviate from that to which he is naturally inclined, but also because, having always prospered while following along one path, he cannot be persuaded to leave it. . . .[14]

Contained in Machiavelli's sixteenth-century treatise are two theories that have come to dominate managerial thinking and practice. What is so intriguing, beyond the contents of these theories, is that most managers do not know they are under their influence.

The first theory, called the contingency model, is that things work in organizations if all the circumstances fit. If you have the right technology and organization to suit the environment, then you will be successful. This model views an organization like a jigsaw puzzle. All the pieces are in front of the manager. The task is to note their size, configuration, color, and texture and then put them in place, one by one by trial and error, until a picture is complete. He or she then can proclaim the program and enjoy the fruits of success.

The problem with the contingency model is that it is vacuous. Of course everything depends on circumstances, but life is hardly a jigsaw puzzle which God, as The Master Designer, has provided.

People must choose and convey to others the substance of their choice. The contingency model exaggerates the manager's conservative tendencies and further detaches him from the substance of the business.

The second theory implied in how managers think and act is behavioral psychology. Unlike the contingency model, behavioral psychology is not vacuous; it is probably the best tool available for predicting behavior. Behaviorism views action as the unit of analysis and hardly concerns itself with studying thoughts and feelings. You observe a stimulus and then watch the behavior. From the results of observation, you derive propositions about the relationship between stimulus and response. One proposition, for example, is that people tend to repeat behavior in the present for which they have been rewarded in the past. If that sounds a lot like Machiavelli's ". . . having always prospered while following the path, he cannot be persuaded to leave it," it is because people have been applying these principles long before the construction of behavioral psychology. In fact, animal trainers reinforced behavior through a reward schedule without ever realizing they were in effect applying behavioral psychology.

Given all of the theories that managers use in shaping their craft of prediction and control, of orchestration and persuasion, the outstanding characteristic of the managerial mind is its programmatic tendency. Once successful, a manager changes thinking and action only after great resistance. Behavior that has been rewarded in the past will be repeated in the present and future.

Because the managerial program asks workers to calculate and respond according to their interests, the result is a state of mind that limits rather than expands emotional involvement in their organizations. As indicated, this limited involvement implies considerable freedom for the individual who continues to calculate and play the roles of the job.

The evolution of management in the United States has been one of extricating business from harsh conflict and tyranny of autocratic leaders. But this history is full of paradox. While moving a long way toward the resolution of external conflict between groups with different amounts of power, the managerial evolution produced inner conflict for individuals. In other words, one source of tyranny has been replaced by another. The earlier tyranny of the autocratic leader consisted of the harsh disregard for the well-being of subordinates. Autocrats have been displaced as the power holders in business. The professional manager has as-cended to the top of the power pyramid. The tyranny, though it may be inadvertent, arises from the logic of calculation and the imperative of control in the managerial mystique.

People in organizations are required to play roles and in doing so to detach their psyche from what they do as performers. The gain derived from this detachment is less overt conflict in the workplace and, at least in the short term, well-run organizations. The cost, however, is the sense people have of being bereft and divided within themselves. This sense of incompleteness affects the manager as well as the worker and staff person, although the headiness of power protects the manager from the ill effects of a divided self for longer periods of time compared with people who have less power.

The malaise of organizations is in one sense a legacy of the past, a product of modernization. The managers may have little awareness of the origins of their roles or the destination to which their activities are leading. There is among managers an optimism, objectivity, and abiding faith in progress, but also a denial of the paradoxes contained in the perfection of their craft. This denial includes the capacity to ignore the errors of omission that result in the slow death of organizations.

Chapter 4

Rationality and Efficiency

*P*robably no figure in the history of management has been more maligned than Frederick Winslow Taylor, the man known as the father of scientific management. Laborers and union leaders, financiers and capitalists, humanists and journalists all attacked Taylor's theories. They perceived in him an evil, which astounded Taylor and his followers. Yet what Taylor proposed through his system of management lies at the core of how modern managers are supposed to think and act. The principle is rationality. The aim is efficiency. And the method is programmatic, which means applying observation, standardization, training, and incentives to achieve efficiency.

Although not a philosopher or an abstract thinker, Taylor held deep convictions about the causes of industrial strife and proposed scientific management as a cure. Basically, he believed conflict was born of ignorance. If neither supervisor nor worker has an objective standard for judging work performance, then their opinions will conflict. Taylor said to them, "The main trouble with this thing is that you have been quarreling because there are no proper standards for a day's work. . . . We make a bluff at it and the other side guesses at it and then we fight. The great thing is that we do not know what is a proper day's work." [1]

Taylor believed rationality could tame industrial conflict and provide a moral principle that would serve humanity well in all aspects of life.

The moral effect of this habit of doing things according to law and method is great. It develops men of principle in other directions. When men spend the greater part of their active working hours in regulating their every movement in accordance with clear-cut formulated laws, they form habits which inevitably affect and in many cases control them in their family life, and in all their activity outside the working hours. With almost certainty, they begin to guide the rest of their lives according to principles and laws, and try to insist upon those around them doing the same. Thus the whole family feels the good effects of the good habits that have been forced upon the workman in his daily work.[2]

Taylor knew whereof he spoke. If it is possible to reduce an individual's life to one theme, Taylor's was the need to control his behavior and his inner world. He suffered severely from an obsessional neurosis and related depressive reactions. But rather than diminishing the man and his works, the fact of his obsessional illness only makes him awesome. He was able to overcome and even use this illness to craft almost single-handedly the monumental work called scientific management.

It is simple for any individual to act rationally under most circumstances. However, it is difficult to achieve and to maintain rational behavior in an organization. Taylor recognized that managing production in large factories depended on establishing a system that would apply rationality consistently. People understood the idea of rationality as it had evolved from John Locke, Adam Smith, and other philosophers of the Enlightenment. For example, Eli Whitney applied principles of efficiency to factory work with his use of the concept of interchangeable parts in the manufacture of muskets. This concept became a cornerstone of mass production and later proved essential to the development of the assembly line. Yet, no invention before Taylor was as programmatically powerful as his system of scientific management.

It is paradoxical that Taylor, who despised philosophers, should implement a program that brought the philosophers' dreams closer to reality than ever before. It is also paradoxical that his elaborate, rational scientific management system evolved from a caldron of irrationality in his inner world and that even today he is denigrated by managerial theorists for creating a program of rationality and efficiency without which professional management could not exist.

Peters and Waterman write about Taylor and scientific management in the management bestseller *In Search of Excellence:* "The old rationality is, in our opinion, a direct descendant of Frederick Taylor's school of scientific management and has ceased to be a useful discipline." [3] They go on to criticize a legacy of false beliefs that they ascribe to Taylor, but that hardly has anything to do with old or new rationality or with scientific management and its inventor. The false beliefs, according to Peters and Waterman, are: To be big is to be better; low-cost producers are the ultimate winners; analysis wins all; plans override zealots; the job of the manager is to make decisions; the job of the manager is to keep things under control; productivity depends on incentives; quality depends on inspection; a manager who can read financial statements can manage anything.

Peters and Waterman are in fact attacking the extremism that grew out of the managerial mystique and led to the arrogance and excesses of post–World War II corporations. There is neither old nor new rationality because rationality is indivisible, timeless, and free of cultural limitations. If their readers were to take the message seriously and discard the principle of rationality and the program of scientific management, real chaos would ensue.

The serious criticism of scientific management is not that it is a program for rationality consistently applied. The problem with scientific management is that managers adopted its program but failed to recognize that it was an incomplete project with unforeseeable consequences. It was neither trivial nor misguided. And it was not without potential for being developed into a humanly acceptable program, although through no fault of his own this aim lay outside the realm of Taylor's system.

Scientific management is a program for increasing productivity through careful organization of factory work. The typical factory of the late eighteenth and early nineteenth centuries was a hodgepodge of activity. Workers performed idiosyncratically. Their supervisors took little responsibility for the design of work methods or factory flow. Instead, they pressed for productivity by intimidation. They assumed it was their right to bully and play on fears in their demands for greater output. To demand greater output without showing a method to achieve it is a situation that can only alienate employees and bring them into unresolvable conflict with authority. This conflict was less concerned with class differences than practical concerns, a fact that Taylor recognized early in his career as a result of his apprenticeship in the factory. He worked shoulder to shoulder with blue-collar employees despite his aristocratic Philadelphia heritage. When he became a supervisor, Taylor refused to engage in the forms of intimidation he had observed. Instead, he proposed to promote superior performance even at the simplest tasks by rationalizing work. He paid attention to processes, tools, jigs, and fixtures in order to simplify effort and maximize results.

Whereas scientific management offers a general program for efficiency, production operations are themselves specific and diverse. It takes highly conceptual thinking to go beyond the specifics of any manufacturing plant to general principles of efficiency. A tour of an oil refinery or chemical works reveals massive physical structures with only a few highly trained employees in the control rooms, who watch instruments to monitor chemical reactions they cannot see. The off-stage activity of the maintenance crew assures steady operation, and their ability to work quickly during emergencies saves expensive downtime and capital equipment.

A food canning operation presents a different picture. Here the work is intensive for a few months of the year when the produce ripens. Seasonal employees arrive at the plant to take up workstations in front of cookers and on conveyor lines. Their productivity depends on the quality of the maintenance crew that steps in after canning season to break down the machinery, clean it, replace defective parts, and put it to sleep until the arrival of the next new crop.

A foundry is a scene of precise worker-machine coordination. When molten metal is ready to be poured, a line of exactly crafted molds must be waiting. The metal shapes that emerge from the molds then go into another production process called machining or assembling. The machining operation is computer controlled today. A programmed tape shifts both the metal object and the cutting tool into a predetermined position. Tool and metal object meet, and metal is removed according to specifications. Assembly operations range from automobile assembly where large parts are fitted onto a chassis that moves along a conveyor to electronic product assembly where micromodules produced at automated workstations are combined.

A walk through a weaving room in a textile mill is a noisy experience. Looms clatter as shuttles shoot back and forth beneath the strands of fiber that make up the warp of the cloth. The looms shut down automatically when strands break. A weaver tends many machines and must constantly move along their banks, repairing breaks in order to resume weaving.

All of these manufacturing operations will be more or less efficient depending on how the work flow is organized. The number of steps must be minimized from beginning to end of the production cycle. Materials must move unidirectionally and should not retrace steps or be held needlessly in storage. The much heralded Japanese method called "just in time" is not a recent innovation; the idea appeared in the methods of scientific management. "Just in time" controls inventories to avoid excess accumulation of parts and work-in-process and to assure the presence of parts when they are needed. Accumulating inventory clutters work space and ties up capital. American producers just forgot inventory control along with other elements of efficient manufacturing.

The genius of any factory is the combination of "hard" and "soft" technology, guided by highly educated engineers, skilled working people, and shrewd supervisors. Hard technology is the useful application of physical sciences. The invention of the steam engine is a historic example of hard technology. The newest example is the development of superconductive materials.

Soft technology is the province of scientific management. It deals with the problems of analyzing products, specifying work methods, designing the workplace, and coordinating the flow of production from its start to finish. Unlike hard technology, which is closely related to the physical sciences, soft technology is only a few steps from artful common sense. For this reason, it may have been a misnomer to call Taylor's work *scientific* management. Science in this case actually refers to observation and motion studies to discover the steps used in manufacturing and to reduce the steps to the minimum necessary. There is no theory and there are no physical laws comparable to, for example, Boyle's law of the relationship of pressure, volume, and temperature of gases that explains the functioning of the steam engine.

People tend to forget that manufacturing is a blend of tradition and invention. The proper blend occurs only when skillful people pay attention to what they are doing, whether they are engineers, workers, supervisors, or managers. When anyone in the human chain loses interest or any technique is inadequate, distortions occur, such as when top managers ignore the care and upkeep of the factory or when sloppy methods produce poor products.

The French have a term for this blending, *bricolage,* and its practitioner is the *bricoleur.* In English it is tinkering done by a handyman. It is learning to make do with what is at hand, finding a better way without requiring a revolution in practice. It is the application of the practical imagination to making things work. An executive of Cummins Engine described the attention to soft technology and its results this way:

> Earlier, we jumped too quickly into robotics on the assumption that the way we got productivity was to eliminate employees. Now we think in terms of work flow: how to reduce the handling of material so that we don't need so much hardware. We found, for example, that we were machining parts, moving them to a warehouse for storage, then bringing them back to complete the motor assembly. We've eliminated the warehousing.[4]

The techniques of efficiency are universal. They apply to all manner of work, whether modern or traditional, performed in the factory or in the individual's workshop. As Professor Theodore Levitt of Harvard Business School argues in a brilliant critique of the theory of postindustrial society, the techniques of efficiency expounded in scientific management can become the means for overcoming the problem of productivity lags in a service economy.[5] He cites as an example the standardization of the work in the McDonald's fast food chain.

> The McDonald's fryer is neither so large that it produces too many french fries at one time (thus allowing them to become stale or soggy) nor so small that it requires frequent and costly frying. The fryer is emptied onto a wide, flat tray adjacent to the service counter. This location is crucial. Since the practice of McDonald's is to create an impression of abundance and generosity by slightly overfilling each bag of french fries, the tray's location next to the service counter prevents spillage from reaching the floor.

While McDonald's aims for an impression of abundance, excessive overfilling could be very costly for a company that annually buys potatoes almost by the trainload. McDonald's therefore developed a special wide-mouthed scoop with a narrow funnel in its handle. The counter employee picks up the scoop and inserts the handle end into a wall clip containing the bags; a single bag then adheres to the handle. In one continuous movement, the employee fills the scoop with the potatoes and then fills the bag—with the exact amount the designers intended.

Nothing can go wrong—the employee never soils his hands, the floor remains clean, dry, and safe, and the quantity is controlled.[6]

Finding a better way is incrementalism at its best. Incrementalism is seeking the next step (not the ultimate step) in improving work flow and productivity. It begins with an observation—perhaps that materials are being produced only to lie in a warehouse, tying up valuable capital and adding costs in double handling and shipping. An observation such as the one the Cummins executive reported produces a sense of unease or disquietude. This emotion does two things. First, it encourages thinking, testifying that emotion and cognition are like two hands washing each other. Second, it encourages communication. The observer with a sense of unease feels urgently the need to talk the problem over with someone, usually an authority figure, but sometimes a peer. The communication leads to effort to define the problem further and to find solutions. A bond is solidified between superior and subordinate to pursue the problem to its conclusion. In that pursuit more work is done and many other people become part of the effort.

But suppose the boss is disinterested and shuts off communication. The result is inaction and a different emotion. Instead of disquiet from a sense that things can be done better, anger arises and then lassitude. People stop caring and lose their capacity to tinker, to innovate, and to search for the next increment.

The reason people in authority lose interest in improvement, and consequently discourage others, is that they substitute the program for the content contained in new possibilities. They lose their acuity for the better way. They fail to observe, and what is more they fail to recognize emotions as a source of information.

The next step never occurs and the tradition of *bricolage* is seriously disrupted.

To his embarrassment, the head of research and development in a high-tech company discovered that his group failed time and again to produce results. He was doubly embarrassed because a special assistant to the president almost single-handedly solved many of the company's critical technical problems in product design and manufacturing. Two conditions accounted for the differences in performance. First, the formal research and development group had become enmeshed in procedural details, such as technical meetings and budgetary reviews, while the special assistant was free to roam throughout the company, tinker in his laboratory, and engage manufacturing people in experiments to help him solve problems. Second, the special assistant had the ear and the confidence of the president of the company, while the research head struggled for time and attention. Talking about work with the president instilled confidence and motivated the assistant to perform, but the research head and his organization lacked these stimuli and suffered as a consequence. As a defensive maneuver, the research head renewed his efforts to build programs and procedures as a substitute for direct engagement in work.

It is an easy step to move from a program fixation to rigid forms of communication. Programmatic thinkers usually like to control the flow of information and require formal presentations, documentation, and set meetings. Their rigidity and formality should not lead to the conclusion, however, that rationality, the quest for efficiency, or scientific management as a rational approach to efficiency is at fault. The fault is in a human failing that is easily overlooked because it is derived from unconscious impulses that subtly affect human relations.

A foreman of a machine shop that was an important arm of an electronic instrumentation company had what seemed to him an eccentric employee on his hands.[7] The employee was a skilled machinist who, in addition, was a master chess player. He wanted to teach other employees the game of chess if they were interested. He posted a notice on the bulletin board and a number of workers appeared at his workplace during coffee breaks and lunch periods to learn. The foreman showed his displeasure over this odd activity by the scowl on his face and other forms of body language.

The machinist observed that the tooling practices were less

than efficient, and he informed his foreman of his views. The foreman took offense and discouraged the man from further analysis of his observation. The machinist became angry, but instead of ceasing to care, he pursued his ideas. When he posted notices on the bulletin board concerning work practices, the foreman told him he could not use the bulletin board for such purposes. The machinist then constructed a small bulletin board near his workstation for displaying his ideas. The foreman and the machinist exchanged angry words and the last word came from the foreman, who said, "You're fired!"

It is probably asking too much of people engaged in production to become acute listeners, sensitive to nuances of expression that might contain new possibilities. For many production managers, perceptions and thinking tend toward the familiar and shy away from novelty. Such is the case with the foreman. What was real for him was authority and the orderliness of expectations surrounding his position. The chess-playing machinist violated these expectations so that the foreman had to cope with his rage and ignore the new possibilities this employee presented to him. Never mind that the chess player might have been correct in his criticisms of production methods and therefore an advocate rather than an enemy of efficiency and productivity. He violated the order contained in position and authority.

Clearly, the machinist had a dual agenda: to improve productivity and to flout authority. Reciprocally, the foreman had a choice, either to focus on efficiency or to contest the challenge to his authority. In either choice there was no real threat to the foreman. What was real was the threat to his sense of order. In microcosm this anecdote from a machine shop reveals the incompleteness of scientific management, which is central to the issue of the managerial role and efficiency. Managers from the time of Taylor to the present day have been unaware that they were using an incomplete system. Had Taylor's work been successfully concluded, the story of America's competitive position would be entirely different from the one we are witnessing today. But to construe the incompleteness as a claim that it should be abandoned is tantamount to throwing out the baby with the bath water.

The great pioneers of management, such as Alfred Sloan, never fully comprehended the intention of scientific management. In Taylor's vision it was a method for resolving conflict in the workplace as well as a means of assuring improved productivity. He would not have one without the other. His passion for industrial harmony and the rapprochement of management and worker is reflected in Taylor's testimony before a congressional committee investigating scientific management.

> I was a young man in years, but I give you my word I was a great deal older than I am now with worry, meanness, and contemptibleness of the whole damn thing. It is a horrid life for any man to live, not to be able to look any workman in the face all day long without seeing hostility there and feeling that every man around one is his virtual enemy. These men were a nice lot of fellows and many of them were my friends outside of the Works. This life was a miserable one and I made up my mind either to get out of the business entirely and go into some other line of work, or to find some remedy for this unbearable condition.[8]

The practitioners of management who followed Taylor construed the project narrowly. They concentrated on the structural aspects of the program and organizational practices, such as decentralization and management control. Consequently, two problems inherent in the modernization of work remained. The first was restriction of output, or resistance to rational programs, and the second was the separation of responsibility and authority.

Taylor's years as factory apprentice and machinist brought to his attention a common practice he called "soldiering," which social scientists later called "restriction of output." Simply put, the practice was to limit output to a level chosen by consensus among workers. Unfortunately, Taylor too quickly concluded what this practice meant. As most rationalists would, he concluded that the practice grew out of a cognitive limitation that affected management and workers equally. He did not believe that workmen were necessarily lazy or that they were trying to cheat their employers. He felt that they simply did not know what was expected of them and there was no objective standard to guide their behavior.

The phenomenon of restriction of output needs a more complicated explanation than worker ignorance. Individual excellence is admired when it seems god-given and individually honed and when it is not a threat to anyone, as in the performance of an athlete. Excellent performance rarely shows in factory work, but when it does, it can easily seem threatening to others. If one worker produces well above the norm, management may calculate that fewer workers are needed to produce a given amount of work and may fire some employees. Or, even if workers are not deprived of their livelihood, they may be expected to perform at a higher level or will look inferior to authority. In the face of this threat, workers form tight groups that practice restriction of output. This solidarity is supportive to the group as a whole, granting it power in relation to authority; it is also intimidating to members of the group, using peer pressure to keep individuals from excelling and thereby harming others.

Taylor identified restriction of output as a factory practice, but it existed long before he put on work clothes. The persistence of the practice testifies to the need people feel to control their environment with whatever tools are at their command. The fact that Taylor encountered resistance to his ideas from factory superintendents as well as blue-collar workers testifies to the ease with which rational programs can become distorted in the politics of control.

The second problem arose because Taylor's program of scientific management reorganized the factory and placed it in the hands of a new corps of specialists, called industrial engineers or efficiency experts. These experts were responsible for all aspects of production methods and seriously shifted the balance of power in the factory away from supervisors to themselves. With the rise of labor unions, the power of supervision deteriorated further and created a disparity between responsibility and authority. Supervisors are responsible for the flow of production, but they lack the authority to give their directives force. They are not permitted to design the plan for work flow, and typically they are not allowed to do more than approve standards of performance, since these activities belong to the specialists. If a supervisor does not go along with projected work methods or production standards, the burden is on him or her to prove error. Most supervisors lack the time and expertise to engage specialists in disputes about methods and standards. Having neither the conviction based on experience nor the tools to control the organization of work, factory supervisors become passive. They usually accept what is presented to them. Their task is their own survival, which further distances them from the people they are supervising.

To make matters worse, the higher echelons of manufacturing management have forgotten about the importance of supervision "in the trenches." They have been so busy defending themselves from marketing people who want more products in the line and from staff people who want reports that the linkage in authority, from front-line supervisors to top management, has eroded even beyond the effects of efficiency experts.

As David Halberstam pointed out in his account of the rise of the Japanese automobile industry and the decline of the American automobile industry, an implicit accommodation between organized labor and management occurred.[9] This accommodation further eroded the ability of manufacturing management to complete the project that Frederick Taylor started. There was no need to solve the problem of worker productivity since it became dormant in the institutional practices of corporations and organized labor. Following World War II, the idea gradually took hold: Instead of conflict, why not accommodation? The cost of labor increases with no concomitant productivity increases could easily be passed on to the consumer who was hungry for goods and services. This accommodation expressed the calculus of rationality in new ways. Figure the cost of conflict, as it has been traditionally expressed through strikes and slowdowns, with loss of income for both the working person and the corporation. Against that alternative, accommodation, with its increased costs and lowered productivity, seemed preferable for both sides, at least in the short term.

In the practice of accommodation, the labor movement was smart enough to stick to economic issues and to relinquish the aim of controlling the workplace. Indeed, Alfred Sloan proudly reflected that in the decade of labor-management accommodation following the 1946 strike at General Motors, management prerogatives remained intact.[10] Beyond preserving these prerogatives, management limited its aim to strike-free business.

In the course of this narrow exchange, the tradition of innovation and improvement fell by the wayside. Neither management nor labor wanted to revive this tradition, if they were even conscious of it. The latent problems resulting from the unfinished project of scientific management may have been repressed, but they have not disappeared. The motivation to work has been transformed from the desire to do better to a struggle for power in which the contending groups have multiplied. It is no longer contention between institutionalized labor and management. Within management itself, power issues dominate interaction. Technologists fight manufacturing people who fight marketing and financial people, and the supervisors make sure that they have a ringside seat, well away from the danger of being struck by a stray blow, but close enough to marvel at the maneuverability of all the contenders.

Perhaps the most devastating aspect of this failure to complete the work of scientific management is the denigration of know-how. Increasingly, top management has engaged in an internal power struggle with its own people who are supposed to be running businesses and factories by placing staff people into line jobs. Typically, top management mistrusts the heads of all operating divisions, including those at plants where products are made. To assure the link to these decentralized power centers, high-level staff people, young but seasoned in corporate maneuvering, are sent out as division heads. In these line positions they are responsible for results. But since they do not have either experience or the expertise in the field of sales or manufacturing, they bring no value to the job, except for the possible claim that they have the ear of top management and can get a fair share of the resources that get distributed for capital investment. This claim is clearly political. While it may induce the appearance of a cooperative attitude (after all, how many people are willing to turn their back on the possibility of more funds?), there is no mistake in the judgment that the alliance comes from politics and not from a shared understanding of what it takes to make and do things better.

Before its transformation from an industrial conglomerate into a service company, the Ogden Corporation experienced the problems typical of a company that relies on staff as a source of line managers and subordinates know-how to the need for top managers' control. Repeatedly, the staff executives sent out to head operating divisions could not overcome their lack of experience with product-market—oriented activities and their personal anxiety in taking charge. As divisions failed to produce results, the division heads became increasingly anxious and began casting about for magical solutions to their problems, such as wild product changes.

In its transformation, the Ogden Corporation did more than divest industrial products divisions. It also changed its philosophy to marry authority and competence, reducing staff involvement and freeing executives at all levels to identify and solve problems. The new Ogden emphasized practical rationality and diminished organizational politics.

Those who criticize scientific management as an outmoded rationality had better take a second look. Even though it is true that Taylorism contributed to the deterioration of factory supervision by centralizing methods in a new function called "industrial engineering," this shift in the balance of power was inadvertent. Taylor was apolitical in his consciousness and had no interest in displacing or promoting power for any particular group. The worst that can be said about the proposal for scientific management is that it was and probably continues to be naive. But it was founded on a love of manufacturing and a humane desire to do things better. And it offered a revolutionary program for institutionalizing efficiency, which before Taylor's time did not exist. Taylor freed productivity from its total dependence on hard technology and, potentially, gave common sense a channel in the large factory.

A revival of the tradition of doing things better is badly needed today, not only in manufacturing, but also in many labor-intensive businesses such as retail goods and services. Those businesses that will make it in the marketplace will do so because they are efficient and have made efficiency congenial to human beings. Learning how to distribute goods and services over large geographical areas and how to please consumers with value at the same time requires the application of knowledge that may at first seem remote from machine shops, foundries, and assembly lines. Yet the origins of those abilities are plain: learning to cut metal efficiently in factories.

Cecelia Tichi, in her fascinating study of technology, literature, and culture, provides a clue that may help explain the distortions that have prevented the generalization and humanization of efficiency.[11] There is an irrational substrate that can easily engulf rational aims and methods. The substance of this irrational substrate is anxiety about time and money. Its crucial theme is the equation that time is money. The fear of wasted time that cannot be recovered and wasted money that will take more time to regain generates at the surface a grim seriousness that is particularly distressful because it is incessantly demanding.

Instead of talking with one another, bosses project their anxiety onto their subordinates, who in turn respond with evasions and off-the-mark excuses. Bosses complain, cajole, and in other ways project their fears that time is passing, money is going down the drain, and bad things are going to follow the inherently sinful waste of time and money. While this fruitless interchange continues, work falters and the ideal of doing things better disappears instead of becoming the force that unifies men and women to find ways to solve real problems.

Some will argue that the conflicts arising from the obsession over the waste of time and money are holdovers from the old world of smokestack industry, with its "gear and girder" mentality. These same observers describe the modern factory as a product of knowledge-based work, in which people at all levels are paid for thinking and not for expending physical energy. In this era of knowledge-based industry, there should be equality in power, and therefore less conflict. While only time will tell, there is reason to believe that this view is naive. Without a change in ideas about human nature and the conditions that bring about productive cooperation, the vision in back of the quest for efficiency will remain just a vision instead of a source of energy in doing things better through mutual effort.

Chapter 5

Cooperation

A merican society is in deep conflict about its industrial and human relations. It values individuality, yet it has crafted an industrial system that requires cooperation to keep the apparatus running. It values equality, yet its corporations depend on a hierarchy to make them effective. Hierarchy works only when a bond of confidence exists among people at different levels of status and power, yet the degree of distrust of authority in business, as well as in other organizations, is high. Given the history of industrial strife in the United States, this is understandable.

In recent studies of the American automobile industry, mistrust between management and labor ranks high as a cause of the decline of productivity and product quality.[1] The narration of the famous battle of the Overpass, with pictures of a bloody Walter Reuther, UAW president, stands as a reminder to students of the industry of the violent struggle in the 1930s between the unions and management over the right to organize. Unlike the situation in Japan, labor relations in the United States were until relatively recently grounded in mutual suspicion and hostility.

Scientific management's solution to transforming conflict into cooperation is not to eliminate hierarchy and inequality in status, but to make all members of an organization equally subordinate to the principle of rationality. Superior and subordinate alike are supposed to be committed to the goal of consistently applied principles of efficiency. Within that frame of reference one person is not exerting power over another in directing behavior, but role and task are defined by the objective requirements of efficiency. Taylor's vision was, and continues to be, formidable. However, for scientific management to succeed in eliciting cooperation, people have to believe in its objectivity and fairness. They have to believe that it advances everyone's best interests. Posing the problem this way shifts the focus from the politics to the psychology of industrial and human relations. The necessity for cooperation remains, but the diagnosis of the failure of cooperation to occur changes, as does the cure.

From the political practice of Mahatma Gandhi, much can be learned about the transformation of conflict to cooperation. When there are deep resentments, mistrust feeds on itself to generate hostility. Gandhi used passive resistance to simultaneously embrace his enemy while engaged in overthrowing a powerful adversary. Perhaps Gandhi learned this lesson from his adversary in the textile mills of Ahmedabad, where he organized a strike in 1918.[2] The Sarabhai family, who were leading mill owners, often helped the strikers by feeding them while opposing their aims. This principle of inclusion applies in situations where an adversary today is also a partner tomorrow in some common endeavor.

In the early 1920s George Elton Mayo, an academician from Australia, journeyed to the United States to lecture on industrial relations and philosophy. Mayo deserves to be called the father of the human relations movement in industry. Like Taylor, he offered a visionary's solution to the problem of industrial cooperation, although his vision differed significantly from scientific management. He and Taylor were also alike in that both men took organized work as the object of their studies, but neither man could live comfortably and productively in real organizations. They were both outsiders and essentially lonely men seeking to solve their personal problems through a vision of harmony in the workplace.

As with many great innovators, Mayo's personal history and conflicts gave energy to his work and probably stimulated his interest in the plight of the working man.[3] His interest in psychology stemmed from his struggles with depression and identity diffusion. Mayo, the son of a physician, studied medicine for two years in Australia and, after another try at medical school in Scotland, abandoned his medical career. Although he never became a physician, medicine formed the core of his professional identity. He was a kind of healer, initially to individuals, but ultimately to society. Colonel Frank Urwick, who was one of the leading management specialists of the 1930s, referred to him as "Doctor Mayo" in discussing the human relations solution to industrial problems. Mayo enjoyed the title.

Mayo had remarkable acceptance among medical practitioners who invited him into their clinics and referred patients to him for treatment of mental disorders. He had little formal training or qualifications for psychotherapeutic practice. Certainly, the first two years of medical school, especially during his years of study, provided little systematic inquiry into mental illness, let alone guided practice in diagnosis or treatment. Whatever he knew came from self-training.

After leaving medical school for a second time, Mayo took work in a home for aged and indigent workmen. His formal job was to teach. His self-defined job was to study the connections between emotional states, patterns of thinking, and people's capacity for work.

To achieve his real purpose, Mayo conducted interviews in which he elicited information on the individual's life situation, personal history, and apparent disturbances in thoughts and emotions. For this work, Mayo was highly regarded by staff and clients alike because of his remarkable capacity to take an interest in another human being. He was naturally gifted as a listener and could easily evoke confidence through his attentiveness and ability to withhold judgment. In clinical psychotherapy, withholding judgment means not registering approval or disapproval of what a patient says. To listen is to accept the other person's communications with the seriousness with which they are offered. Sensing such unconditional acceptance, the speaker will feel increasing interest in exploring and presenting inner thoughts and feelings.

Mayo discovered other consequences of his skill in listening. The relationship of the interviewer and the interviewee, particularly when it has the overtones of a medical situation, produces effects that may go well beyond the ostensible reason for conducting the interview. For example, the interviewee may experience a kind of cathartic release, or "blowing off steam." The idea of catharsis was not new at the time that Mayo conducted his interviews. Although it was discredited as a method of curing mental illness, Mayo, along with other practitioners of psychotherapy, found that it did provide temporary relief.

Another aspect of the interviewing method, which Mayo perhaps understood but did not make explicit in his theories, is the influence a sympathetic listener may gain in the life of the other person. Long before Mayo, this influence had been recognized first as "suggestibility" and later as "transference." In certain cases the interviewee responds to the attentiveness of the listener by vesting confidence and even power in him or her. The interviewer can make suggestions and the interviewee will be inclined to follow these recommendations, sometimes with beneficial, if temporary, results. The power of suggestion is particularly strong when the interviewee is attracted to the interviewer. Sometimes the attraction is induced because the interviewer seems like a kindly parent who stands ready to grant permission to the interviewee to do what he or she is aching to do, but cannot do because of personal restraints and inhibitions. In other cases the attraction is sexual, which frequently leads to the idealization of the interviewer. Whatever the source of attraction, suggestibility results in one person's gaining considerable influence over the thoughts and actions of another.

Mayo believed that the interview method could be applied to industry as a means of promoting cooperation at all levels of the organization.[4] On the surface, it would appear that Mayo's proposal for introducing the interviewing method in industry was intended to tranquilize the work force by the seduction of sympathetic listening. Indeed, many labor leaders and sociologists attacked Mayo's theories and called the practical application of his work "cow sociology." There was only one attempt to use interviewing in a personnel program. Western Electric Company introduced it under Mayo's general direction, but it was abandoned, probably because it lacked clear purpose, showed few results, and came under severe criticism as an antiunion practice.[5]

A more detailed examination of Mayo's work presents a subtler picture of his aims and methods. It is a case in which research and theory leap far ahead of practical application. Mayo's purpose in conducting interviews became part of a larger effort to understand, as well as to promote, the conditions that would bring about cooperation in the workplace.

Mayo's research linked the human relations of employment to the causes of mental disturbances in individuals. These disturbances appeared in the form of reveries accompanied by feelings of guilt and diminished self-esteem. The basic causes of these disturbances were the social isolation of work and the repetitiveness of physical activity in mass production. A single worker was part of the overall labor crew, but without requiring concentration or the use of well-developed skills, the work induced a sense of detachment in his or her consciousness. As a result, the normal tendency for cooperation fell victim to the pathology of the isolated individual.

For Mayo, spontaneous cooperation was the normal condition for individuals engaged in the division of effort. Its absence represented illness, which appeared in the form of symptoms such as individual depression (more commonly recognized as boredom and fatigue) and collective unrest and strife.

Mayo's argument began with the problem of worker fatigue. Mayo's experience in interviewing and his reading in psychiatry had already convinced him that one could not isolate a single phenomenon such as fatigue and correlate it with levels of production. Fatigue is not a simple result of the expenditure of physical energy. The notion that the workers are a reservoir of energy that they expend as they perform and that could be managed to produce higher productivity and well-being ran counter to Mayo's perception of work as a complicated mental process grounded in self-image and social membership.

The procedure for eliminating symptoms of malaise, such as fatigue and boredom, and for restoring the natural tendency for cooperation was to strengthen the ties of membership in the small group and the larger corporation. Interviewing was an indirect method of creating a tie between the individual worker, the group of which he or she was a part, and the company as a whole. Another method was introducing rest periods in which workers were encouraged to communicate with one another and, more important, to establish a positive link to authority.

This positive link could result from more effective supervisors. As the immediate representatives of authority, supervisors could represent rationality, fairness, consideration, and competence as images with which workers could identify. To identify means to incorporate within one's own psyche the representation and images that may be portrayed in another individual, a group, or a corporation. An identification with authority would evoke the cooperative tendencies inherent in human beings.

The case files of the Harvard Business School are bursting with studies that show the consequences of failed identification with authority. One in particular is a classic case involving the introduction of a new method of core making in a foundry.[6] The new method, consisting of innovations in hard and soft technology, was introduced before the workers were prepared for the changes. The company had a history of disputes over work standards and piece rates, and the workers immediately opposed the new methods because they felt the rates were unfair and would result in lost income. The supervisors withdrew from the conflict. They feared taking a position about the rates, although interviews with them revealed that they, too, believed the time studies to be faulty and the rates poorly set. The worker opposition led to job transfers, shutdowns, poor quality, lower production, and loss of promising technological improvements. The company began with an antagonistic relationship between management and workers, and the experience with new methods threatened to encase these relationships permanently in a mood of dark hostility.

Participation is also a method for inducing cooperative attitudes. Quality circles, used extensively in Japan, begin with favorable attitudes toward authority. All employees identify with the company which, in turn, is supposed to look after its employees with programs such as guaranteed employment. Assembling work groups into quality circles helps to reduce the isolation inherent in mass production, and participating in improving the quality of output potentially enhances self-esteem and status in the immediate group. An already strong foundation of cooperation in Japan is expanded through participatory practices.

Mayo's grand vision of spontaneous cooperation never became a reality in the United States. It is an oversimplification to suggest that the reasons for this failure lay in Mayo's psychiatric orientation. Although neither management nor labor officials viewed the problem in the same terms, Mayo sufficiently disguised his basic ideas so that he appeared as a humanistic social scientist rather than a psychiatrist. His sparse writings were mainly addressed to a general audience, including managers, and he tried to write in a popular style. In his one technical book he discussed his theory of work and mental illness, but it is doubtful that the more general audience associated his ideas with modern psychiatry.[7]

Other social scientists appeared to advance ideas similar to Mayo's, certainly with many of the same aims of promoting cooperation, although with varying theoretical orientations. The topological psychologist Kurt Lewin, for example, advanced his ideas of participation through studies of democratic, autocratic, and laissez-faire leadership.[8] This work led to the formation of the National Training Laboratories and the use of training groups (T-groups) to teach supervisors how to establish a democratic group culture and leadership style. Other social scientists proposed new models of management, such as McGregor's Theory X and Theory Y, the former fostering rigid patterns of behavior and the latter participatory and democratic patterns designed to encourage co-operation in the workplace.[9]

The models of participatory management gave birth to the movement called humanistic industrial relations, with advocates such as Abraham Maslow, who suggested in his needs hierarchy theory that any level of satisfaction is bound to produce frustration because of the activation of higher level needs.[10] If Maslow's theory were to be proven correct, then the problem of cooperation would indeed be a never-ending challenge to management.

Management in the United States barely responded to the vision of Elton Mayo and the humanistic psychologists who came after him. Similarly, management turned a deaf ear to the plea of the prominent author of management books, Peter Drucker. In his early book, *Concept of the Corporation,* Drucker subscribed to the ideal of cooperation and urged management to develop industrial citizenship: "It is perhaps the biggest job of the modern corporation as the representative institution of industrial society to find a synthesis between justice and dignity, between equality of opportunities and social status and function." [11]

Concept of the Corporation resulted from Drucker's observations of General Motors, which was until recently the model American corporation, with its well-designed programs of decentralization, incentive compensation for executives, and market segmentation. Industrial citizenship was to be the program for providing opportunities for status and meaningful activity in industrial work. Following Elton Mayo, Drucker rejected the theory that monotony is the simple cause of industrial unrest. Using observations of morale in factories during World War II and the results of the Western Electric studies at the Hawthorne works, Drucker concluded that cooperation depended on reconceiving the idea of mass production in factories. In this conclusion Drucker did not reject Taylor's scientific management, as did many humanistic psychologists. Rather, he believed that studies done at Hawthorne "showed clearly that it is not the character of the work which determines satisfaction but the importance attached to the worker. It is not routine and monotony which produce dissatisfaction, but the absence of recognition, of meaning, of relation of one's own work to society." [12]

Continuing in this same vein, Drucker concluded:

> The major problem, however, is not mechanical but social: in mass-production industry the worker has not enough relation to his work to find satisfaction in it. He does not produce a product. Often he has no idea what he is doing or why. There is no meaning in his work, only in a paycheck. The worker in his work does not obtain the satisfaction of citizenship because he does not have citizenship. For as very old wisdom has it, "a man who works only for a living and not for the sake of the work and of its meaning, is not and cannot be a citizen." [13]

The appeal for cooperation, whether couched in psychology or political theory, evades certain economic and political realities in America. Pragmatism and individuality are values deeply ingrained in the American character. Cooperation in either the language of humanistic psychology or the principle of citizenship contains images of dependency and subordination of individual interests to the corporation. Indeed, General Motors and other corporations, in concert with the labor unions, established formal contractual relationships on the grounds that there is no greater form of mutual respect than that contained in hard bargaining that acknowledges institutional power. A contract negotiated with faith in that institutional power and with the vigorous pursuit of opposing interests offers dignity to both sides and a basis of mutual respect.

Economic incentives are a part of contractual cooperation. The piecework incentives in scientific management generated suspicion that management was out to exploit the work force with the lure of higher take-home pay. Workers suspected that once income rose, management would cut the piecework rates; there was evidence that such practices did occur.

To overcome suspicion of motives, advocates of economic incentives, such as Joseph Scanlon, author of the Scanlon Plan, and the Lincoln Electric Company, which offered large profit-sharing bonuses, tied their incentive programs to group effort and total

corporate performance. Such programs gained only limited acceptance. For management, part of the problem in accepting incentive programs was loss of control over costs and benefits. It was
far more consistent with management practices to predict costs
within an acceptable range of productivity than to face the fluc-
tuation of unusually high benefits one year and reduced payments
another.

Furthermore, management believed that the structure of payments would be less controllable under incentive plans. They
feared arousing expectations that could not be fulfilled consistently and fostering the perception of unfairness in the wage structure. Management was unwilling to risk the possible discontents
arising from these problems, even though the advocates of economic incentives promised more than adequate returns for the
risks incurred.

The truth of the matter apparently lies in the pragmatics of
administration. Why strive for large goals, such as those contained
in humanistic psychology and political theory, when it seems possible to establish an acceptable balance within the legal framework of collective bargaining? There is an inherent conservatism
in management that cannot be overcome by the promises of therapeutic intervention, participative cooperation, and corporate citizenship.

Industrial reformers such as Douglas MacGregor, Abraham
Maslow, Rensis Likert, and Peter Drucker were dissatisfied with
the accommodative approach and the pragmatics of management.
Undoubtedly, they were influenced strongly by the demonstrated
performance of industrial workers and managements acting in
concert during World War II. Their writings reflect the euphoria
resulting from the enormous production that poured out of American factories to support the war. It was easy, and probably correct, to correlate the productivity of that period with the unity of
purpose that produced such dedication and high morale.

Taking the successful example of industrial America during
World War II, these industrial reformers tried to create conditions
that would ensure high morale and cooperation as a permanent
aspect of industrialization. The idea of cooperation transcended
contract and justice narrowly defined. For some theorists, cooperation provided the means to tame impulses and to achieve personal stability and rationality.[14] Drucker ended his chapter "The
Corporation as a Social Institution" with this challenge:

To understand that the modern large corporation is the representative institution of our society; that it is above all an institution, that is, a human organization and not just a complex of inanimate machines; that it is based upon a concept of order rather than upon gadgets; and that all of us as consumers, as workers, as savers, and as citizens have an equal stake in its prosperity, these are the important lessons we have to learn. To make it possible for this new social institution to function efficiently and productively, to realize its economic and social potential, and to resolve its economic and social problems, is our most urgent task and our most challenging opportunity.[15]

The ideal of cooperation in industrial relations should have taken urgent priority following World War II. As Drucker correctly stated, the example of what high morale could do to productivity should have been enough to propel management to duplicate the conditions that characterized the wartime industrial scene—identification with authority and unity of purpose. The work of Elton Mayo and other psychologists provided various theories and techniques for implementing a program of cooperation. Finally, managerial spokesmen such as Peter Drucker offered the rationale for cooperation that it creates meaning and consequently citizenship in the workplace.

One of the most tested occurrences, but least amenable to duplication, is the cooperation achieved in companies where there are charismatic leaders. There are numerous examples, unfortunately, found most frequently in small enterprises rather than large corporations, of the power of identification with the charismatic leader that results in subordinating personal and group interests.

Chomerics, a chemical specialty company in Massachusetts, is one example. Robert Jasse, founder and chief executive, until he sold the business to W. R. Grace Company, was widely known for his hard work, creativity, and dedication to the success of his business. He attracted many able executives and workers who were devoted to him and his ideals. Although he was often harsh in his demands for performance, employees from high-level executives to factory workers accepted the eccentricities of his personality along with his almost fanatic demand, on himself and others, for product excellence and innovation.

Apart from the charismatic effects, the vision of business as cooperative systems and of institutions engaged in responsible and harmonious relations with their environment became meaningless. It was not a vision that appealed to managers. Instead, the appeal of narrow pragmatism, controlled performance, and economic contract has guided managers' actions through most of the last forty years. Since business was providing only basic economic satisfaction, not psychological fulfillment and the sense of citizenship, these needs had to be satisfied outside the job, at least for lower level employees. It is not clear where citizenship is expressed, but the path to fulfillment in the workplace was blocked as an outgrowth of modernization.

Americans have learned to look outside their work for psychological fulfillment. Consumerism is perhaps the most visible form. People have learned to spend beyond their income by taking advantage of installment buying, credit cards, and bank loans. While difficult to document, there is good reason to view consumerism as a nostrum to alleviate psychological depression, the mood that is more popularly understood as boredom and fatigue. Work may be depressing, but as a means to consumerism, it becomes tolerable.

Work without ego-involvement does not require citizenship or participation. The trade-off is clear and only an extension of the contractual arrangement. The only requirement in meeting the obligations of the contract is to perform in the role assigned with minimum competence.

This trade-off worked for a long time but finally collapsed with the decline of America's competitiveness relative to Japan and West Germany. Managers may have become aware that the skeletal contract in place today does not use the potential capacity of people to make things better and to make technology work. The idea of cooperation is to increase people's involvement with the work situation so that they use their know-how to perfect the ideas derived from hard technology.

Paradoxically, this renewed awareness of the importance of cooperation comes too late to permit reviving the old ideas from psychological humanism and political science. When Chester Barnard presented his theories of cooperation in *The Functions of the Executive*,[16] he assumed that corporations were institutions. Barnard described the institutional character of business as cooperative systems. The critical element in this description is continuity. "The conception of organization at which I arrived in writing *The Functions of the Executive* was that of an integrated aggregate of actions and interactions having a continuity in time."[17] Events have overtaken this definition of institutional character. Instead, the portfolio concept dominates thinking about business. A corporation as a portfolio of assets implies just the opposite of continuity over time. Assets may be acquired and divested with an eye on the economics of return. The basic requisites of cooperation are a belief in the permanence of the business and a potential for workers to identify with it and its aims. But this identification would conflict with individual interests when the belief in continuity over time is lost.

The acquisition mania of the 1960s became rationalized as conglomerates in which diverse businesses could be assembled under one corporate umbrella. But almost by its definition, a conglomerate operates in a marketplace where buying and selling businesses are dictated by price-earnings and debt-to-equity ratios. The activity of raiders in the 1980s was a response to undervalued stock prices, a condition that Boone Pickens, one of the prominent raiders in the oil industry, ascribed to poor management.[18] Pickens was probably correct in his explanation of conditions that made raiding profitable, but the effects on cooperative enterprise were devastating. The phenomenon of corporate raiding nailed the coffin shut on business as an institution.

Large takeovers, such as Allied's acquisition of Bendix and Campeau's successful bid for Federated Department Stores, involve massive amounts of debt which require sell-offs to reduce debt to more acceptable levels. To improve the benefits of economies of scale, duplicate staffs are eliminated. Employees in the swirl of takeovers and mergers often live in suspense as to who will be their new employer, if indeed they continue to be employed. Whatever identification with the corporation existed soon disappears in the face of the dissolution of independent enterprises as they are absorbed, divested, and reabsorbed in new forms of association.

In earlier times, for example, when Elton Mayo was writing about spontaneous cooperation and Peter Drucker was advocating corporate citizenship and statesmanship, the problem was how to bring the blue-collar work force into membership. Today, the resistance to cooperation has broadened to include white-collar workers, staff people, and middle managers, groups that have been harmed in the practice of managing businesses as portfolios of assets.

A new elitism has emerged from portfolio management. Top management and their staffs have enjoyed an unprecedented period of reward in the form of salary, bonus, stock options, retirement benefits, and termination guarantees. Executives who are displaced as a result of takeovers walk away with awesome sums of money. For many, work is no longer an economic necessity. Pride of membership in a major corporation ranks at the bottom of the values at stake in employment. As a consequence, the concern for cooperation and corporate statesmanship has diminished.

In his epilogue to *The Concept of the Corporation,* written in 1983 (almost forty years after its original publication), Peter Drucker reflected on the negative response to his book from Alfred Sloan and other high-level executives in that corporation. Drucker stated that Sloan decided to write *My Years with General Motors* because he felt the Drucker book did not tell the General Motors story as it should have been told. Evidently, Sloan and his associates perceived in *Concept* an implied criticism of General Motors, despite Drucker's admiration for the company and its people.

With a modest reading between the lines, it is apparent that the General Motors executives reacted to an implicit attack on the company's two-tiered structure of cooperation. The first tier consists of institutional cooperation between General Motors and the United Auto Workers. This level of cooperation separates the obligations of management and labor and designs a contractual relationship that promises fair market value for employment in exchange for compliance with management.

The second tier presents a more subtle aspect of cooperation, involving management in general and the upper levels of the executive ranks in particular. Here, the concept of membership and identification has taken hold. Institutions do provide narcissistic gratification for members. This source of self-esteem is exemplified by membership in a corporation such as General Motors, recognized as the giant of industry, the exemplar of modern management practice, and the dominant force in an industry that has impressed itself upon the American psyche.

That General Motors was the insiders' corporation where executives were recruited almost exclusively from within the organization and that it offered fabulous economic rewards for moving up the ranks amplified the value of membership. Yet, as Drucker pointed out in his 1983 epilogue to *The Concept of the Corporation*, something went awry. According to Drucker, part of the explanation was the smugness and self-satisfaction of the executive group. When the press supposedly quoted Charles E. Wilson, the former chief executive of General Motors, saying in effect that "What's good for General Motors is good for America," it captured a reflection of institutional narcissism that was embedded in the mentality of GM executives.

Evidently, there is no means to escape the dilemmas of the modern corporate life. On the one hand, without an institutional character, it is extremely difficult to elicit cooperation, which is a necessity of the division of labor in our economic society. On the other hand, the presence of an institutional character fosters a kind of narcissism that is group derived and institutionally supported. Executives in institutions are not only in the organization, but they are of it. And here lies the heart of the dilemma. People who serve the interests of the institution must have clear vision and must think beyond the boundaries of accepted ideas to serve its purposes over the long run. Yet this institutional narcissism may obscure vision and limit thinking to the long-range detriment of the business.

The reason corporate raiders are so successful lies in their independence from membership. They do not belong and evidently don't need to belong. Yet the problem of cooperation remains.

Unfortunately, despite the threat of competitive disadvantage and despite all the talk about introducing quality circles and other ritualistic forms of participation, the problem of cooperation and the consequences of the deinstitutionalization of business have not yet penetrated the consciousness of American managers. To penetrate consciousness requires the reeducation of a management that turned fear into the technology of control and turned strategic thinking into a kind of game. The entry fee for competing in this game is a demonstrated shrewdness in the mechanics of control and an almost cold-blooded determination to know its psychological foundations and master its techniques.

Chapter 6

Control

*T*he human relations movement failed in its effort to reform management practice and bring about spontaneous cooperation in business. The reasons for this failure lay in the misinterpretation of agenda on the part of both human relations specialists and managers. Human relations specialists implemented a program of psychological conversion aimed at changing managers from task- to people-centeredness and from autocratic to democratic orientation. Managers focused on improved methods of correlating prediction and performance. At first, the two groups' activities traveled in opposite directions. But soon managers discovered that they could use some of the psychological techniques to improve management control. Thereafter, human relations as a discipline and practice changed to suit managerial practices.

The ideas of the late Douglas M. McGregor, a notable figure in the human relations movement, are an example. McGregor, a professor at MIT's Sloan School of Management, was a leading proponent of humanistic psychology's mission to convert management. The book that brought McGregor to management's attention, *The Human Side of Enterprise,* presented, in almost mythic form, a struggle between two opposing world views, Theory X and Theory Y.[1] Although called "theories," the ideas contained in them are not scientific explanations derived from a logical sequence of evidence and inference. Instead, Theory X and Theory Y present two stark pictures of how very different mythical personality types perceive other people.

Theory X types see a world in which people, usually blue-collar workers in factories, are stupid, lazy, and out to cheat their bosses. Naturally, if a manager held the Theory X world view, he or she would behave toward people *as though* they actually were stupid, lazy, and out to cheat their bosses. Sensing these unfriendly assumptions, the objects of this world view indeed behave that way and confirm Theory X.

Theory Y types act from an opposite standpoint, believing that people are good, industrious, and more than willing to trust others, especially authority figures. In response to this benevolent attitude, people behave in a way that confirms Theory Y. They are good, industrious, and trusting of their bosses; they cooperate and act to promote the interests of the organization.

The concept on which McGregor's Theory X and Theory Y are based is that life is a self-fulfilling prophecy. Relationships develop from the assumptions people bring to the situation. Because authority figures from the start have more influence than their subordinates, their assumptions are more controlling. Managers get back the result of what they put in. Conflict results from Theory X; cooperation is the fruit of Theory Y. The prescription that follows is to change the X types into Y types through a conversion experience such as "sensitivity training."

McGregor's *The Human Side of Enterprise* presented a popular short-lived message to managers. The book offered an upbeat homily, implicitly religious in tone and content, although couched in the language of humanistic psychology. But as with similar appeals, the popularity of Theory X and Theory Y faded. Its strongest advocates warmed to the message because it helped them deal with their guilt feelings, which were more related to their personal history than the objective circumstances of their professional life. It seemed to touch a nerve especially in some middle-aged managers who felt uneasy about their power. The conversion from X to Y relieved their sense of guilt, and the training programs offered at least the form of intimacy, if not the enduring content.

Theory X and Theory Y, however, missed the point. These theories were not in harmony with the evolution of the managerial mystique. Most managers are not the simple-minded authoritarians caricatured in Theory X. Neither are they the loving and trusting figures portrayed in Theory Y. The crucial change that had occurred with the advent of the managerial mystique was the development of a new attitude neither authoritarian nor egalitarian, suspicious nor trusting, hostile nor loving. Managers had adopted what Richard Sennett, university professor of humanities at New York University, called "authority without love."[2] The authority is detached, emotionally neutral, and grounded in the pragmatics of using people to get things done. It is thoroughly professional.

This new authority expects people, especially managers, to guide their behavior by rational calculation of self-interest and to have goals that promote the organization's and the individual's interests simultaneously. This new philosophy of management also provides a clear path to achieve goals. Add to this formula the crucial elements of measurement and reward to complete a structure guaranteed to link prediction and performance. This structure contains the essential elements of managerial control as they evolved from the fusion of accounting, statistics, and behavioral psychology. Following World War II, managerial control became the most powerful force directing organizations because it co-opted and dominated the human relations movement and acted as the new advocate of cooperation.

Professional management borrowed an important idea from scientific management and applied it to gain control over the corporate enterprise. In personal power relations one individual directs and commands or reasons with and persuades a subordinate to act in a predetermined fashion. In professional managerial relations, the control structure is itself the object of direct attention, detached from any vestiges of a personal relationship between superior and subordinate.

All elements of the control structure are clearly intended to dominate the consciousness. Although seemingly neutral in emotion and independent of power differences, the control structure dictates the framework for communication and the metaphors used to communicate. If language affects the way one thinks—and there is much evidence to support that hypothesis—then managerial constraints on language are powerful tools for regulating behavior. While denying the legitimacy of personal dependency in the relationship of superior and subordinate, the control structure forces a new kind of dependency. Self-esteem becomes closely linked to performance, which is measured in the shortest time intervals possible. In effect, everyone has a report card almost as compelling as the stock market quotations for corporate shareholders. Self-esteem rises and falls in direct correlation with the comparison of actual to expected performance as shown in the report cards issued daily, weekly, and monthly, according to the level in the organization.

Strangely, modern managerial control equivocates. According to the principles of control, no one issues orders anymore, and everyone is free to act in accordance with his or her own evaluation of what needs to be done to further collective and personal goals. But this self-determination is illusory, particularly at lower levels of the organization, and even at the higher reaches of power. The overshadowing presence of the managerial control structure, with its formal budgeting process, financial plans, monthly reports, quarterly reviews, and capital expenditure planning and projections, determines how an executive thinks and what he or she does. Intentionally or unintentionally, the effect is to make authority relations revolve around the management process rather than the content of the work.

In most modern corporations the budgetary cycle begins at least six months before the end of the fiscal year. For corporations on a calendar year the summer months mark the flow of papers from staff to line profit centers. It is a bottom-up, inclusive process. Every unit capable of being measured by profit performance conducts meetings to complete performance objectives for the next year. As papers are sent up the hierarchy, negotiations ensue in which margins of safety become the centers of attention. No one wants to project at top performance, yet outrageously exceeding budget casts suspicion on the integrity of the process. The process culminates in the fall, often with marathon meetings in which major divisions and groups that represent agglomerations of profit centers present consolidated budgets. During this process communication is framed by the structure of reports. Anything else on the manager's mind, such as quality control, impending changes in the marketplace, and new technologies, lacks a context or a language to permit exploration. After this exhausting ritual, ceremoniously concluded with presentations to boards of directors, managers promise themselves that someday soon they will sit down, let their hair down, and talk about what is important in running their businesses.

Not atypically, in one large consumer products company, a newly appointed chief executive officer discovered that her subordinates were meticulous in participating in budgetary and strategic planning, but were emotionally uncommitted to the process.

The driving repetitiveness of the cycle and its stultifying language and modes of communication had turned off the top and middle managers. Although she recognized the importance of budgets and planning, the CEO's problems were how to get people committed to the businesses they were managing and how to provoke discussion of the concrete events masked behind, and badly represented in, the figures. In her words, "I need the numbers, but more importantly, I need executives with a fire in their bellies to accomplish something in their business that will make them and their people proud."

Control is the core of modern management. It has been seen misleadingly as a set of tools, which people may or may not use wisely. After all, you cannot blame the hammer if it falls on a finger instead of the nail. Managerial control, however, is much more than a set of tools. It is itself a world view, which has been integrated into the thinking of a powerful new elite.

Managerial control is also a form of organization, which allots power and carefully defines the uses of power. The decentralized organization is subordinate to formal control and would not have been feasible without it. Decentralization serves control rather than the reverse. Dividing organizations into centers of initiative, or profit centers, became a possibility when managers realized that they could exercise control through a process in which people were left alone, relatively speaking, and still conformed to expectations.

Despite its mundane roots in accounting and statistics, in the final analysis managerial control is social engineering. Accounting is an old art, a medieval invention that provided mercantile capitalists with records of transactions as well as a summary of the state of the business. Modern accounting is divided into two parts, financial and management.

Financial accounting provides information on the state of the business to outside constituents, including investors, lenders, and suppliers, who are making investment decisions of one form or another. If bankers are considering lending to a business, they have to have assurances that the loan will be repaid. In deciding to invest in a business, the community of investors forms a judgment on how the business has fared. Without reliable financial information, capital allocation would grind to a halt, particularly now that investment decisions are based on numerical analysis rather than assessment of the character of the chief executives.

Financial accounting provides the universal language for describing the state of the enterprise, with the accounting profession serving as the arbiter of how this language should be used. Even government regulatory bodies, such as the Securities and Exchange Commission, rely on the accounting profession to provide standards to assure accuracy of financial reports.

Management accounting is used primarily to help executives run their businesses. Where financial accounting intends to describe the state of the enterprise as a whole, management accounting seeks to separate the whole into the smallest units for measurement and evaluation. From the standpoint of management accounting, the enterprise as a whole is of little interest; if the parts are controlled, the whole will be in good shape.

As H. Thomas Johnson and Robert S. Kaplan point out in their history of management accounting, when exchanges were totally market-oriented, there was little need to make periodic measurements of revenues, internal costs, and profits.[3] For example, it would have been senseless to measure profitability, and hence cost allocations, by periods within a trading expedition from Italy to India and back. When the expedition returned to Italy and sold its imported product, the investors could calculate revenues, subtract costs, and recognize profits. The cash was available to restore the investment and distribute the profits to the investors.

Similarly, when factory production relied on contract labor, cost accounting was simple indeed. Labor cost represented the direct payments to contractors, who in turn paid laborers. Only when production became integrated in the factory, and particularly when business shifted away from the manufacture of a single product for sale in a single market, did it become necessary to develop sophisticated cost accounting that allocated fixed costs.[4]

According to Johnson and Kaplan, the elements of modern cost accounting were in place in the 1920s and progress soon ceased. Even the shift from manual to automated systems brought little or no change in the concept of management accounting. The authors argue that while the distinction between financial and management accounting is vital, only financial accounting, or the fiduciary aspects of record keeping, dominates the business scene. Little change occurred in management accounting to keep pace with and to recognize the information needs of managers in global enterprises, in multiproduct businesses, and in businesses where direct labor is becoming a significantly smaller part of cost and investment. It offers no help to businesses that operate with shorter product life cycles and firms that require heavy front-loaded investments in research and product development. The argument explains the title of their book, *Relevance Lost: The Rise and Fall of Management Accounting.*

That the outside constituents' needs have come to dominate accounting in recent times is plain. But it is also apparent that outside constituents, such as fund managers and security analysts, do need the same type of conceptual information as managers to arrive at a real appraisal of the health of an enterprise. The investment community not only wants to assess the current well-being of the corporation, it also wants to predict the future, in stability of performance, growth from within and from acquisitions, and probable payoffs of internal investments in plant, people, and research and development. For these purposes the investment community needs to understand the chief executive officer and associates in top management. Financial accounting reports are not useful in this exercise in prediction.

To aid investment decisions, outsiders must penetrate financial statements to determine the effectiveness of the organization. The security analyst working for investment bankers, brokerage houses, banks, and other financial institutions generates and transmits information to the investment community. Inside the corporation, information can be power; to outside investors, information is wealth. A good security analyst who has a knack for accumulating and interpreting information well ahead of competitors will make a large sum of money for clients as well as for him- or herself.

When they developed the system of internal controls to support decentralized management, the executives of Du Pont and General Motors did not envision the resulting dependency, if not symbiosis, between chief executive officers and the investment community, with the security analysts playing a crucial role in it. The CEO's report card is quarterly earnings and, consequently, the price of the stock. This narrow time span often limits the chief executive officer's vision of where the company is heading, but the report card cannot be ignored. Too many independent investors, such as Asher Adelman, Ronald Perlman, and Boone Pickens, stand ready to make money by acquiring undervalued companies, thereby forcing managements to focus on quarterly earnings and stock prices. Unfortunately, the result of this dynamic relationship between the heads of corporations and investors has been to tighten controls to force the short-term correlation between prediction and reported results. As many writers have observed recently, looking out for the short term runs the grave risk of depleting the long-term earning power and value of corporations.[5]

For operating purposes a corporation consists of multiple responsibility centers. The more clearly these centers are defined and used for planning, supervision, and evaluation, the more managers feel confident in their ability to control them. However, management accounting in organizations with well-defined responsibility centers does not assure control. Management accounting can be just as inert for control purposes as financial accounting. There may be a clear definition of responsibility centers and of measurement of performance, but the result can be the mere accumulation of information rather than control.

What transforms management accounting into control? One answer is in management's state of mind. If the heads of corporations think in reaction to, rather than in anticipation of, events, they are not control-minded. The object of control is to meet problems in their incipient stages. Furthermore, this attitude must permeate all levels of the organization to avoid a situation in which the only active center of control is top management.

Professor Robert N. Anthony, who has been influential in formulating and disseminating managerial control, emphasizes the differences between control as a system and control as a management process. According to Anthony, control as a process is a psychological event activated by top management. As an example, he cites Ernest R. Breech on the reorganization of the Ford Motor Company after World War II.

In the course of reorganizing Ford Motor Company, by 1948 we had set up a modern cost control system and a supplemental compensation plan. Having done so, we were startled to find that nothing in particular happened. We had built, or so we thought, a log fire under the company. But we had not, up to that point, applied the torch of internal competition.

In the fall of 1948 we called together several hundred of our top management men. We analyzed and compared the profit performance of each key operation, and showed how performance was reflected in the supplemental compensation fund. It was quite a show, and each man went out of that meeting determined to put his own house in order. Each man in turn set up a similar meeting of his own supervisors and the process continued on down the line. These meetings were held, and still are, at regular intervals. The results were almost unbelievable.

Our direct labor costs were reduced from an off-standard of 65 percent in July of 1948 to only 6 percent off-standard in 1951, and manufacturing overhead improved 48 percentage points during the same period. We never could have achieved that performance without a real incentive program and internal competition that reached deep into our management structure.[6]

Professor Anthony concluded from the Ford case that:

Action is a sure signal, probably the only effective signal, that management is interested in the control system. Basically, this action involves praise or other reward for good performance, criticism of or removal of the causes for poor performance, or questions leading to these actions. If, in contrast, reports on performance disappear into executive offices and are never heard from again, the organization has reason to assume that management is not paying attention to them. And if management does not, why should anyone else?[7]

All managers have some understanding of accounting, financial statements, and the nature of planning, budgeting, and operations reporting. Managers also have a grasp of descriptive statistics and know how to use averages and ratios for comparative analyses of operations. But knowing accounting and statistics is not equal to practicing control.

In their history of management accounting, Johnson and Kaplan conclude that Du Pont and General Motors brought managerial accounting to its maturity in the 1920s.[8] However, much of the credit for management control's active posture and ascendancy in the corporate power structure must be given to the Air Force's program to manage its huge logistical and operational problems during World War II.[9]

In March 1942 General H. H. (Hap) Arnold of the Army Air

Force ordered Colonel Byron E. Gates to establish a management control system for the Air Force. Gates, in turn, enlisted Captain Charles B. (Tex) Thornton to help him.[10] At the time the Air Force had no system for tracking, on a timely basis, the status of planes, engines, crews, spare parts, and other inventory necessary to keep planes in the air. When World War II began, the Air Force, then part of the Army, consisted of about 50 airplanes. General Arnold called each of these planes by name, to suggest the informality and intimacy of logistics and support.

President Franklin Delano Roosevelt projected a monumental expansion for the Air Force. The problem facing Gates, Thornton, and Robert Lovett, the assistant secretary of war for the Army Air Force, was how to manage this expanded force. The problem was of such magnitude and importance that it could only gladden the hearts of systems analysts. The Royal Air Force of Great Britain had faced a similar problem and had launched an effort to apply formal analytic methods to making tactical as well as logistical decisions. The U.S. Army Air Force also used scientists for formal decision analysis using probability theory, but this body of knowledge, in its rudimentary state of development (Von Neumann and Morgenstern did not publish their classic book on game theory until 1947[11]), did not address the organizational and administrative aspects of decisions. Evidently Tex Thornton believed these aspects were crucial for effective planning and control and that a new approach would have to be taken to solve the problem of managing the expanded Army Air Force.

While Lovett, Gates, and Thornton were studying this problem, a number of people at the Harvard Business School wanted to apply their ideas about business administration to the needs of national defense. Professor Edmund P. Learned and Associate Dean Cecil Fraser traveled to Washington to find out where the talents and experience of the business school's faculty could help the Air Force. They were eventually referred to Thornton, who had been appointed chief of the newly organized Statistical Control Unit of Air-Staff. This meeting soon led to the formation of the Army Air Force Statistical School at the Harvard Business School.

The school was established to train, in a short period of time, new officers who would be the statistical analysts assigned to operational units in the field and elsewhere. They were to become the equivalent of controllers in business. The job of the statistical officer was to go beyond reporting quantitative information on personnel, aircraft, and equipment. The job required "the presenting of facts from these reports and from special studies of other staff officers in such form as to emphasize the meaning of the data and to bring out the significance of the facts."[12]

With this definition of the job, it became evident that the newly trained officers, although young and inexperienced, would wield great power. Their office was the collecting station for important information. But the statistical officers added value to this information by presenting to line officers, who had to make interrelated decisions concerning personnel, material, and operations, interpretations of what this information meant. In presenting their information and interpretations, these statistical officers had to be bright, tactful, unassuming, yet progressive. They had to be sensitive to personalities and politics. One officer, for example, presented a report to General LeMay in which he had concluded that it was inefficient and costly in both men and machines to use fighter planes as escorts for bombers. General LeMay read the report and scrawled an expletive broadly across it. Another statistical officer recalled an incident at a depot in England in which he told another officer to work late on a project that was under way. The next day, the commanding officer of the depot called in the statistical officer to remind him that orders came from the CO and not the statistical officer. Because this new role required the ability to work well with people, especially since little formal authority went along with the job, the training program at Harvard included cases on human relations. The intention of these case discussions was to sensitize the new officers to the subtle relationships between information as power and formal authority and to the multiple perceptions of rights and responsibilities in initiating action.

This work in the Air Force attempted to build a management point of view into the command structure. The statistical officers, who were either catalysts or "point men," acted as day-to-day controllers. It was change without precedent, challenging tradition and practice in the military. It would be foolish to attribute the success of the Air Force during World War II to the management point of view, but its contribution through the work of the statistical officers should not be minimized. The benefits the Air Force derived and the controllership approach taught at the Statistical School and practiced in Washington and in the field had a profound effect on management practice for the generation following the war.

Tex Thornton saw the implications of his experience in the Air Force. He had assembled his own brain trust, and when the war ended, he wanted to keep the core of his group intact. To do so meant finding a place to apply the knowledge and skill put to use in the war effort. Thornton must have scanned business opportunities to replicate the situation in which the Air Force had found itself at the beginning of the war: a large need with little available resources within the organization for meeting it.[13]

He approached Henry Ford II, who was young and inexperienced but by virtue of family lineage was in charge of the foundering Ford Motor Company. The company had been traumatized by the elder Ford's erratic and paranoid approach to running the business. Once the leader in the automobile business, the company had slipped badly and was saved from disaster by the onset of the war and the need for mass production of armaments. To make matters worse, the organization was in shambles, having been run by the autocrat Charles Sorenson and the hoodlum Harry Bennett. Before the grandson of the founder reformed it, the Ford Motor Company was as close to a corporate police state as Nazi Germany.[14]

After taking office, the young Henry Ford fired Harry Bennett, brought talented people on his board to help him, and later hired Ernest Breech from General Motors to be his operating chief. Along came Tex Thornton who shrewdly had surmised the plight of the Ford Motor Company and its need for the talents he had assembled and used in the Air Force. Ford hired Thornton and his group, which included Robert McNamara and Arjay Miller, both of whom would become presidents of the company, and Edward Lundy, who became the power behind the throne.

Thornton's group at the Ford Motor Company became known as the "whiz kids" for their youth and brainpower. The whiz kids exercised clout to a degree unusual for young people, heralding the end of a tradition of business that correlated power with age. Their rapid advancement in the company also violated the tradition that for emotional as well as intellectual seasoning, a person should move through the levels before exercising a great deal of power. If the whiz kids accomplished little else, they helped bring to life the managerial mystique.

Equipped with a few analytical tools and the willingness to use these tools actively rather than passively, bright young men and women can wield enormous power. The staff's source of power lies in their proximity to someone with general management responsibility. In due course this "borrowed" power amplifies because of the curious objectivity that surrounds the tools of control. The very fact that these tools are objective and depersonalized, yet vital in the communications of the chain of command, gives the one who is expert in their design and use extraordinary ability to shape what other people are thinking.

David Halberstam describes the use of managerial controls in the hands of Robert McNamara.

> At Ford it was clear very early that McNamara was not just a brilliant man but a formidable one as well. His special ability was using numbers to tilt a decision in the direction he wanted, which was almost surely the direction his superior wanted. McNamara was devastating in intramural arguments, so sure of his own facts that he seemed without bias, the ultimate rational man wanting only the rational decision. The arguments were often with the product men, who usually wanted to spend money that McNamara wanted to save. Anytime he and his disciples wanted to, they could make a product man feel inadequate, make him feel he had failed....[15]

Turning tools that appear passive in design to active in use is the essence of managerial control. But this turn from passive to active may also threaten the integrity of authority and its intelligent use in organizations.

Tex Thornton left the Ford Motor Company possibly as a result of rivalry with Ernest Breech. General Ira Eaker, who had retired from the Air Force, brought Thornton to Hughes Aircraft, which badly needed his talents for managerial control. Thornton left soon after to head Litton Industries, an early entry into conglomeration. Conglomeration on the scale of a Litton Industries or an ITT could scarcely have succeeded if it had not been for the invention of managerial control as a methodology.

When Robert McNamara became secretary of defense in the Camelot of President John F. Kennedy, he brought the ideology of control. To be an active secretary of defense required some leverage that was foreign to the traditions of the military. It did not take long before McNamara had all the generals and admirals and their staff talking the language of control. Cost-benefit analysis became the watchword as it was popularized in "more bang for the buck." The influence of cost benefit analysis became the center of controversy: What is the ultimate cost of instrumental effectiveness if it masks the crucial issues in making policy decisions? The continuing debate about U.S. involvement in third world countries is part of the larger debate on means and ends in the uses of power.

Managers tend to deny that they rely on power to implement the process of control. With this disclaimer they appear much like President Lyndon B. Johnson who invoked Isaiah, "Come let us reason together," while using power of position and personality to get his way.

How do people reason together under conditions of inequality of power? There is nothing inherent in power that prevents people with unequal status from listening as well as talking, from making themselves available for persuasion as well as attempting to persuade. The fact remains, however, that communication usually flows in one direction: from the top down. Rather than reasoning together, more often than not the superior is trying to channel subordinates' thoughts and perceptions toward a predetermined end. Channeling the content of another person's mental activity is part of managerial control. Paradoxically, the more successful the channeling becomes, the greater the risk that control will break down, because information becomes limited to what the power figure or control mechanisms dictate. Crucial material is, therefore, left out.

Harold Geneen provided an interesting example of how information can be distorted and even omitted in reaching important policy decisions while maintaining all the necessary forms of management control. ITT was considering a large capital expenditure to build a new plant for its Rayonier division. The proposed expansion was to take place in Quebec, Canada, which presumably offered advantages in its proximity to trees and hydroelectric power, both crucial resources for manufacturing. After the company had built the plant, management discovered it had made a blunder. Because of the climate in Quebec, trees could not grow large enough to reach the diameter needed for efficient operations. The new plant had to be closed, and ITT took a write-off of $320 million.

Geneen described this "mistake" as an example of "making the 'right' decision based upon 'facts' which are mistaken, misleading, or overlooked." [16] Geneen also wrote,

> Rayonier's plans were checked and rechecked, the risks and rewards were carefully analyzed, and we decided to go ahead . . . but that $320,000,000 loss could have been averted if someone had actually gone up and looked at those trees before we had begun. Instead, we had relied upon some very shaky "facts" indeed. We had seen the forest, the plant, the profits and not the you-know-what. [17]

A description of this same event in Robert J. Schoenberg's biography, *Geneen,* throws additional light on how facts can be overlooked and distorted within the most highly organized management control system. [18] Schoenberg provides evidence that Geneen pressed this decision on his subordinates who then accumulated the "facts" necessary to support the investment. The management control system did not encourage, or for that matter enable, subordinates to think independently of the boss.

The same conclusion can be reached in the use of information to make decisions concerning the United States's involvement in the Vietnam War. Cost-benefit analysis produced "facts" to show we were winning the war until the famous Tet offensive proved decisively that we were not.

The point is that management control systems easily produce the illusion of control because top management vests great confidence in them, because they are imposed from the top, because they become a lever by which staff people increase their power at the expense of line people, and because the control system is subject to manipulation by those who feel coerced by their relationships with authority.

The process requires reports and documentation to meet the standards supposedly issued in the name of the chief executive, but which staff people engineer under the umbrella of the CEO's power. To cope with this process, line executives create their own priorities. Heading the list is the urgent need to dominate their staffs.

Management control seems to demand the presence of parallel staffs, one at the corporate and another at the field level. Both staffs try to guarantee that the control structure will channel the line executive's thoughts and actions. The two staffs are in constant communication. The local staff, as the "early warning device," alerts headquarters about problems as soon as they surface, whether or not the officers responsible know about it. Staff people in the field no longer suffer the conflict of serving two masters at the same time—the line executive to whom they report and the staff counterpart in headquarters. In practice, the headquarters staff dominates. They are the role models of the field staff and have more to say about rates of promotion than line executives. The path of promotion follows from field staff to headquarters staff and then to line executive positions.

A staff is as powerful as it is near real power holders. Staffs also gain power through expertise in the instruments of control. To complicate matters, the relationship between staff and the line executives who run profit centers for large corporations produces anxiety for line people.

The control systems in corporations are universal in design, language, and use. They exist apart from the language of products, markets, and manufacturing methods. They are so powerful in framing problems and perceptions that they can easily take on a reality they do not deserve. It is astonishing to observe the reality ascribed to these reports and the numbers on them. Control systems easily assume an awesome quality, and the individual who can quote the numbers assumes an awesome presence. It is understandable that Harold Geneen is perceived with this sense of awe, but quite different when a young staff person is perceived in the same light. The presence of the young staffer contains marked incongruities that generate considerable anxiety in line executives.

One of the most formidable methods for resolving inconsistencies in status (and consequently power) is to attempt to gain the upper hand in a relationship. Young staffers enter this struggle with the advantage of proximity to the center of power and expert knowledge in formal controls. Line officers in the field seek to co-opt the staffers and make them singularly loyal to them rather than headquarters. The management control system produces a rift in the fundamental structure of authority, the one-to-one relationship between superior and subordinate. By avoiding direct relationships, chief executives substitute impersonal but coercive structures for personal ties. For line executives to acquiesce and accept a subordinate position in the power relationship is to make them ultimately worthless in their jobs. By acquiescing, executives relinquish responsibility for the generative thinking that makes a business strong over the long run.

But acquiescence is not the only method of dealing with the anxieties that result from the control structures and the incongruous relationships that seem to develop around them. And here lies the crux of the dilemma of modern managerial control. By investing interest and confidence in control structures, chief executives operate by the illusion of control. They are inviting a Machiavellian response in which cleverness takes the place of loyalty and self-interest dominates mutual obligation and responsibility.

The cardinal rules in modern management are to be active rather than passive and to master rather than acquiesce to events. If a manager remains passive in an authority structure, whether in relation to an immediate superior or to a surrogate staff executive, the manager relinquishes autonomy. And in relinquishing autonomy, the manager jeopardizes integrity and career. Those reporting to him or her lose respect, and his or her identification with accomplishment will change. But in seeking to remain in the active position, a line executive must learn to avoid direct competition with either the boss or the staff who represent the boss. The first step in this contest, therefore, is to assure loyalty below to make certain that all of the key players are beholden to the line executives rather than to headquarters staff or some other agent of the headquarters. The temptation in achieving this loyalty is to promise large rewards at some future date and to monitor closely the communication between subordinates and representatives of the central staff and headquarters.

Another rule in this Machiavellian game is to avoid confrontation over different interpretations of policy and management practices. Clever line executives know that the best way to avoid confrontation is to agree to investigate an initiative or proposal from the headquarters or staff.

In one instance a group president was ordered by headquarters to change the name of his group and its various operating divisions to provide a consistent image to the public, to increase the visibility of the corporation and ultimately the price of its stock. The group president believed that a uniform name through-out all the businesses would work against the best interests of the group and the company, because of the value of local identifica-tion in regional markets. Instead of refusing outright to change the name, he invited the corporate headquarter's staff to discuss the program and how to implement it. The group president also initi-ated a survey to accumulate data on the importance of local rec-ognition with diverse names. In the face of a series of delay tactics and the president's capacity to endure meeting after meeting on the subject, the headquarters group ultimately gave up the re-quest. But through all this maneuvering the president appeared compliant and cooperative with the initiative. The cost of the maneuver in time consumed cannot be measured easily, but nevertheless it should be taken into account in considering the effects of this struggle for autonomy between headquarters and field and between line and staff.

Control systems do not simply provide instruments for mea-suring, describing, and evaluating information. They provide the forms for directing the behavior of people. The principle of avoid-ing passivity and assuming the active role causes a rift in the bond between superior and subordinate. Instead of cooperation, there is conflict. But the conflict over control will never be played out in direct terms. The stakes are too high. Because modern mana-gerial control has almost become an ideology, it invites indirect resistance while masking overt conflict. What is illusory about control systems is that the manipulation engendered by the game of gaining autonomy through indirectness ultimately undermines the loyalty and responsibility that are the bases for effective au-thority.

Chapter 7

Professionalism

People exist in a kind of double consciousness, where they act in a situation while maintaining the ability to observe themselves acting. Erving Goffman, observer and analyst of social interaction, suggested the theater as a convenient metaphor with which to analyze this dual awareness of self as actor and audience in social situations.[1] The purpose of the dual awareness is to regulate conduct according to the norms prescribed by the situation. According to Goffman, there are two regions of consciousness when people interact. In his metaphor the first is the region "on stage," where behavior must follow the script, the norms of the situation. The second is the region "off stage," where the players can relax and act spontaneously.

The metaphor of the theater has special significance in those aspects of worklife dominated by professionalism. Nowhere is professionalism more pronounced than among managers, and nowhere is performance judged so relentlessly by the standards of "appropriateness" than in the corporate scene. No remark will bruise the ego of a manager more than the bland comment "You behaved in an inappropriate manner."

For the corporate professional *control* is the key word to describe the expectations governing behavior. In this context control means to regulate action and to be "on stage" at all times, so that what the audience, usually made up of other professionals, sees is the role more than the performer. To control performance means more than dressing appropriately and speaking in the affectless tone so characteristic of managers. It means holding one-self in check and showing no emotions, especially not anger. Max Weber, the sociologist who taught us so much about bureaucracy, understood the requirements of performance. He understood it so well that he described organizational membership as life in an iron cage, life in which individuals are constrained to control their emotions.[2] The purpose of professionalism, with its premium on self-control, is to remove extraneous matters from attention so that work and the discourse related to work can proceed without wasted energy. Even under the most difficult circumstances, such as when a promotion doesn't materialize, the professional is supposed to behave appropriately. Never show hurt, never grieve in public, and never get angry.

Displaying feelings is a gaffe that causes embarrassment to others because their tendency is to respond with emotion. The gaffe is a lapse in professionalism which, if continued, shows a disregard for the standards by which professionals judge others and themselves. Never mind its justification or the spontaneity or the human quality presented in this display. It is still a blunder and a breaking of the code of professionalism, as the following incident from a corporate boardroom indicates.

On a warm spring evening the directors and senior officers of a large corporation assembled for their annual dinner meeting. The penthouse suite, with its rich decor and breathtaking view of the city, traditionally had been the place for celebrating the conclusion of a good year and for reaffirming confidence in the management. This year, instead of a celebration, the scene turned into what was memorialized in the lore of the corporation as "The Last Supper."

After a round of cocktails and a sumptuous dinner, the chairman and chief executive passed cigars and began a morbid recital. A corporate raider had seized control of the executive offices and the board of directors. The CEO was to relinquish his post to the financier and become the president and chief operating officer. More than half the board would not be on the upcoming slate of directors, and one of the corporation's senior officers and long-standing "inside" directors would be required to resign immediately to make room for the financier.

The deposed senior officer was well aware of the code of professionalism. He managed to keep a tight lid on his feelings, and in a deadened voice he began to ask some technical questions about the changes. The chairman responded in an equally flat tone and expected to move on to other matters. But the senior officer persisted and began speaking loudly and quickly with obvious breaks in his voice. After he had devoted years to the service of the corporation and loyalty to the chairman, he now felt he was having his head handed to him. The senior officer used an expletive. At this point the chairman reprimanded him, his colleague and presumed friend, with the Victorian retort, "We don't use that kind of language here."

Work in America is an unsettling experience. The blue-collar ranks, the people who operate the factories, have long accepted technological change, periodic layoffs, and other dislocations as a way of life. What is new is the extent to which disturbing changes have come to affect white-collar workers, middle management, and senior executives. Although corporate America never guaranteed employment and group membership in exchange for loyalty to the company throughout the ranks, as is done in Japan, it traditionally did take care of its management and staff.

A new mentality has infiltrated the elite groups. Instead of taking for granted the many perquisites, both economic and social, that had been intrinsic to their employment, they are now wary, insecure, and angry. The recent rash of mergers, acquisitions, and divestments has destroyed corporate identities and, along with them, the assurance of rewards and the identifications that used to support the egos of the white-collar and managerial ranks. Even the routines of life in corporate offices have been overtaken by technological change. Executives are expected to show hands-on competence in using computers for their own analytic work and for communications through electronic mail. Previously, executives merely dictated to a secretary or used the telephone. While these changes improve efficiency, they also produce stress and subject people to the numbing effect of having to respond to initiatives that occur outside their sphere of influence.

Because of shifting premises and violated expectations, people today are vulnerable to a greater degree to the phenomenon psychoanalysts call "narcissistic injury" and other social scientists call "felt injustice." People are angry and are faced with the problem of coping with a degree and quality of emotion new to them. As the executive who was abruptly kicked off the board rediscovered, angry words are taboo in the corporate office. The lawyers' advice "Don't get mad, get even" might work in the courtroom, but it is hard to imagine in a corporate situation without the use of low-down politics.

The net effect of this emotional state in the offices of America's corporations is further erosion of group cohesion and loyalty. Typical of this erosion is the case of a young middle-level manager who found himself in a business that had been acquired by a large corporation. He was initially angry at having to go to school to learn all the new forms for submitting budgets and operating results that emanated from the new parent. He was further angered by having to explain the business he was in to corporate officers who knew far less about it than he and who also seemed to care less. This young manager understood the corporate taboo and kept his anger to himself. He said, "If you let go, you can count on being bumped from the fast track to the side track, so why hurt my reputation by letting them know I'm angry?" Instead, he became less involved in his work, began looking for a new job, and started a rigorous physical fitness program training for a marathon.

A chairman of a large New York Stock Exchange company confirmed the caution of the young executive in inhibiting display of angry feelings. This chairman said, "If someone gets angry, we are not going to promote him. That's the way of the large corporation today. In the old days when we were entrepreneurial, it was not at all unusual for someone to let go without worrying about hurting his career."

Although there are no objective measures of the degree of anger in organizations today compared with earlier periods, the changes under way suggest that the conditions precipitating anger are increasing. Yet, from another perspective, these conditions are all part of the development called "modernization," which began in the eighteenth century and continues today under the rubric of "professionalism."

Professionalism describes a particular state of mind that supports the modern structure of economic activity. It is difficult to say which came first, the state of mind or the structure. But whichever came first, modernization and professionalism are closely interlocked. The state of mind is an awareness of one's place in the various layers of society and of how one should act and react when confronted with opportunities and problems. In the premodern consciousness, which still affects the blue-collar ranks, the normal state of mind was passivity, acceptance, and fatalism. What is, *is,* and the individual has little capacity to change events that are under way, let alone cause things to happen. In the consciousness of modern management, the professional state of mind is action, where the individual expects to make a difference in outcomes.

Professionalism in management is essentially elitist. The elite are self-defined individuals known by their achievements. An integral part of this elitism is the scientific and rationalistic ethos. Nature is knowable, predictable, and therefore potentially controllable if the individual can adopt a rational attitude. The rational consciousness involves making choices. To choose is to feel independent and capable of looking after self-interests in modern economic and social life, to weigh alternatives, and to compare costs and benefits. To choose rationally, the individual must learn to suppress impulse and emotion. Hence the cultivation of dispassion and the separation of thinking from feeling.

The rules of rationality as they apply to more personal choices elicit uneasy reactions. Utilitarianism is easy when it comes to choices of what car to buy. It is easy to open a *Consumer Reports* and study the costs and benefits of owning a Ford as compared with a Chrysler. But what about "choosing" a spouse or "deciding" on a career? In the personal choices of life the individual soon discovers that pure rationality leaves something to be desired. In fact, calculation in such instances soon appears ludicrous. Beyond that fact, however, there may be an important truth to the notion that in the large decisions of life, a solution can appear only as a synthesis of an intuitive grasp of the problem and the trust of inner reactions. Despite the need for an intuitive grasp of a problem, the expectation of rationality has taken hold for all aspects of life. Therefore, the critical rule "Do not react emotionally" has become pervasive in the professional's existence.

But professionalism goes beyond the rule of individual choices. It is expanded increasingly in relatively new structures. Hierarchical organizations became the rational means to achieve social and economic control over the environment. For this collective control, the individual is supposed to subordinate individuality, at least to the extent of suppressing impulse and emotion.[3]

The modern organization, Weber's "iron cage," constrains individuals to learn their roles and fulfill them without extraneous communication or content, without emotion of any kind, and most especially without display of anger. However, life in the iron cage does not necessarily mean that the individual does not experience emotions while engaged in the work of the corporation. Certainly a person can avoid trouble by not experiencing emotions, but the important requisite is not to express them. In other words, the premium is on suppression of feeling in order to permit the organization to function at its highest level of efficiency.

Weber's work brought forth a large number of studies that showed that organizations are not as completely rational or as devoid of emotion as Weber suggested. Besides being rational, or perhaps because of rationality, large organizations train people to become incapable of seeing beyond the limits of their prescribed roles. Thorstein Veblen called this condition "trained incapacity."[4] Or consider the tendency of bureaucracy to give such weight to its own procedures that people lose sight of the goals which the procedures are supposed to help attain. The sociologist Robert Merton called this tendency the "displacement of goals," where ends and means are thoroughly confused.[5]

These pathologies of organizations arise when thinking is not informed by feeling. If feelings were allowed to enter into play, people would not be as prone to tunnel vision, valuing how things are done as more important than what things are done.

The gap between Weber's description and the sociologists' discoveries revealed much more than the simple notion that the description of an ideal or theoretical type is bound to miss many aspects of reality. The concepts of trained incapacity and displacement of goals reveal more of what Weber's iron cage is all about. The habituated tendency to isolate thinking from feeling finally diminishes the capacity to be realistic. If anything would appear to overcome this separation of thinking and feeling, it would seem to be the combination of professionalism and politics in organizations.

Politics in organizations defines self and group interests that are more important to the people involved than the good of the organization as a whole. People in organizations, particularly at the higher levels of the hierarchy, will dedicate themselves to making certain that they and their group gain power or at least maintain parity in the distribution of power.

At first, it would appear as though the presence of politics in organizations finally undermines the principle of cold rationality and the suppression of feelings. After all, what could possibly engage people more than their commitment to power and its preservation for themselves and their cohorts? But playing politics successfully requires the coolest of temperaments and exquisite ability to keep feelings out of the game.

Machiavelli said it first, and perhaps best, in his treatise, *The Prince*: "... for a man who wishes to profess goodness at all times must fall to ruin among so many who are not good. Whereby it is necessary for a prince, who wishes to maintain his position, to learn how not to be good, and to use it or not according to necessity."[6] Today, society consists of hierarchical organizations as a means for doing business. Friend and foe, colleague and antagonist, are not marked off by boundaries, but can exist alike within the organization. Given the tendency to politicize, the organization becomes a site for rivalries, coalitions, and collusive behavior, all of which are central to power. It takes a cool head and a numb heart to play that game well and to win. Instead of allowing feelings to inform thinking, the politics of organizations force emotions out of the picture. The rule "survival of the fittest" tends to prevail. For those ill-equipped for the coldly rational approach to power, survival becomes difficult indeed. Those who prevail become the role models for successive generations, whose representatives become similarly attuned to guarding their feelings.

The same analysis applies to professionalism in organizations. Although it introduces the ideal of doing one's work well and even contributing to better practice, professionalism also establishes lines of demarcation within organizations. In addition to the hierarchy of authority, professionalism introduces hierarchies of expertise, which tend to fragment rather than bond people's relationships. Professionals think of themselves as performing services for others who are by definition clients. To be a client is not to be an associate or a colleague, least of all a friend. While the professional-to-client relationship, with its reserve and distance, serves many useful purposes in medicine, psychotherapy, and law, it is detrimental to human relations in organizations. The code, either implicitly or explicitly, fosters the suppression of feelings and, consequently, communication.

Implicit in the professional attitude is the notion that the work atmosphere devoid of emotion provides freedom for the individual. Work for a corporation leaves the psyche untouched. A person works hard and follows directives, but is well paid and left alone in a quest for self-fulfillment. The professional's life in the organization also has its compensations. Even though it suppresses emotions and the fantasies that accompany feeling, it does provide the means for attaining the good life as measured by standard of living. But the trade-off is obviously without closure. There are too many instances of individual and social pathology which can be related to the suppression of feelings to let the iron cage stand without further examination. Even in Japan, where emotions of loyalty and group identification are fostered, there is evidence of a lack in the lives of individuals as a consequence of professionalism in large organizations.

A psychiatrist practicing in Japan described what, to him, seemed a new syndrome in Japanese mental illness. He reported a growing incidence of depression accompanied by a loss of motivation in middle-aged executives. Life once rich in purpose and attachment had lost all meaning. The patients felt bereft and seemingly without a method for finding their way back to their roles in business, family, and society. Perhaps these executives-turned-patients could find their cure as the standard of living rises in Japan, encouraging them to be consumers rather than savers. This alteration in the Japanese culture, however, will take a long time. But even when, and if, it occurs, it will provide only a tenuous cure, as we are discovering in western societies. The pressures to choose, to trade-off, and to calculate increase stress, particularly if the route toward self-expression is blocked.

It appears that the conditions that promote emotional reactions are increasing. Would it not help the quality of life in corporations for people to express what they feel? Would it not also be beneficial to mental health, if people allowed their anger to show instead of repressing it with damaging consequences for the individual and the corporation?

Anger arises when a person feels injured in a relationship to another person or to an organization. The expression of anger is not merely a reflection of this personal injury. Giving vent to anger —through words, changes in facial expression, body language, and symbolic forms—has a purpose, which is to repair the injury and forestall its recurrence. If people feel a situation is unjust and their expression of anger leads to beneficial changes, the result is to ensure their continued participation and enhance their self-worth.

Anger seldom appears in situations in which people feel indifferent. Caring about a relationship, common purposes, quality of work, and personal well-being in association with like-minded people leads to anger when people feel they have been injured. The injuries range from having status ignored to hearing unwarranted reflections on competence to being fired. In the workplace an injury can occur when someone is passed over for promotion, or when a corporation decides to sell a profitable division because it no longer fits long-term strategy. If people remain placid under such circumstances, they either are living in fear or suffer from psychological inhibition. Fear that their expression of anger will lead to further injury will surely restrict people in expressing emotion. But it will also cause them to limit their personal investment in the job and the organization in order to prevent the arousal of anger and other feelings. For talented people the solution of withdrawal is unsatisfactory and will propel them to find alternate employment. Those people who have few alternatives survive by becoming apathetic and doing the least necessary to hold their jobs.

Inhibited people face a different problem. They are so fearful of their own emotions that they do not experience anger when the provocations exist. For example, a young corporate attorney once complained that his career had not progressed as he had hoped. As he spoke it was apparent that his wife felt the dissatisfaction and anger, but that for him the complaint was an intellectual exercise. No matter how provoked, he remained bland, soft-spoken, and seemingly without angry feelings. Yet, he described without self-awareness how he withheld information from his boss that would have made a crucial difference in certain decisions. Although he did not experience anger, he used it passively to sabotage his own career, as well as his company in its ability to compete. With neither the awareness of the harm he was causing nor the psychological capacity to take responsibility for repressed feelings, this individual remained suspended in a life of unfulfilled hopes and fading dreams.

Not all anger is beneficial to communication and group solidarity. Some people will invent causes for anger if the real world does not provide provocations. The actual cause for their perennial anger is found in their personal history, resulting in an inability to distinguish between indignation and envy.

Another type of harmful, angry display results from learned behavior. A vice president of manufacturing freely let his anger out in displays both humiliating and out of proportion to provocations. His subordinates were completely exasperated and protested to the chief executive about the abuse they had been taking. This vice president was almost a textbook case of the authoritarian personality, obsequious to those above him and demeaning to those below. He was born and raised in a culture in which authority figures seemed at liberty to treat their subordinates harshly. He had identified with this type of authority figure and became the aggressor when he achieved power. He followed the cynic's golden rule: "Do unto others as you have been done unto." Counseling with him seemed to produce some awareness of what caused him to display anger so freely, and he appeared to be changing his attitudes and behavior.

People who are always angry cause a great deal of damage in any situation that requires cooperation. As a result, organizations impose several restraints on the expression of anger. Anger can flow down the power structure, but seldom up, according to the norms of corporate organization. But the expression of anger downward has to be indirect and symbolic. A manager who has a reputation for showing anger directly soon develops a reputation for being unpredictable, like a loose cannon on a rolling ship.

A manager became angry because his group was not meeting the schedule he had established for the introduction of a new product. Instead of calling the group together, telling them how he felt, and listening to their responses, he avoided any direct expression of anger. Instead, he had his group stay beyond normal working hours on a Friday, spoiling dinner plans and the weekend for many of his subordinates. The message was not lost on his subordinates who knew he was angry. But the symbolic expression left them without a way to communicate what was affecting them and the performance of the group. The manager had complied with corporate expectations of remaining in control of his emotions.

With the entry of women into the corporate world, an experiment began which will give us insight into the pliability of codes of conduct. Women have been raised to experience and express their feelings, while men have been taught to repress and suppress their emotions. One of the mechanisms on which repression depends is reaction formation, or turning an emotion into its opposite. Many men strive to appear masterful, congenial, and unflappable. They are also monotonic in their emotional response, undoubtedly fostering the corporate stereotype of the man in the gray flannel suit. To the individual who almost never acknowledges to himself that he is angry, reaction formation keeps the lid on anger. He smiles too much, appears too solicitous, and wears a face that has not been lived in.

With women joining the managerial ranks, we should see changes either in loosening the codes restricting emotions or in women becoming emotionally constricted like many of their male colleagues. All the evidence is not in, but it appears as though the change is in the direction of their adopting the corporate code. A woman who achieved the position of vice president in a corporation learned that it was suicidal to express anger and worst of all to cry while trying to suppress her feelings. She learned whom she could trust among her male colleagues. One of these colleagues cautioned her to sit on her feelings and learn to "button down." He advised her to come to him when she needed to ventilate her feelings. She followed his advice and remained grateful to him, both for helping her to understand the code of the corporate world and for supporting her in her need to let down her guard from time to time.

The presence of women in the managerial and staff ranks often poses a problem for men in dealing with their anger, particularly when women provoke the anger. Whereas much has been written about problems that may arise because of sexual feelings, anger may be the more important issue in determining whether there will be good working relationships between men and women in the office.

A veteran middle manager had every reason to believe that he was secure in his job and would continue to enjoy professional respect in his immediate office and the wider organization until retirement. Life for this manager changed suddenly from security and self-confidence to anxiety and doubt. He had appointed to his office a young woman whom he had trained in the technical crafts of the job and the methods for getting work done in the organization. She had been a conscientious student and apparently felt grateful for his teaching and support. He had promoted her with the approval of his superior until she had reached the position of second in command of their department.

Without consulting him, however, she began to build independent relationships with department heads throughout the company, leaving the impression that they should deal directly with her for the services the department normally performed. Her boss lost his visibility, which led to questions about his performance and discussion about splitting the department in half, giving him the part with the lesser power and the remainder to her.

The department head claimed he was unaware of his assistant's desire to build a power base independent from his. He did not want to know what was going on because he did not want to confront her, express his anger, and try to reestablish their working relationship. He allowed her to overextend and as a result, she violated the important norm that cautions people to support rather than undermine their bosses.

It is important to recognize that proportion is the key to putting anger to good use. Studies of primate behavior show that the head ape instinctively uses the right amount of what is the human equivalent of anger to bring a lesser ape into line. The purpose is to maintain cohesion, not to destroy it.

Without necessarily relying on instinct, human groups also depend on proportion in the constructive use of anger. The trouble in most cases in the corporate world is that the rule about verbal communication of anger is so restrictive that people adopt a survivor's mentality of withdrawing emotional investment from the situation. The less an individual cares about a situation and a relationship, the easier it is to withhold emotion and communication, and withholding provides safety. To urge the corporate mentality to become more free in emotional expression, especially anger, is to heighten risks. But with risk goes the possibility of gains, in this case, cohesive organizations with people who are committed to the substance of the business.

One of the consequences of the cultural revolution of the 1960s was to make people aware that the suppression of anger and other emotions in the workplace is not necessarily the natural order of things. In earlier generations the expectation that emotions should be separated from thinking and acting in work roles was ingrained and habitual. In fact, this separation appeared to be an achievement of modernization, the triumph of organizational order over individual chaos.

For example, running throughout Chester Barnard's classic *The Functions of the Executive* is a vague unease concerning the tenuousness of cooperation given the frailty of human character.[7] For Barnard, individuals are all too ready to lose control, to victimize others, and to become victims themselves of primitive emotions. The latent objective of organizations is to broaden the capacity of people to work together by constraining them to suppress primitive emotions in the interest of cooperation. Barnard's aim was compliance rather than commitment, because commitment entails the risk that once people begin to care about what they do, they may feel frustrated, angry, and deprived, leading who knows where with the outbreak of emotion.

Barnard did not recognize the secondary and even tertiary effects of repression and suppression of feeling. The secondary effect is the dampening of active thinking about what one is doing. The tertiary effect is either displacing feelings, which often in the case of anger means victimizing someone who is innocent and relatively powerless, or becoming depressed and emotionally ill.

Barnard's advice to the executive seeking cooperation in organizations was to expand and play on the zone of indifference. As we have seen, it is widely understood that people cannot care about everything in their lives; they would be overwhelmed by their emotions and incapable of acting on anything. People, therefore, sort and select. They are willing to let someone else make decisions about activities that fall within their zone of indifference. The principle is to get along, go along, and trust that somehow needs will be met. A sly administrator who is worrying about gaining consensus, which is often mistaken for active cooperation, will try to get people to expand the zone of indifference. As this zone expands, more decisions are within the discretion of the administrator.

Without a zone of indifference people may collapse from stimulus overload or, short of that, become totally inefficient. People who have no zone of indifference have more mental disturbance than heroic involvement in all aspects of life. They suffer because they care too much. But most of us go too far toward the other extreme. We care too little when we should care a lot. The absence of commitment follows from the twofold concern that, first, people's emotions cannot be trusted to remain within their control and, second, that cooperation is so fragile that it is worth the sacrifice of human involvement to secure it.

An idea still attributed to psychoanalysis is that anger bottled up invites mental illness and that releasing the anger purges the individual of noxious material, in a process called catharsis. Freud used the notion of catharsis in the early phases of his work, but he soon abandoned it as the means for curing mental illness because he observed that patients did not recover and that it provided at best temporary, symptomatic relief.

While catharsis is an antiquity of the early days of psychoanalysis, there is some truth to the more generalized notion that to bottle up feelings leads to bad consequences. When an individual airs anger, he or she, along with whoever else happens to be listening, becomes an audience to the material that is being ventilated. Some people are sufficiently reflective that they learn independently, but most of us need to voice our feelings. A sympathetic listener is sometimes helpful, but it is the display of anger, even to an antagonist, that is important because the observing ego of the individual is also a witness. The observing ego becomes the instrument, built into all of us with varying degrees of efficiency, for using feelings to grow as human beings.

A head of a major department in a company expressed her anger to the chief executive officer. She was angry because she believed another department head was not doing his job. As she talked, she became more angry, giving some credence to the notion that anger expressed begets more anger. "I would never," she said, "sit in the same room with this man." Later that day, she said to the chief executive officer, "I thought a lot about what I said and it was stupid. No matter how much I dislike him, and how much he nauseates me, I still should be able to be in the same room with him and conduct our business. I feel ashamed of myself."

Catharsis is a limited concept that does not justly convey the complicated mental act of expressing anger. The presence of an observing ego does not eliminate the need to put the anger people feel into words. Responsible individuals express their feelings in proportion to the stimulus and in the aim of trying to preserve and even enhance human relationships. The function of anger in the corporate context is to right wrongs and to improve relationships, thereby helping to turn businesses into hard-hitting and efficient organizations.

If business organizations continue on their present path of restricting the expression of anger, our society will have to endure two consequences. The first will be reducing cooperation and effectiveness of organizations. The second will be constricting individuals in their ability to grow. The observing ego will be forced to withdraw during work. Without the aid of an active observing ego, people will stop thinking and feeling, resulting in our collective impoverishment.

During the 1960s a rallying cry of the counterculture movement was "to let it all hang out." Anger found ample expression, culminating in street demonstrations in Chicago during the 1968 Democratic party convention. Even the most conventional corporations were not immune to cultural changes that accompanied the movement. Dress codes eased and even emotional expression became more acceptable. Some corporations, including mainstream establishment types such as Exxon (then Esso), began sensitivity training for management and staff to help them become "open" to their own and others' feelings. It was also the time when humanistic psychology, exemplified by Douglas McGregor and Abraham Maslow, was popular in management circles.

On the whole, these cultural currents have had little enduring effect on the corporate code. People in corporations are trying to be even more controlled as a result of a belief that work as a professional activity should be conducted with a minimum of emotion. It therefore becomes more important for individuals to take responsibility for keeping their observing ego functioning. Toward this end, family relationships and friendships outside of work should be cultivated in order to allow people to express and listen to their anger as well as the doubts and anxieties that arise in competitive corporations.

There are places where people can work and expect to communicate with considerably more freedom than that allowed in large corporations. People whose defenses allow greater acceptance and access to their anger will fare much better in entrepreneurial businesses than in the corporate world. Entrepreneurial businesses find it more acceptable for people to express anger both up and down the hierarchy. Relationships are more flexible, people are more tolerant, and the atmosphere is more volatile, as a result of the strong personal investments in these businesses.

Western civilization places great stock in civility in human relationships. At the same time cohesion in organizations and society depends on the expression of anger to remedy those situations that undermine active cooperation. The political arena has various channels for expressing discontents. The corporate world, however, has a long way to go to understand the uses of anger in human relationships. It should take heed of the Duke of Albany's words in *King Lear:*

> The weight of this sad time we must obey
> Speak what we feel,
> Not what we ought to say.

Chapter 8

Molding Managers

*P*eople interested in a business career face competitive pressures. How can they gain access to the job market and make themselves visible in it? In earlier times the main access was through a personal network of family and friends. A family friend would introduce a candidate, the candidate would expect to start at the bottom of the ladder, but knowing he was part of a network gave him assurance that he would not get lost, but rather would be watched and advanced. The personal network placed at a disadvantage members of the "out-groups" who found it extremely difficult to enter the executive ranks of corporations. For an outsider, the favored, and perhaps only, ways to enter management were to join entrepreneurial companies or to become an entrepreneur. The outsider could try to enter business by becoming an expert. Capitalizing on expert knowledge allowed an individual to overcome some of the disadvantages of operating outside of a personal network, but it seldom allowed for entry into management ranks.

Professionalism in management entered a new era in the 1960s when America fell in love with the MBA degree. In 1965 some 5,000 students received MBA degrees; in 1986, 67,000 men and women were awarded the degree.

An optimist might cheer this development, believing that MBAs are better prepared to serve American business and industry than their predecessors who rarely acquired an advanced degree in business. A pessimist might argue that the MBA phenomenon is another piece of evidence that American society has shifted values from productivity and performance to status and credentials. The pessimist might also note that the adoration of the MBA degree coincides with America's industrial decline and with the rise of the service sectors in its economy.

There are some signs that companies that helped make the market for MBAs are beginning to question both the public and private benefits of this push for the degree as a prerequisite for a career in business. In preference to hiring exclusively MBA graduates for management positions, General Electric and ITT now hire large numbers of college graduates and give them in-house training. These companies may save between $5,000 and $10,000 in annual starting salaries. More important, they may be suggesting that they can do a better job preparing young people for the human aspects of a career in business than the typical MBA program.

Economic factors favor an MBA over other advanced degrees, but not necessarily over direct entry into business after graduating from college. A college graduate might even have an advantage over a competitor with the MBA degree. He or she will not have to deal with exaggerated expectations and grandiose beliefs that form part of the aura of the MBA degree. The college graduate who is well educated will also not have to unlearn the trivia that goes along with much of business education, and in particular, the professional aura that foolishly teaches people to treat others as clients, not as human beings.

Besides the reevaluation under way in companies, individuals are taking a second look at the value received from the investment in an MBA degree. MBA programs teach analytical techniques, provide familiarity with business functions, provide some experience making decisions, and, on occasion, offer an opportunity to discover interests and talents for business. Armed with what they have learned, MBA graduates probably have an advantage in adjusting to the business environment. This advantage, however, costs time and money.

By 1986 the cost of the MBA degree in elite institutions had approached the $50,000 mark. This figure includes tuition, books, and living costs for a single person, but it does not include opportunity cost in forgoing income while studying. The only sure thing that can be said about the degree is that its economic benefits exceed the benefits that can be realized from most other advanced

degrees. The humanities especially suffer by comparison, and undoubtedly much of the attraction of the MBA degree reflects the
adverse position of alternative careers in teaching, social services,
and, more recently, law.

The idea of business as a profession is generally appealing but
only loosely applicable. There are no legal credentials for a business career as in law and medicine, nor are there prerequisite
qualifying procedures for practice.

The popularity of the MBA degree reflects two deepening
trends in society. The first is the democratization of the corporate
world, which increasingly allows outsiders to join the managerial
ranks. The second, which in part grows out of the first, is the need
for a market in which employment transactions can take place
efficiently. A senior in college who elects to go into business has
a difficult time presenting herself to an employer so that she is
differentiated from her competitors. Choosing to endure the expense of getting an MBA degree is one significant way to stand out
from the crowd.

Michael Spence, now dean of the faculty of arts and sciences
at Harvard University and formerly on the faculty of the Harvard
Business School, seriously considered the problem of information
flow in the job market. In his doctoral dissertation in economics
Spence called the market aspects of getting an advanced degree
"signaling behavior." At the very least, the decision to get an MBA
degree is a signal to prospective employers that the individual
wants to be a manager. While the degree does not carry assurance
about the individual's ability to perform, because it does not define the areas within which the employer can look for expertise,
it does represent a specific commitment. Given the time and
money invested in acquiring the degree, there is an expectation
that the individual is serious about advancing in a business career.

From the employer's position, the problem is to gain access
to a pool of candidates not only to find people, but to reduce the
risks of making bad choices. It is impractical to hire a person,
determine his or her level of productivity and performance, and
then adjust job title, salary, and perquisites to match the individual's economic worth. The employer increases confidence in employment decisions by relying on various market signals, one of
which is level of education. On the basis of common knowledge
and experience, employers develop beliefs about the relationship
between level of education and productivity. If experience after

hiring seems to support these beliefs, they are reinforced; if not, they are reevaluated and modified. Although the MBA degree is now subject to such a reevaluation, it still appears to be a prerequisite for a high-level job in business. Because it signals the individual's intentions, it not only presents credentials but, as with conspicuous consumption, contains a hidden message. In conspicuous consumption, the message is wealth and by inference power and status; with the MBA the message is ambition and the desire for corporate power and prestige.[1]

All advanced degrees act as signals in the career market, but they vary considerably in the amount and kind of importance they have. In medicine, for example, the signaling value of the degree is far less important than the intrinsic value of the training and evaluation of performance. A person's reputation in medicine grows out of evaluations that result from careful observation and supervision, first during medical school and second during the intensive period of internship and residency training. What the person intends to signal must stand against rigorous evaluations made from supervision in the clinic. Information about the individual is highly reliable because it involves many years of observation by many seniors. When the time comes for fellowship and junior staff appointments, the hard information available about candidates' performance and ability is much more important than any latent message about image and ambition.

When employers begin looking over MBA candidates, the most reliable information they have concerns the school attended rather than the individual. In the United States about 700 schools grant MBA degrees. To distinguish among them, business schools are ranked in a three-tier structure by deans, faculty, graduates, and other groups. The first tier consists of 15 private, elite schools, such as the University of Chicago, Columbia, Dartmouth, Harvard, MIT, Stanford, and the Wharton School of the University of Pennsylvania. Most have offered the MBA for a long time.[2] The second tier consists of some 100 regional schools, many of which are part of state universities. The third tier consists of more than 400 schools that serve a local constituency of students and prospective employers.

The desire of employers to gain access to a select pool of people places the elite and some regional schools in a strong position. They have marked advantages in recruiting able students and a strong faculty. They also have the prospects of continuing financial support from a strong and loyal alumni group. These advantages ensure the future for these top tier schools, in contrast to the position of many of the regional and local schools.

That many of the second- and third-tier schools exist at all attests to the ease of entry into the MBA field of education. When the demand for MBAs grew in the 1960s, it was relatively easy to mount a program. At least for a time, the business schools enjoyed financial surpluses, and universities were able to use these funds to support other branches. Law schools also tend to produce budget surpluses because they typically have large student bodies and a low faculty-to-student ratio, but it is not easy for a university administration to siphon funds from its law school to other faculties. The American Bar Association closely oversees the use of funds, and a university president tempted to use the law school as a cash cow soon encounters resistance from the dean of law and the law faculty, with the American Bar Association supporting this resistance. The funds raised from business schools are not similarly restricted.

The American Association of Collegiate Schools of Business has little clout since there are more business schools offering MBA degrees without AACSB accreditation than with it. If graduates can be placed, the school has good assurance that it will be able to recruit a student body.

The strongest and perhaps most immediate market factor affecting business schools is the need of business to have access to a pool of managerial level employees. These companies are certain when they arrive at the campuses of the top-tier schools that they will be seeing the best and the brightest. They can count on seeing prospects who are fully conversant with the technology of modern business and who have been thoroughly indoctrinated into the social aspects of their career. This indoctrination guarantees that new employees will have internalized the style of behavior that goes along with professional management, will know how to fit into a group, and will know how to participate without being disruptive. This style has its own signals and language code familiar to all managers with MBA degrees—men wear only blue and gray, never brown suits; women wear tailored clothes, especially suits, and avoid feminine display; everyone addresses everyone else by first name, regardless of age or status; vocabulary and expression are bland, not highly charged; people use buzz words, such as "to dialogue," "input," and "feedback," and technical

terms and jargon, such as "cash flow," "product and market segmentation," and "decision tree."

Employers can be certain that the indoctrination of the MBA
will stick. Most business school graduates participated in the MBA
culture even before they enrolled in a course of study. At least 90
percent of MBA candidates have had at least two years of work
experience before entering an MBA program. In the elite schools
most of that experience involved work with people who have
MBA degrees, and therefore indoctrination is well under way by
the time the student steps into the first class.

Indoctrination continues in the classroom, in social relations,
and in the frenzy of job hunting stimulated by company recruiters.
In the classroom students compete with each other knowing that
the grades they receive will have a strong influence on their ability
to interest "fast track" companies in hiring them. Students in discussion classes fight for "air time" and seek visibility in the eyes of
their professors. Students are so anxious about this visibility that
they make it a point to visit their professors in hopes of gaining
recognition. These students may be so focused on visibility that
they have little to say about the content of the course, their problems in dealing with difficult material, or their reactions to business and the world in general. They may be intelligent, but have
somehow lost their grasp of common sense and human relationships under the sway of competitive pressure.

One of the most frustrating aspects of teaching through participative methods, whether it is the case method or some other
form of instruction that elicits active involvement, is the difficulty
students have in listening to what others are saying. Aware that
the professor is interested only in comments related to the flow
of discussion, students often make embarrassingly studied attempts to be relevant in relation to what other people have said
during the class discussion. Various forms of posturing are used to
give the impression that the speaker has been listening attentively
to what his or her colleagues in class have been saying, as when
they gaze up at the ceiling as though deep in thought, before
uttering what often turns out to be a ponderous and vague opinion on what has transpired in the class.

There is a decided MBA style. The latent aim of a good part
of the MBA education is to inculcate this style as a way of ampli-
fying the signals the students cast out onto a waiting world. More
than a few irate executives write to business school professors to

record their disappointment in the MBA student as executive material. These executives really are not complaining particularly about one school's MBAs. Unknowingly, they are writing about the whole movement that has propelled the MBA degree into prominence as a ticket to success in business.

In one letter a chief executive listed these characteristics of MBAs that he thought created problems.

> First, MBA graduates treat everyone alike. Every associate is just an "erg" and [they] don't understand the need to know the idiosyncrasies of an individual. Second, they usually don't speak to their employees when coming to work in the morning. ("Why should I show interest? I'm here if they want me.") And, then, they have very little interest in anyone's career but their own.... [MBA graduates] have a personality that's centered on self, feel that they have something of a God given eliteness, and ... have the overblown mindset that they can bring a unique, extra special message to the business world.

Whether or not the MBA gave its graduates anything special to bring to business, it became popular among students selecting a career because there was a considerable demand for it among employers. Investment banking and consulting firms, which have little need for managers, stimulated the demand even more. The stated purpose of the MBA places little emphasis on the qualities that these industries want—specialists who are bright, sophisticated, socially adept, capable of working long hours, willing to accept the toll of excessive travel and long absences from their homes, and driven by the ambition to earn large sums of money early in their careers.

We hear stories about the explosion in starting salaries for MBA graduates. These stories need to be put into perspective. Comparing starting salaries for graduates over a 15- or 20-year period and correcting the data for the effects of inflation yields a surprising result. With a couple of important exceptions, the real salaries remained fairly flat over that period. The exceptions were investment banking and consulting, where starting salaries increased in real dollars, reflecting the rise in demand for MBAs in these two industries. The starting salary figures do not tell the whole story about grim competition between the banks and consulting firms for the bright graduates. The figures need to be supplemented by bonus guarantees, special sign-on premiums, and contracts to liquidate the educational debt of the graduates over a stipulated period of time as an inducement not only to take the job but also to stay on it. Entry salaries can be augmented by as much as $10,000 to $20,000 by bonuses alone, reaching $70,000 or above for the premier graduates of the elite business schools.

Investment banking and consulting firms are, reputedly, the employers with the golden track. But what these industries need from the MBAs is not what most of us think of as management talents, let alone leadership abilities. Instead, they look for specialized cognitive skills along with certain social skills and a particular motivation. The cognitive skills are the ability to analyze strategies for corporations and the ability to apply the methods of financial analysis in considering strategic alternatives. Although these are formidable abilities, they should not be confused with running a part of a corporation and being judged by results. The human aspects of the executive's job rank among the most important challenges, and these responsibilities are precisely what are not required in investment banking and consulting. In addition, working as an investment banker or consultant is a long way from taking responsibility for making decisions and dealing with the resulting anxieties.

Investment bankers and consultants bring certain social skills to their job. They often work in task groups and with representatives of client organizations. Because these relationships are not hierarchical, more often than not, the client holds more power; therefore, the ability of the investment banker or consultant to satisfy the client depends on his or her ability to persuade. In addition, the members of the banking or consulting firm are often significantly younger than the people they work with in the client organization. To overcome this disparity in age and relationship, the specialists rely on the clout of their firm and on a certain mystification that goes along with their work. They become adept at making presentations and learn to rely on process, hoping thereby to engage members of the client organization. In many cases, especially in consulting, the process is intended to make the engagement a participatory relationship so that the age and experience disparities between professional and client fade into the background. It is commonplace, particularly in consulting, for the professional to view his or her task as facilitating a process rather than as solving problems, making decisions, and leading people. Such abilities stand in sharp contrast to the work of professionals in medicine, law, and architecture and also in contrast to what the executive does in leading an organization.

Even when MBAs take jobs outside of banking or consulting, they often avoid direct responsibility for making decisions and the well-being of other people. Procter & Gamble invented the job of product manager during the 1920s, and since then it has been widely adopted in business, although it is under scrutiny. The job carries no formal authority but a great degree of opportunity for interacting with people who do. In companies that produce many products aimed at distinct segments of the market, the product manager in charge of a brand is supposed to "manage the process" for the development of a marketing program for that brand. The product manager coordinates, expedites, and troubleshoots among people in functional fields such as market research, advertising, selling, and manufacturing. But because brand managers have no formal authority, they must use their superior intellectual talents, communication skills, and the ability to persuade other people to get things done. Using their brains and charm, they may accomplish much, but it is doubtful that what people learn in these jobs prepares them for leadership.

The terms manager and leader were once synonymous. Both terms implied the responsibility for getting things done by directing peoples' efforts. The relationship was vertical, and superior and subordinate understood that they were in an unequal power relationship. Ever since the 1960s the vertical relationship has been enveloped in a more complicated structure in which facilitators and staff specialists play a more compelling role in the procedure. The emergence of this new role, along with the growth in the investment banking and consulting industries, has generated the growing market for MBAs. Although the market may shrink overall, it will continue to provide brisk business for the first tier of business schools, leaving the regional and local schools to scramble for both students and companies to hire them.

The elite MBA programs make a claim on society: They are training the future general managers of business. To a remarkable degree, these elite schools are polarized in their relation to the markets they serve. Some elite schools are captives of their market; others eschew the market and allegedly represent superior values. Although business schools have undergone studies and self-analyses since the 1950s, business education has yet to confront the implications of either the symbiosis with or indifference to its primary market.

That some business schools mirror business is not necessarily cause for alarm. It is to be expected that professional schools will be closely tied in consciousness and purpose to the communities they serve. But the symbiosis between corporate business and several elite business schools poses a number of complex problems that other professions escape.

A business school professor put the following question to his colleagues: "What have been the major contributions of business schools to significant innovations in business practice?" The silence was embarrassing. Yes, the theory of capital markets and mathematical decision making could be viewed as a contribution from the academy, but if the truth were told, these contributions came from people who consider themselves economists and mathematicians rather than business school professors.

The nature of the contributions were clearly set forth in a *Fortune* article entitled "In Defense of MBAs."[3] The author, Joel M. Stern, is managing partner of a consulting firm in New York that specializes in corporate finance. He holds an MBA degree from the University of Chicago, which is widely regarded for its economics and finance faculty. Stern wrote the article as a rebuttal to critics of MBAs who claim they are "too ambitious, too impatient, and not worth the high salaries they command."[4] Stern argues that the market properly evaluates the best MBAs from the best schools. The problems that firms have had with MBAs have occurred with graduates from the lesser schools or with mediocre students from the best schools. What differentiates the best schools from the others? The best schools, according to Stern, rely on economic science and statistics to teach capital-markets theory. The lesser schools teach descriptive practice in different kinds of business. Without a theoretical foundation, this teaching of practice probably conveys as much false information as it does useful information.

Capital-markets theory aims at providing answers to questions about how corporations should deploy their assets to yield the greatest value in the stock market. By applying theory to quantitative data, modern finance provides answers that often fly in the face of conventional wisdom on Wall Street. According to Stern, conventional wisdom says that company stock prices are a function of earnings-per-share. The decision to increase dividends communicates management's belief about future earnings-per-share. The nonconventional view of the economists is that the stock market values cash flow. The principle of maximization, therefore, should be applied to after-tax cash flow and not earnings-per-share, which often is an accounting fiction dependent on, for example, the way inventories are valued and reported.

Stern goes on to criticize the case method for perpetuating the apprenticeship method of training which, he argues, should be supplanted by the scientific approach. What distinguishes the scientific from the apprenticeship approach is the use of theory derived from applications of the scientific method to the study of business.

This argument seems to have merit. Medicine provides a prime example of the way in which science can transform a profession. The hope that the revolution that occurred in medicine would eventually be duplicated in business stimulated criticisms of business education in the 1950s. At that time the Carnegie and Ford Foundations separately sponsored studies of business education in the United States and recommended a program for its reform.[5] One of the inspirations for these studies was the Flexner report of 1910, a report that played an important part in bringing about reform of medical education.

Abraham Flexner, who lived from 1866 to 1959, was a prominent American educator who devoted his life to comparative studies of European and American educational systems in the hope of raising the standard of education in America. On behalf of the Carnegie Foundation for the Advancement of Teaching, he studied medical education in the United States and Canada.[6] The results, published in 1910, presented a disturbing picture of a society bent on overproducing badly trained doctors who ignored the scientific revolution in medical practice, which was already well under way and soon to provide the foundation for the great advances of the twentieth century. Flexner's report gave focus and visibility to the scientific revolution in medicine, a revolution that continues today in outstanding medical faculties, research laboratories, and teaching hospitals.

The business school studies sponsored by the Carnegie and Ford Foundations were influential, but neither produced results comparable to the Flexner study of medical education. Although the authors of the Ford and Carnegie reports recommended that business education be placed on a more scientific foundation, they were careful to point out that the problems of business education in the 1950s were different from those confronting medical education in the early twentieth century. American business education in the 1950s was "heterogeneous and pioneering," whereas by 1910 there was a firmly established model of scientific medical education set by such universities as Johns Hopkins. Although this standard was widely breached in practice, it presented an ideal toward which other institutions could strive. In business education there was no established ideal. Business education, at the time these reports appeared, had a model in the case-method approach of the Harvard Business School. Although Stern and many educators disdain the case method essentially for being "nonscientific" and not grounded in theory, in its best applications it is analytical, oriented to solving problems, intellectually demanding of faculty and students alike, and the closest business education comes to the clinical method that has worked so well in medicine. It need not lack a foundation in theory, provided its practitioners understand the difference between inductive and deductive logic and permit the two to work together.

Another difference between the state of business education in the 1950s and medical education in Flexner's times, according to the Ford and Carnegie reports, was the difference in the development of science relevant to the two fields. The social sciences of the 1950s were in an embryonic stage of development in comparison with the well-advanced stage of the natural sciences in Flexner's day. Nevertheless, both reports recommended that mathematics, economics, and the other social sciences should be made the bases of business education and research at the best business schools. Only by providing a rigorous scientific training along with a broad liberal education, they said, could business schools at the upper level prepare managers who would no longer have to rely on methods and procedures that would soon become obsolete. Both reports strongly recommended developing doctoral programs in which candidates for the highest degree would be trained in scientific methods of research to investigate significant problems relating to business.

As the reports quite rightly noted, business exists in a state of flux. Current practice, whether taught through a descriptive or case method, is an unreliable guide for managers in the present and future. The ideal of establishing a scientific foundation for business education rests on the belief that there are basic propositions to be discovered that are not bound to a certain culture or to particular business institutions and that can be applied to solving problems. If this ideal should become a reality in business education, its proponents believe that students would be critical, objective, and capable of mentally leaping out of familiar contexts into a changing world.

The scientific promise outlined in the Ford and Carnegie reports is far from being fulfilled. But, even if science were to dominate business education, there is serious question about whether or not the individual who was a product of this education could lead people. Even now, one can discern a major weakness in the scientific ideal in preparing people for what Douglas McGregor called "the human side of enterprise" and what others call leadership.

The job of the executive is to accomplish valuable work through the cooperative efforts of people. But many efforts to apply the scientific method to organizations through the behavioral sciences have resulted in excluding people as the object of study. The majority of academics specializing in organizational behavior as a branch of the behavioral sciences focus on form and process and not on people and relationships. This focus fits in well with the managerial ideal of establishing structures to get people to do the appropriate tasks. It is not surprising, therefore, to find that in courses in organizational behavior students do not study people at work, but rather events, such as budgeting, performance evaluation, and compensation, that are a part of a process in organizations. Generally, organizational behaviorists assume the variable abilities and personalities within an organization average out. This assumption is merely a statistical truism, particularly in comparing large organizations, but it leads professors of organizational behavior to neglect personality. It is assumed away, therefore it does not exist.

When organizational behaviorists attempt to focus on executives, distortions appear because they avoid personal and institutional history. It is as though there were no continuities in the life of individuals and the traditions of corporations. The reality is that people are continually absorbed by their inner world as well as the world outside of themselves. Making decisions is nothing less than the drama of linking these inner and outer worlds. But because of their occupational bias, organizational behaviorists stubbornly refuse to acknowledge that what people do may be closely connected with their particular personalities and life stories.

Many organizational behaviorists share with managers a strong antipathy to history. Managers are biased toward the here-and-now and are disturbed by the way forces in the past determine the present, for both the individual and the institution. Ignoring history in research and especially in teaching reflects the current ethos of management, which is never to look back because the past deflects attention from the present. But perhaps more to the point, looking back frequently evokes guilt, particularly when people come to see their own mistakes.

In their urge to appear practical and capable of helping managers solve real problems, many organizational behaviorists have become directed by their audience. If managers appear action-oriented, the organizational behaviorists will stress action programs in their teaching. Students come away from such courses with a deadly combination of mechanistic and magical thinking. The mechanistic side appears in the attitude that an organization is a system of parts related to the whole, and the goal is to find the malfunctioning part and fix it. This mechanistic approach blinds the actor, whether manager or organizational behaviorist, to the reality of people. Organizations reflect the characteristics of human beings, the most prominent of which is their innate and well-developed defenses. With the aid of these defenses, employees singly or collectively learn how to look after their interests and are less taken in by action programs than their proponents realize.

Magical thinking also dominates the perspectives of organizational behaviorists and the students who follow their approaches. It is cause for wonder to observe people who follow a profession whose substance they abhor. Imagine a doctor who hates people with illnesses or a psychiatrist who cannot tolerate people with emotional disturbances. These unfortunate professionals spend many years and a great amount of money pursuing the career and denying their abhorrence of the substance of their profession. Many organizational behaviorists have the same problem. They do not find people interesting and they may choose to avoid them rather than understand them. What do they do under these circumstances? They contrive a universe in which, through magical thinking, they are able to shut from view the complicated and turbulent world of people with their emotions, needs, and defenses. Being action-oriented, they fall into the manager's trap of believing that if you mount a program, then you have solved the problem, even though you don't know what the problem is.

Managers are often crafty in their substitution of programs for thinking. Some call it adroit and compare it to leaping off the horse about to be shot out from under you and then quickly mounting a getaway horse. Organizational behaviorists, as captives of their market, often lack this craftiness. More often they are innocents, seduced by the world of management, who try hard to appear relevant and yet are constantly beset with doubts arising from the questionable intellectual content of their field.

Another solution to the problem of fulfilling the promises held out to business and management is to avoid being captive to the market by remaining steadfast in the belief that science will win out and sway the market. Aloof social scientists hold strictly to the tenets of science and run the risk of discovering how little one really knows about the subject. Academic social scientists often make no pretense that what they are studying has practical application. They believe that by toiling in the vineyard, they are adding to the storehouse of knowledge. They believe also that from time to time a genius appears who is able to transform this storehouse into a castle. But geniuses appear rarely, and in the waiting, pseudo-scientists make themselves heard. Caught up in the jargon, they substitute ponderous language for knowledge.

When the authors of the Ford and Carnegie reports stated that the behavioral sciences, along with economics and mathematics, would transform business education, they may not have given sufficient weight to the crucial variable: talent. The fields concerned with the application of the behavioral sciences to business have not been successful in attracting gifted students. Yet the problems in business that behavioral scientists should be studying are extremely complex both in their theoretical and practical dimensions. These problems demand exceptional rather than average talents.

Behavioral scientists face strong competition in gaining a grasp on problems in business. The competition comes from the ranks of managers who apply practical know-how to the solution of these problems. Even though these solutions lack a theoretical foundation or scientific validation, they often work, if only because taking some steps to solve problems unfreezes an unsatisfactory situation. Beneficial results occur often when someone in a position of authority takes an interest in the problems other people are experiencing. But this phenomenon, known popularly as the "Hawthorne effect," easily gets out of control and leads to faddism in management.

Business Week devoted a cover story to business fads.[7] The lead idea was that "Executives latch on to any management idea that looks like a quick fix." Unfortunately, too many organizational behaviorists become the generators of the quick fixes and contribute to the debilitating effects of a succession of fads. To disdain fads is to respect practical know-how. Yet, behavioral scientists should not try to be the source of practical know-how because they do not have the experience or the inclination for it. Behavioral scientists should study the application of practical know-how to discover the effects on human motivation and behavior. Their contribution depends on their ability to see the underlying forces, to uncover the dynamics of behavior, and, as a result, to be in a position to improve what they offer as educators.

Behavioral sciences will soon discover that the problem of the dynamics of behavior arises as a result of a fact about people: People not only act, but they have awareness. This awareness does not include unconscious motives, but it does provide a link to motives that enables people to benefit from reflection. Scientific knowledge enriches, but does not substitute for, this awareness and its reflective possibilities. In their studies of people in organizations, scientists have to take into account subjective experience. As a consequence, these studies invariably require observation of individuals and their inner world. To think of organizations as behaving misses the point that the proper study of humankind is the human.

The problem of generating new knowledge about people acting in situations carries over to teaching MBA candidates. After World War II the Harvard Business School began an experiment in MBA education that made students' subjective experience the central consideration in the curriculum. Specifically, students were encouraged to learn how to see themselves in the context of problems in business organizations. Among the faculty, whether in the fields of marketing, finance, and production or in the courses most centrally concerned with the human aspects of managing such as human relations, control, and business policy, there was surprising consensus: The individual in a position of responsibility can make a difference. The case method of teaching, which came under scrutiny following the publication of the Ford and Carnegie reports, was ideally suited to this consensus. It turned the initiative for learning over to the students, made them responsible for everyone's progress, and, particularly in the business policy course, provided a brilliant opportunity to fuse form and substance, subject matter and process, and to learn about the world while learning about oneself.

In the case method, in order to analyze the situations presented, students must first learn to project themselves. They have to identify with the person who has the problem to solve, but they must also maintain objectivity. In addition, they must apply certian analytical tools that will enable them to deal with the facts in order to arrive at a solid understanding of the problem. This simultaneous identification with a key person and objective analysis brings urgency and practicality to their work. At best, it allows students to move imaginatively beyond the strict confines of their analytical tools. Analysis enriched by imagination leads to a vision that can go well beyond the limits of the problem set forth in the case.

Because the case method is a powerful and evocative way to teach and learn, it is subject to many abuses, for example, reducing interesting problems to common experience and, worse, making a caricature of teaching. One social scientist, who spent some time trying to teach a so-called case method course at the Harvard Business School, compared it to a cocktail party conversation. In this instance he was probably correct. But he may not have realized that the particular course he was teaching and the materials he was using reflected misuse of the method. Such experiences give the case method a bad name.

Abuses of the case method of teaching occur when it is used as a "consciousness-raising experience" and also when unqualified people are allowed to enter the classroom. Not by chance, these two abuses appear together and usually in the "soft" subjects involving human behavior. As a result, courses with well-developed analytic techniques dominate the MBA curriculum, leaving open the question of how managers of the future will understand and use their reflective ability.

As with most professional education, business schools face many ethical problems in deciding what and how to teach. The most significant ethical problem today is a consequence of giving potential managers technical competence without serious regard for relationships with others. Even where people are considered, more often than not, they are regarded as members of constituencies rather than particular human beings. The key idea seems to be "managing" these constituencies, which places human relationships narrowly within the scope of technical competence. The area of personal responsibility now emphasized in training managers refers to advancing their own careers. Courses in career development appear in the curriculum and emphasize maximizing one's own opportunities rather than concern for other people. Business schools that establish counseling programs may be unintentionally contributing to self-centeredness. By encouraging students to seek professional help for problems ranging from uncertainty in career to anxiety, people lose the experience of friendship and community as a source of personal growth.

The trend in MBA education is decidedly toward a technical orientation. The primary focus is on subject matter, relegating the subjective awareness to a subordinate or nonexistent position. Business strategy has overcome business leadership, while concern for self has displaced the urge to make a difference in the lives and well-being of other people. The MBA has become a symbol of the twentieth century belief in manipulation as the means for running organizations and governing society. We are fabricating managers not educating leaders.

Part III

Consequences

Chapter 9

Politics Prevails

That American business has lost its competitive edge is clear. The underlying cause is less clear. Many observers of the business scene mistake the symptoms for the cause of the deterioration of America's ability to match, let alone best, foreign competition. Emphasizing short-term results rather than long-term growth, managing corporate assets as though they were a portfolio of investments, ignoring manufacturing and marketing while emphasizing financial manipulation, and concentrating on marketing stocks instead of products are symptoms, not the root cause.

Describing the effects of financial manipulations, economists Walter Adams and James J. Brock point out that funds spent on corporate mergers exceeded funds spent on research and development from mid-1982 through 1985. In 1985 the combined expenditures for research and development and net nonresidential investment were below the value of mergers, which in 1986 reached the record sum of $190 billion. These economists state that the measure of the cost of the merger mania fails to include opportunity cost, or the cost of forgoing investments in other activities, such as research and development.

> Thus, two decades of managerial energies devoted to playing the merger game are, at the same time, two decades during which management has been diverted from the critically important job of building new plants, bringing out new products, investing in new production techniques, and

creating jobs. The billions spent on shuffling paper ownership shares are, at the same time, billions not spent on
productivity-enchancing investments.[1]

Other economists argue that responding to undervalued assets is rational and beneficial. When it is cheaper to acquire oil
reserves than to drill, of course the pull will be toward acquisition.
Similarly, when a whole corporation is worth less than the sum of
its parts, the stage is set for raiding and corporate dissolution.
Nevertheless, more fundamental factors explain why corporate
management allows a situation to arise such as the Allegis case,
cited by Adams and Brock. Under its chief executive, Richard
Ferris, the company made major acquisitions in order to transform
itself into a full-service travel company. Starting with United Airlines and the Westin Hotel chain, Ferris acquired Hertz, Hilton
International Hotels, and the Pacific routes of Pan American World
Airways. The corporate name changed from United to Allegis to
symbolize a new identity, which had been acquired rather than
built. The financial world began to view Allegis as worth more
dead than alive, and Ferris found himself embroiled in efforts to
avoid a takeover. As his financial tactics approached the bizarre,
his board ultimately fired him. His successor immediately reversed
course, announcing a planned sale of all nonairline businesses and
the restoration of the corporate name United Airlines, thus moving back to the business where it had deep experience.

Managements have a peculiar tendency to imitate. Merging
could not have become a mania were it not for the outgrowth of
professionalism, which, combined with ego, leads managers to run
with the pack. But beneath this compulsion to imitate lies a
deeper problem, which is the major disaster of the managerial
mystique. In applying the principles of efficiency, cooperation,
and control, along with the compulsions of professionalism, managers engross themselves and others in politics.

A professional manager newly appointed to the chief executive position of an international corporation immediately set out
to build an orderly organization structure. He drew and redrew
charts to achieve on paper an organization that exemplified the
principles of decentralization. Although his key subordinates
could not quarrel with his logic, they recognized that the problem
he chose to fix was far less important than stimulating a corporate-
wide product development and marketing program, which the

company sorely lacked. Considering how clearly the subordinates saw the real problem, it was astonishing how reluctant they were to tell the new CEO that he was on the wrong track. Perhaps jealous that he, and not one of their own, had been named to the position and perhaps hesitant to appear negative in the face of their new boss's enthusiasm for organization charts, they watched him blunder into a project that needlessly aroused anxiety about areas of responsibility and relative power. By his choice of problem and the methods he used, the CEO heightened political consciousness in the organization and, therefore, hindered the company from confronting the real issues of the business.

This CEO had fallen into the trap many managers set for themselves of creating political anxieties in their subordinates while failing to establish what value they are bringing to the enterprise. This situation is not unlike the case of an academic dean who sought to change the emphasis of a school without first having in hand the money necessary to fuel the program. The professors reacted as though they were being threatened politically because they could interpret the dean's actions only as the start of a venture aimed at "eating off their plates." It was clear that existing programs and power bases would be seriously disturbed while the newer programs the dean favored would benefit. Not only were the merits of the new program questioned, but also the tactics the dean chose to implement it. The faculty became preoccupied with defending their beliefs and the power positions through which their ideas were made known and implemented.

Political behavior is often defensive in motive and aim. People form alliances and trade off their power bases to avoid trouble, at least in their perceptions. When the person in charge appears to be the enemy, goals are displaced. Instead of dealing with goals, people are activated by their fears and fantasies, which often amplify conflict beyond its usefulness.

Political consciousness heightens whenever individuals have cause to rethink the elementary questions of membership. It is as though opposing voices in the psyche debate three nagging questions: What are the chances that I can satisfy my needs working in this organization? Who are my friends (and my enemies) as I go about getting my job done? What are the standards I should meet and the ideals I should emulate to establish who I am in this organization? These questions lead to different answers at different stages of the life cycle, but they should be answered and "put to bed" for significant periods of time to allow the individual to get on with work. If they remain open to continual debate as a result of heightened political consciousness, energy is displaced from where it belongs.

Executives especially are vulnerable to preoccupation with these questions: Highly sensitive to power and personal ambitions, they are easily diverted from the substance of their jobs to political concerns. The diversions are a regular feature of corporate life largely because top managements have not learned how to diminish politicking and how to provide focus for substantive thinking.

The chief executive officer of a company that supplied industrial equipment pondered the question of what to do in the face of a severe industry depression in the early 1980s. His executives were restless and felt a lack of direction in the face of dismal industry prospects. The CEO hired an outside consultant to begin a process of strategic planning. Coupled with the fact that the chief executive was approaching retirement, the decision to begin a formal program in strategic planning aroused political anxiety. First, it made little sense initially to bring in outsiders to do a task that executives believed they should do themselves. Second, the timing was poor. Many executives believed that the first order of business during depressed economic conditions was to cut costs and restore profitability at much lower levels of production, as the Chrysler Corporation had done in reducing its break-even point to about a million cars a year from a level more than twice as high. Third, they viewed the entire effort as theater, the appearance of doing important work. In fact, the real drama had to do with management succession and the mystery of who from within the company were the contenders for the CEO post and how they were faring in the competition. The succession problem should have been addressed directly, but the CEO was reluctant to give up his post to a younger person, especially with the implication that in the face of a critical situation, it was time to transfer power.

For organizations to work best, they require commitment from individuals. Yet political consciousness brings forth the ability to calculate and, consequently, diminishes commitment. Furthermore, it isolates people at different levels of the organization and ultimately destroys the integrity of authority.

It is worth pondering the problem of power and politics in hierarchies, or, as Leo Tolstoy put the issue in his epilogue to *War and Peace,* the bonding, if any, that holds together the few who plan and the many who implement.[2] The usual bond between the few and the many is the expectation that people with power will express the aims and desires of followers. Yet often the few who plan intend to inflict pain on the many who implement, leading one to wonder at the persistence of hierarchy. Evidently, people can be fooled into following directives not in their best interests for a considerable period of time, but over the long run they bring an end to oppression by refusing to do what their leaders direct them to do. The Vietnam War is an example of what happens when the actors in the lower levels of the power structure simply withdraw their compliance. Junior officers viewed the war as a career opportunity, rank and file soldiers sought to survive, and civilians balked at serving.

The presence of hierarchy is a universal fact. The explanation for its existence is that hierarchy is the best available means for organizing power so that it can be used to further the interests of people. But this utilitarian truth is evidently difficult to accept. Utopians who seem to ignore human nature are constantly devising means to overcome the imbalance of power between the few and the many. Despite experiments with the equalization of power, the fact of hierarchy persists, demanding a deeper understanding of its functions than we now have.

Ranging from the animal kingdom to human groups, relationships form into a hierarchy. In primate groups the hierarchy consists of a dominant male followed by a cadre of females with whom the male copulates, followed by weaker male animals. The weaker males gain the protection of the dominant male and, in return, abide by rules of the status arrangement as expressed in the distribution of rewards. As the dominant male gets older and weakens, his place is eventually taken by another male who assumes both the benefits and the costs of power in the group.

In recent times primatologists and ethologists have adopted the explanatory models of economics and game theory to account for their observations of the hierarchical arrangement of power.[3] Cost-benefit analysis may at first glance seem absurd in application to animal studies, since there is no basis for a calculating mind in animals. This utilitarian model, however, provides the best fit between fact and theory. The theory does indeed work, leading to the inference that there is probably an innate characteristic of animals that leads to an economy of power among primates. The dominant animal, for example, will not use more force than is necessary to maintain the power structure. When challenged by a subordinate, threats are usually all that is necessary to push the subordinate back. One can conceive that it is in the best interests of subordinates to wait and accept lesser rewards than to challenge for dominance. The point is that the hierarchical arrangement has the support of the group since threats to the hierarchy create instability that is generally unacceptable. There are cases reported where animals will cheat and thereby threaten the dominance hierarchy, but only under circumstances where they are probably not going to be discovered. Dominant animals are constantly alert to the possibility of cheating and are careful to block its appearance.

In human groups hierarchy in the distribution of power is a general tendency that has been verified in many observations and experiments.[4] In study after study of group formations in work and "natural" groups, leaders and followers align themselves into a remarkably predictable relationship with few at the top and many at the bottom of the power pyramid. The pyramid can be manifested in various ways. In experimental groups the pyramid appears in the amount of talking that power figures do and in the direction in which responses flow. Leaders in such groups talk more than followers, and when followers talk, they generally address people above them in the hierarchy. And, it is not simply in overt behavior that a ranking system appears in human groups. The arrangement of power affects the way people think and feel, which in turn affects the way they act. Low-ranking members tend to establish coalitions with people who are of higher rank, but who are not too distant from them in the hierarchy.

In work groups typically found in factories, the hierarchical arrangement defines the informal group structures that seem to appear spontaneously quite apart from the intentional designs of technology and formal organization. There are leaders and followers in the informal organization and interaction tends to occur among people who are fairly close in rank. Low-ranking members often desire to improve their standing in the group, but they display remarkable patience, taking care not to jeopardize whatever position they hold by aggressively vying for status. What is worse, perhaps, than being a low-ranking group member is to be an isolate who has been excluded from the group.[5]

Hierarchy serves various purposes. If a structure is efficient, it will give power to the members most capable of directing the group to achieve its goals. The members of the group who come closest to representing the characteristics and values most admired by others will find their status elevated. If these characteristics correspond to ability, then the power structure will be clearly defined and less susceptible to rivalry and contention.

Hierarchies stabilize as the rewards distributed to members of a group or organization correlate well with rank in the group. Power figures usually try to establish an equitable arrangement for the distribution of rewards. Nothing will undermine the stability of a power structure more than a sense of injustice members feel in the distribution of both tangible and intangible rewards. Members of a group who receive more pay and esteem than their rank deserves will elicit resentment and instability. What people get out of a group will need to balance with what they put into it.

When hierarchy is absent, social relations are subject to the pains of anxiety. The basic motivation then is to eliminate the apparent cause of the pain. In so-called leaderless groups, which have been used as training devices in group psychotherapy and group dynamics, behavior becomes immobilized upon the first appearance of anxiety.[6] Carried to the extreme, anxiety produced by a power vacuum can easily lead to reactions that resemble the psychological effects of sensory deprivation and isolation. If groups are unsuccessful in alleviating status anxiety, ever more regressive defenses will appear, including hostile projections of malevolence onto various group members. In other words, the state of power relations in a group affects significantly how people think and feel. Motivations are strong to create a hierarchy of power as a means of avoiding the sense of chaos characteristic of a disorganized crowd.

Hierarchies work when organizations prosper and people have confidence that the few have the best interests of the many in mind. When organizations no longer meet these two conditions, people reopen the three questions about satisfaction, belonging, and identity. The heightening of political consciousness, along with defensive behavior, follows.

The chief executive of a large conglomerate developed a reputation among his executives and middle managers as a man obsessed with the short-term movement of his company's common stock. It was well known throughout the organization that he had borrowed heavily to buy shares. He also had a reputation for passing on the responsibility for corporate mistakes, while he covertly supported and in some cases forced division heads to take risks to support quarterly earnings. Because he held a tight grip on the corporation and controlled the board, there appeared to be little anyone could do to change his behavior. But the operating heads of the various businesses in this conglomerate lost respect for him, and while outwardly compliant, they became critical among themselves. They stopped communicating with him and turned their attention to survival. For example, they took steps to ensure the loyalty to them of their own people. They insulated their operating businesses from corporate staff and steadfastly refused to voice formally any objections to the policies of their boss.

Situations need not deteriorate so completely for politics to undermine the integrity and effectiveness of hierarchy. Even the slight suggestion that power figures are operating with a personal agenda that excludes the interests of others will produce countermoves to protect well-defined individual and group interests. These countermoves employ the methods of calculation, which go right to the heart of the managerial mystique.

What do people do when they become wary of their bosses? They apply three principles of power economics to protect themselves: First, reverse the normal dependencies in hierarchies; second, enhance power bases by forming alliances; third, manipulate to advantage the relationship between personal investments and organizational rewards.

Hierarchy means inequality. Its justification is that it is the best way to get things done and to provide maximum returns for members. At its best hierarchy involves mutual obligations as well as differences in power and reward. Power holders are expected to look after the interests of people with lesser power. But in modern times the legitimacy of any dependency relationship in organizations has come into question. Employees have limited job security. They win maximum security by reversing the dependency, that is, by making the boss need them more than they need the boss. This principle has dominated labor relations in the United States since the inception of collective bargaining.

The notorious Jimmy Hoffa, the late president of the teamsters' union, was without peer in his ability to gain power by making himself indispensable. When still an adolescent, he led his fellow loaders on a strike at the Kroger grocery warehouse just when fresh strawberries had arrived and would rot if left on the trucks or the loading platform. He followed the principle of reversing dependencies during his rise in the union movement and employed it as well in constructing contractual agreements in the trucking industry. Under the tutelage of older union leaders, he refined the principle of dependency reversal to the point where, as president of the teamsters, he defined the vulnerable points in his industry and pressed them until employers needed him to maintain stability. The structure of the trucking industry made his tactics work, but without his sense of what happens when hierarchy has failed, it is doubtful that the union's total dominance of the industry would have been possible.

Collective bargaining provides an undisguised case of the strategy and tactics of dependency reversal. But within the many forms of authority that exist in an organization, subtler actions with similar aims unfold. These actions range from the minor deceptions of managing a boss to the major rivalries in decentralized organizations.

The decentralized organization fosters the development of dependency reversal unless strong psychological bonds link people together in common cause at all levels of the hierarchy. The decentralized organization is especially pertinent, since after Alfred Sloan put it in place at General Motors, it became the ideal form of organization in the management lexicon. Indeed, management consulting firms thrived on prescribing decentralization, although recently strategic planning has probably replaced it.

A decentralized organization establishes independent profit centers, each under the direction of a general manager. Depending on the size of the business, profit centers can be aggregated into divisions, and divisions into groups, with each layer of general management reporting to the next highest in the hierarchy. Following this definition, no organization is completely decentralized. Several autonomous units might share research and development, marketing, financial, legal, data processing, personnel, and other staff activities. But the aim of decentralization is to ensure that an accountable general manager has under his or her control the resources necessary to get the job done. Otherwise, if resources were outside his or her control, the general manager could excuse failure to meet projections.

No matter how high or low in the hierarchy, general managers frequently become obsessed with the need to turn the tables. Instead of the manager's being dependent on her boss, she wants her boss to become dependent on her. The simplest and probably most useful method is to become reliable. By following the golden rule of management (Say what you are going to do and do it), an executive increases her value to the organization. Her bargaining power rises, enabling her to dodge the dangerous dependency feelings, which are self-limiting and in violation of the ideals of managerial professionalism.

Beyond cultivating a reputation for reliability, an executive can engage in a number of tactics to ensure that his boss becomes dependent on him. For example, while known for his reliability, the executive may try to hide his method of performance. The more the executive keeps his boss's eye on the prediction, the less he has to reveal about the process.

One chief executive officer in a decentralized corporation was keenly aware of the contest underway to make the dependency feelings flow down rather than up the hierarchy. As in many corporations that are both diversified and decentralized, the corporate staff played a key role in this contest. The corporate financial officer and staff tried to establish direct lines of communication to counterpart staffs at the divisional and group levels. The corporate staff played much the same role that the president's staff plays in the White House: protect the boss and maintain his power. The heads of the operating units were on the whole successful in preventing corporate staff intrusion. Out of frustration, the chief executive officer announced the appointment of one senior corporate staff person to work closely with each divisional president. Perhaps to disguise the intent, the CEO announced the plan as "the buddy system." But the operating presidents were not amused and the plan met the same fate as other devices intended to infiltrate the so-called autonomous divisions. The CEO reluctantly scrapped the buddy system when it became evident that no one planned to treat it as a serious initiative.

Another tactic in this battle of dependency is to inculcate the habit of trading-off where it will do the most good. Loyalty is a sentiment that, unfortunately, has gone out of fashion, but trading-off is very much in vogue in the practices of corporate managers.

Writing in *Fortune,* Roy Rowan posed the question "What became of loyalty?"[7] Rowan talked to people in the corporate world and discovered that the answer was "It doesn't pay." It has fast disappeared in the executive ranks, because to be loyal is to relinquish one's hold on calculation as the way to make it to and stay at the top rungs of the corporate ladder. To be loyal requires that an individual invest emotionally in an organization and the people who best represent its ideals. Managers avoid making, and asking for, emotional investments. They would rather establish their relationships on the basis of calculation and exchange. If a manager can show immediate subordinates how their interests are served best by casting their lot with him in organizational politics, then it becomes easier to maintain his and his followers' independence.

For the many in the hierarchy, the sentiment of loyalty presupposes a commitment on the part of the few to accept obligations inherent in dependency. For the few, these obligations violate managerial calculus, because it soon becomes apparent that ordinary dependencies turn into entitlements; the fixed expectations entail both emotional and monetary costs, without necessarily providing commensurate returns in the short run.

A chief operating officer of a company expects someday to succeed the chief executive. However, the chances of linear succession in modern corporations are becoming slimmer as organizations become more professional. For example, the CEO of Rubbermaid, Inc., told Robert E. Fowler, Jr., the chief operating officer, that despite his being second in command, he would not be named successor upon the CEO's retirement. When asked about his reaction, Fowler said, "I'm disappointed. I feel that I certainly have the abilities to be the CEO of Rubbermaid, but that's not my call. . . . I came to Rubbermaid with the objective of becoming chairman when Mr. Gault retired."[8] Among the notable features of this example is the absence of expressed bitterness.

To express bitterness reveals the existence of dependency and expectation. There is little room for either emotion in corporations and, in conjunction, there is little room for loyalty. Once having accepted the ideals of calculation in choosing a career in management, people soon realize that investing needs and expectations in an organization can reduce the chances of satisfaction. The individual who is intent on maximizing returns must adopt the attitudes of a temporary worker. While here today, he could be gone tomorrow; in either staying or leaving, the aim is to keep the initiative in his own hands. The gains available in changing jobs exceed the prospect of gradual advancement usually available in staying with one company. The more loyal an individual, the less she will be able to maximize her returns.

Executives reach the top rungs of the power ladder in managerial-oriented businesses by good calculation and expert negotiation, especially on their own behalf. Once they reach the top, what they can expect from their subordinates is what they are able to negotiate. There is little right to expect loyalty. Managers who try to elicit loyalty and support will be seen as hypocrites or seducers luring people into relationships which offer them no advantage. Shrewd negotiations while climbing the ladder of power sooner or later produce a gross contradiction between what professional managers espouse and what they exemplify. The lesson learned in corporate politics is that loyalty is for suckers or for the unfortunate many who have not yet learned to look after themselves.

To command loyalty requires the acceptance of dependency as a legitimate aspect of human relations. People at the top feel no guilt concerning their power if they recognize that along with power goes responsibility for the well-being of subordinates. Like other emotions that create cohesion and morale, loyalty is generated by example. The willingness of people at the top to take responsibility for others engenders attachments to them and to the organizations they lead. The danger, of course, is that the acceptance of dependencies can burden the corporation with the sense of the many that they are entitled to compensation and security simply by virtue of their membership. But to reject dependencies means that organizations rely exclusively on utilitarian principles. Work then becomes an endless routine of bargaining, ultimately draining the vitality from human enterprise.

In the tactics for reversing dependency, the players are all sophisticated. They understand the tactics and, moreover, they recognize that one does not acknowledge this understanding to others, especially about the ultimate tactic, which is to terminiate the relationship.

Realizing that termination is a possible option reduces dependencies, but it also reduces commitments. For those who cannot exercise this option, dependency become real, and possibly frightening, particularly where calculation is the accepted way of doing business. Therefore, the managerial orientation produces its own paradoxes in creating an atmosphere that heightens political sensitivity. By fostering utilitarianism, organizations become two-class societies. The upper class consists of the people who are expert, or on their way to expertise, in the arts of calculation. The lower class consists of the dependents, the people who either do not understand the tactics of calculation or who emotionally cannot participate. The experts are the least committed people, who operate out of a packed suitcase, ready to leave the organization when circumstances and opportunities dictate. The product of this paradox is that an organization over time tends to lose the people who should be the most capable in handling power, but who cannot see the moral justification of hierarchy.

What do people do who seek to create advantage? In the lower classes of the hierarchy, what do people do who seek to overcome their inherent weaknesses in the power structure? They follow the pattern established from time immemorial—they form alliances. The combination of power in an alliance may successfully reverse dependency, when operating alone maintains a relatively weak position. Therefore, alliance politics is the second principle of power economics that comes into play when organizations politicize.

Chief executives in the modern decentralized corporation form alliances mainly with their staff. This alliance with people who have had limited or no operating experience draws the line of contention in corporate politics. This line pits the CEO and the CEO's staff against divisional and group executives who have bottom line responsibility. In defense of their interests, line operating executives try to build strong alliances to prevent infiltration and domination from corporate headquarters. The line executives support one another, share information on the foibles of the CEO and staff, and develop common approaches to dealing with budget battles. Since the balance of power depends on meeting expectations, the people who run profit centers prefer conservative forecasting rather than aggressive targets. Often, their incentive compensation is calculated to meet and exceed forecasts. The more conservative the forecast, the better the chances of handsome bonuses. These heads of profit centers not only are looking out for their own interests; they also realize that their subordinates will become resistant if they are forced to work against aggressive budgets, thus risking incentive compensation. Instead of encouraging bonds between CEOs and operating heads of businesses, the politics of the large, decentralized organizations create rifts.

It is strange to observe this weakening of the authority structure when protective alliances with staff people define the informal power structure in corporations. The problem is especially pronounced in multidivisional corporations that are highly diversified in products and markets. The homogeneous companies are less prone to the divisiveness of alliance politics because common interests, backgrounds, and concerns bring executives, line or staff, into closer working relationships.

In Wal-Mart Stores, Inc., the highly successful mass retail chain, the unity of purpose and commonality of understanding begins at the top. Sam Walton, who founded and runs Wal-Mart, is a retailer. He joins his associates in visiting stores and related retail operations in markets other than his own. He sets an example of attending to substance rather than to politics and process. In corporations that engage in unrelated businesses, operating executives complain of the frustration that results from talking to someone who has authority, but knows little and may care even less about the business.

Perhaps the most pernicious effect of corporate politics appears when people engage in mental maneuvers to make their situation bearable. People are most dissatisfied when they expect much and realize little from their work. The most obvious solution is to go to another place where rewards are greater. But except for the great calculators, people tend to stay on. In staying, they adapt to reduce the level of frustration. They invest less of their ego and yet get greater rewards through honing their political skills. If they maintain their investment and endure the frustration, stress illnesses are sure to follow. Those entrenched in the management ranks avoid stress by identifying with their profession, turning their attention inward to learning, and then manipulating the ropes to climb as high as the situation allows. Events inside the organization become a contest that provides excitement, not unlike the thrills politicians seek in constituency politics and government process.

This psychological introversion that occurs with the dominance of politics in organizations undermines business. It diverts attention from products and markets, from customers and competitors, where the attention really belongs. It fosters interest in tactics and promotes people with tactical imagination. In the end corporations become mediocre and inhospitable to creative people.

Organizations shape people's thoughts and feelings. Because hierarchies exist in business and other large organizations, people who join them look to power figures for the standards to meet and the ideals to emulate. For the utilitarian, standards and ideals are embedded in their pursuit of personal interests and therefore broader values become irrelevant. But the issue will not go away.

When power is real, it will evoke fear and envy, love and dependence, admiration and respect. These emotions cause people to begin to tend to themselves, either out of motives of self-protection or of satisfying deeply felt needs. In the lower levels of the hierarchy, the evocative aspects of power are not usually evident. The reason is that managers at the lower levels have little clout. Subordinates, therefore, do not respond to them as power figures. But the organization as a whole represents power, and people at the top evoke all the reactions to power, both good and bad.

In response to these emotions people absorb the standards implicit in the organization and words and actions of its power figures. When people actually work for someone who has power, either through the weight of position or competence, they make attachments and identify with the power figure. Power figures have the potential to influence people in profound ways and therefore assume a responsibility which they may neither enjoy nor understand.

Some power figures prefer to remain neutral in their influence on people's thoughts and feelings. They make a claim derived from the utilitarian policy of seeking a fair exchange without involving values beyond those necessary to complete a transaction. "A fair day's pay for a fair day's work" may be all there is to a relationship between employer and employee. The utilitarian operates according to the principles of least harm, if not of maximal freedom. Other power figures consciously or unconsciously make a larger claim to control the hearts and minds of their subordinates. Those who accept this kind of influence become totally dependent and therefore dangerous to themselves and other people. Their conscience becomes submerged in the will of the power figure, and their moral capacities eventually atrophy. Yet if hierarchies are to function, some other grounds for attachment and identification in work life must be found beyond the neutrality of fair exchange and the ego deprivation of total dependency.

The place to begin searching is the substance of the business and the activities that make up the work of the organization. Linking power to substance is simultaneously rational and personal, because it makes a demand on people to recognize value in what they are doing and in what the organization is to accomplish. At the same time it subordinates politics to uphold the standards of the business rather than to perpetuate personal advantage. People at the apex as well as those at the bottom of the hierarchy dedicate themselves to the broader standards and ideals. They join forces to accomplish valuable work. They gain self-respect regardless of power and position in the hierarchy.

Hierarchy is a reality of organization. To deny it is to ignore a fundamental fact of power. People distrust hierarchy because the inequality of power leads to abuse. But what is the source of this abuse? Is it to be found in inherent imperfections of hierarchy or in the motives and character of people in charge? Can the abuses be corrected by finding more suitable forms for distributing power and by erecting controls over power holders or by reaching a deeper understanding of the human psyche and trying to improve the quality of leadership?

Chapter 10

The Corruption of Power

*M*ore than ten years ago, Richard Nixon resigned from the presidency of the United States. Rather than resign with grace and a sense of remorse, he waited and then launched a deliberate campaign to erase Watergate from consciousness. With a shrewd sense of how to use media, and an unerring instinct for making money in the process, Nixon tried to sell the following message: Judge a power holder by the decisions he makes on the big issues (such as war and peace) rather than by his oversights and errors on the smaller issues (such as campaigning for office), and, above all, ignore matters of character and concentrate on results. By implication, the message is societies survive by the ends achieved and not by the means used to pursue them. The message is tempting, but morally corrupt.

Leaders affect societies and organizations profoundly in their impact on morality, morale, and the fundamental attitude toward authority and power. Americans approach authority with deep ambivalence. Major scandals, such as the Iran-contra affair and Watergate, and events on a smaller scale, such as the failure of the Continental Illinois bank in 1984, make people less inclined to cast their lot with those who gain power, either by election or appointment, making the job of leadership more difficult. Future generations may approve of Nixon's policy that opened the door to renewed relations with China, but they cannot ignore the long-term effect of dishonesty on the willingness of people to trust and work with their leaders. The ability to lead depends, in part, on what leaders face in popular attitudes toward authority—the people's willingness to cooperate, to withhold judgment, and to help leaders prove their worth.

Power holders in government and business would do well to contemplate what Lord Acton said in his inaugural lecture on assuming the Regius Professorship of Modern History at Cambridge:

> I exhort you never to debase the moral currency or to lower
> the standard of rectitude, but to try others by the final
> maxim that governs your own lives, and to suffer no man
> and no cause to escape the undying penalty which history
> has the power to inflict on wrong.... Opinions alter, man-
> ners change, creeds rise and fall, but the moral law is written
> on the tablets of eternity.[1]

This stern exhortation to historians to judge leaders is based on the fear that the possession of power has a corrupting influence on people. Acton's words are well known: "Power tends to corrupt; absolute power corrupts absolutely.... Great [to be read powerful?] men are almost always bad men...."[2]

Do great men and women become bad because power makes them arrogant and unfeeling for their constituents, and yet grandiose about themselves? Or do individuals seeking greatness often carry with them fatal flaws that corrupt power, which in itself is neutral, amoral, and a force awaiting goals and direction? Flaws in judgment, and ultimately in character, convert power from a constructive to a destructive force. When powerholders corrupt power, they often tell a story of a deeply personal need for control, fear of being dominated by others, and doubt about their legitimacy as powerholders.

In examining cases where authority fails, it appears at first blush that incompetence at the top is the root cause. For example, when the history of the Continental Illinois bank is written, competence of top management will be a major issue. It is obvious from the departure of the lending officers that they were being blamed for the bank's troubles. Blaming lesser executives, after the fact, could not undo the damage done by the reckless granting of large loans to questionable oil ventures. Some observers said that competitive pressures and faulty incentives tied to new standards of performance were the cause of the Continental Illinois failure. But these observers overlook the fact that structural defects result from the ideas, motives, and actions of top management. The chief executive of Continental Illinois must have fostered recklessness, either by misplaced delegation or by outright collusion, in a risky course of action which board members either did not understand or chose to ignore. Blaming subordinates attempts to preserve the power of the chief executive despite blatant evidence of incompetence. Although the shift of responsibility downward may affect the perception of outsiders, to insiders the truth is out: The chief is incompetent and the enterprise is in peril.

In one company suffering from an incompetent chief executive, subordinates were outwardly loyal (perhaps compliant is a more accurate term) but inwardly seething over their chief's poor judgment. The CEO adroitly managed to pass the blame for failure on to others and nearly convinced outside constituents, such as lenders, that he was not at fault in the misfortunes of the business. But subordinates understood the situation differently. Morale suffered throughout the organization; some of the best people left, while the less able and more dependent individuals clung to their jobs, hoping only to survive.

Incompetence, not a simple failure of intellect or just plain bad luck, frequently is a reflection of immaturity. The fantasies of youth that drive the ambition for power will hardly ever entertain the stark fact that power is burdensome, that it involves accountability and responsibility. In some cases immaturity appears as arrogance, the belief in the omnipotence of one's ideas. In other cases the immaturity shows as a lust for power. Fantasies associated with power are often infantile, grandiose, incapable of being fulfilled, and intricately involved in the individual's neurotic struggles.

Problems in holding and using power also arise frequently from the individual's psychological conflicts rather than from external frustrations. More often than not, the fights people have with others or problems in handling difficult conditions result from, rather than cause, their psychological problems. Conflicts within the personality express themselves in strong desires that cannot easily find outlets in productive activity, whether solitary or cooperative. Strong desires remain unfulfilled and turn in on themselves, thereby affecting the individual's actions and emotional reactions.

Facing the end of his active career, the head of a business found only empty choices in his search for someone to whom he could pass the mantle of power. His was a history of friendships, partnerships, and associations lost or destroyed. For him, power was a means of getting even, and life was a repetition of episodes of revenge. Even vacations amounted to acts of retribution rather than of renewal and pleasure. The only people who seemed able to work for him were of two types. First there were those who were too young and too insecure to understand that they were being beguiled into a relationship by promises that were never going to be fulfilled. Once they understood that fact, they would depart, leaving their chief executive further embittered. The second type understood his motives, but chose to get as much as they could from the relationship by extracting concessions from him in constant haggling over salary and other cash incentives.

This businessperson was aware of his conflicts. He could attribute his attitudes to the death of his father, which occurred just when the two were to begin working together to fulfill a dream both father and son cherished. After his return from the service to join his father in the business, the older man succumbed to a sudden heart attack. Never fully able to mourn his loss, the executive played out his bitter dream of revenge. He could take little interest in younger people because, without realizing it, he could not bear the thought that they could, or should, benefit from the kind of fathering he wanted, but never felt he really had.

It is not unusual for people to have understanding within their grasp, but be unable to comprehend and use it. As with this executive, the key idea is not beyond consciousness. Rather it is suspended at the top of a pyramid of associations that contains at its base some deep emotions. This foundation of emotions, which is well beneath awareness, affects character and supports the conflicts that prevent intelligent and humane uses of power.

Power is the potential of an individual to alter the behavior of other people. Whether or not this potential results in actual change depends on many conditions, not the least of which is the ability of other people to assess their interests and to act accordingly. In other words, having power does not mean that one automatically gets what one desires. Executives often feel frustrated and angry because of discrepancies between what they want and what they get. The problem sometimes arises because of unrealistic expectations that exist as an outgrowth of prior frustration and overwhelming need or that persist from defective relationships with other people. People become obstacles rather than helpers; they block rather than facilitate fulfilling desires. The sense of people as obstacles or as helpers conditions attitudes and behavior toward them, and in a self-fulfilling prophecy, what one believes tends to become actuality.

Harold Geneen worshipped facts. The search for certitude was a deeply embedded aspect of his character. As chairman and chief executive officer of ITT, while ostensibly delegating, Geneen erected a structure of control to ensure that he could maintain a hold over this complex, worldwide corporation. Commenting on his management style, Geneen said, "If I had enough arms, legs and time, I'd do it all myself."[3]

Geneen tried to achieve certitude by creating a system of monthly reports from his profit center managers and his controllers. By the time he left ITT, the company employed 375,000 people involved in a wide diversity of operations. To control such an ungainly company, Geneen broke it down into 250 profit centers. Except for August and December, the manager of each profit center had to submit a monthly report citing all the conditions affecting the performance of the unit.

The monthly reports had to contain financial analyses of sales, profits, return on investment, and every other relevant measurement, as well as a description of possible problems and how they arose. The information presented in the monthly report had to be "unshakable facts," and all potential problems had to be "red-flagged." The reports sometimes were as long as twenty single-spaced typewritten pages.

To ensure that his staff distinguished "unshakable facts" from "so-called facts," Geneen wrote a memorandum:

> There is no word in the English language that more strongly conveys the intent of incontrovertibility, i.e., "final and reliable reality," than the word "fact." . . . However, no word is more honored by its breach in actual usage. The highest art of professional management requires the literal ability to "smell" a "real fact" from all others—and moreover to have the temerity, intellectual curiosity, guts and/or plain impoliteness, if necessary to be *sure* that what you do have is indeed what we will call an "unshakable fact."[4]

The reliability of facts in the reports was tested at monthly meetings. Each profit center manager was expected to have read all the reports and to be prepared to defend his own and criticize others. Geneen seemingly read all the reports and made notations in red ink at passages that raised questions in his mind. He presided over the mammoth meetings, which sometimes lasted up to fifteen hours at a stretch, with a firm hand.[5] Having no respect for the old theory of not criticizing a person in front of others, often he would grill a manager to get at the "facts." Although he might sometimes forgive an admitted error, Geneen was infuriated when he suspected fudging or covering up.

Many people found Geneen's questioning technique almost sadistic in its intensity, and many managers were crushed at each session. Most people, however, felt that Geneen did not attack just to exercise his power, but because he genuinely felt that it was a necessary procedure. As he described it himself:

> I'm no laissez-faire, let-me-know-how-things-are-in-six-months guy. I want to know what's going on. I don't want some proud guy to get into his own Vietnam and then suddenly hand me his resignation. Hell, his resignation can't bring back the $10 million he'd lose. That's why I make everyone tell me about red flag areas—spots where trouble may be brewing.[6]

At another time he said, "I believe in pushing and pulling and kneading and whittling until you finally get those two purple drops."[7]

Geneen introduced his system of reports and monthly meetings while he was at Raytheon. As an additional check on the content of the managers' reports, Geneen swamped the company with controllers who were required to submit a detailed monthly critique of a unit's progress directly to the corporate controller. Since prior to Geneen's arrival controllers and division managers had cooperated together in running their divisions and reporting to higher management, this was an innovation that was resented. At Raytheon the reports were nicknamed "yellow peril" reports (only partly because they were bound in yellow paper). Progress in a division was measured solely by profit performance—the objective to which Geneen directed all his energies.[8]

Attending general manager meetings on a monthly basis required a huge expenditure of time and energy. Geneen once estimated that he had a total of 2,400 years of business managerial experience on hand for each meeting. At another time he added up the hours spent attending such meetings and found that it took 35 weeks of his and his managers' time. After subtracting vacation and holiday time (never taken by Geneen), this "left a scant 13 weeks of 'other' time in which to run the company."[9] The scantiness was made up by working weekends and nights.

Geneen justified the amount of time spent on meetings by saying that "It was truly at our meetings and the face-to-face meetings down the line in our subsidiaries that we ran ITT."[10] It was thus that ITT and Geneen, to use one of his favorite phrases, had "no surprises." "There's no substitute for getting the facts, because," he claimed, "when you're aware of the problems, you soon think in terms of the solutions."[11]

For Harold Geneen, the need for control and reliance on "facts" instead of people was a recurrent theme. Executives frequently seek power in perpetuation of early childhood fantasies about how to gain control over parents so that they may become predictable. Dominance over people rather than control of situations can be the driving motive for seeking power. These fantasies can poison the sense of power one achieves in reality and can lead to an outbreak of irrational behavior which so often produces disastrous results for the individual and the organization.

Geneen was relatively isolated from his parents, who were separated early in his childhood, and he learned to counteract feelings of loneliness and dependency. In his memoir Geneen reported an early memory from the time he was a boarding student in a convent school.

> I have a vivid memory of myself at age six, sitting at a desk alone in a large empty classroom reading a book. The Mother Superior came by and, concerned over my apparent loneliness, asked me what I was doing. I told her simply that I was reading a book. She smiled at me sympathetically. Perhaps I noticed the pity in her expression. What remains with me is the feeling that she was wrong, that I never felt uncomfortable about being alone. I thought that I could always find something to do, even at that tender age. Per-

haps the isolation back then taught me to be independent, to be able to think through my small daily problems, and to achieve a sense of self-confidence.[12]

For someone who professed independence and who "never felt uncomfortable being alone," Geneen managed through his system of controls to have people around him almost constantly. Yet, these contrived associations never attacked directly Geneen's rejection of his need for people. He used power to get what he needed while disguising to himself and others the dependency that lurked beneath the image of a powerful and self-sufficient person.

As Geneen's career with ITT demonstrated, his need for power finally absorbed him and involved him and his company in a variety of questionable dealings with Chile and inappropriate contributions to the Republican party in order to gain justice department approval of significant acquisitions. The string had run out on his phenomenal program for building "the number one size corporation in the world."[13] Even before his troubles with the government surfaced and his image to the public was marred, Geneen's frenetic pace with acquisitions (ITT acquired twenty domestic companies in 1968) revealed a compulsive need for power that was out of his control.

One of the ways people regulate their needs and tolerate frustrations is by believing that satisfaction is possible and that once appropriate action is taken, the desire will diminish. Eating food abates hunger; sexual activity provides satisfaction and eliminates sexual tension. This expectation of satisfaction appears in a person's character as the ability to delay gratification and provides an enormous resource for self-control. With it one can wait for power or for power to produce results, as one can wait for food on the table.

A perverse need works in the opposite way. The more one gets, the more one needs. Greed for power appears contradictory to the apparent self-assurance executives display. But beneath this self-assurance lurks emptiness and low self-esteem. A perverse need for power can never relinquish its control over the human mind. Greedy people are angry people who, if the anger turns inward, will become clinically depressed. Acquisition of more power may ward off depression, but the perverse need encourages self-destructive behavior. If the perversion is isolated, kept secret, and stops short of illegal or unethical actions, the individual may be protected from depression and may in fact be able to function well. The uncertainty, however, is how firmly the anger encapsulated in the perversion will remain contained. When the capsule breaks, destructive behavior flows out.

Blatant violations of law or ethics may result from a desperate need to stabilize one's inner world under stress. But actions need not be illegal or unethical to call attention to the relationship between motives and role. When the role calls for exercising power, people with power conflicts will pursue aims that are egocentric, defensive, and usually out of touch with reality. Despite their massive need for control, they themselves are out of control.

The ability to reach decisions and to act includes a good sense of timing. One must be able, when appropriate, to implement associative thinking and to provide closure. The timing of thinking and acting can be disturbed when power needs become perverse. The disturbance can take the form of impulsiveness, the inability to think before acting, or the form of circularity, the inability to bring thinking to a conclusion and take action.

An executive assumed the position of general manager of one operating division in a large corporation. This division, in serious financial difficulty, needed decisive action to form a plan for a turnaround, to organize and staff key positions where weaknesses appeared, and to enact the turnaround plan. Because of the circularity of his thinking, the executive could not function in his job. When, for example, questions of divesting unprofitable units were considered, he would return to the possibility of making them profitable. He felt that he had to be absolutely certain before he could take action. Providing the certainty he needed was impossible.

Another characteristic of his circular reasoning appeared in his approach to establishing organizational structure and assigning jobs. He could not distribute authority cleanly and insisted on overlapping responsibilities because of his reluctance to express finality and closure about organizational structure. He rationalized his reluctance by extolling the merits of "open-ended" organizational structure.

This executive inspired loyalty and personal devotion of subordinates. He was placed in his assignment for his ability to motivate people and consequently to create a cohesive organization dedicated to reversing the division's misfortunes. The ability to achieve loyalty stemmed, in part, from his attractive personality, his ability to express ideas interestingly, and, above all, his aversion to making other people unhappy. This last characteristic was one of the causes of his inability to decide and to act. He was deeply afraid of offending and hurting others. As head of a failing division, however, he could take little action that would not cause some discontent, particularly in altering job responsibilities and assignments.

His fear of hurting others originated from two sources. First, he felt, but suppressed, competitive feelings toward a younger brother who was also a business executive. The younger brother had a reputation for toughness, leading one to suspect that each brother unconsciously cultivated different character traits and styles to dissolve their rivalry. Second, he wanted to make more of his life than his father. In fact, much of the rivalry with the younger brother arose from the displacement of competitive feelings from his father to his brother. This executive, in short, was guilt stricken over the prospect that his decisions could prove hurtful to other people even though the motives and reasons were not intended to hurt. He leaned over backward to avoid offending, and his caution manifested itself in overelaborate thinking, as though he had to be completely certain of every action he took.

At one time the conventional wisdom about abilities for successful management placed decisiveness at the top of the list. A subtle change, however, has taken place. Increasingly, ambiguity and the ability to devise and work in open-ended forms of organization are being extolled. The shift is away from straight-line organizations, executive responsibility, and the ability to make decisions as individual acts of commitment. This shift may be an error.

This change is partly directed at overcoming rigidity in thinking—the inclination to see things as black or white, right or wrong. Rigid thinking, found in authoritarian personalities, indeed can adversely affect decisions and organizations. But before becoming too enthusiastic about a new wave of management practice designed to correct one set of problems, be aware of the potential problem of circuitous and even duplicitous thought patterns that the new practice may encourage. Cerebration can be a manifestation of character conflicts within individuals. Once these conflicts are rationalized and extended into an organization's practice, they can paralyze will and the ability to act. Circularity through the elaboration of thought and manipulation of words is not an improvement over the rigidity of authoritarianism.

Perhaps managerial organizations encourage the elaboration of process and the convolution of ideas in reaction to the potential for corrupting power. However, when this occurs, communication difficulties soon appear. Rather than remedy the problem by simplifying the process, the response is often to engage in more process.

Behind this emphasis on formal process is a psychological defense: the isolation of thinking and feeling that may be at the heart of the difficulties certain executives face in making decisions and in communicating with others. In one organization, a high executive found that when she tried to present her views in meetings, no one really listened to or absorbed what she had to say. The first conclusion that came to mind was that she aroused competitive feelings among her co-workers, especially the men, who ignored her because they envied her brilliance. Closer observation suggested another explanation. Her participation was entirely verbal and totally lacking in emotional value. One could sense an earnestness on her part, but she had so successfully isolated thinking and feeling that her words lacked color, relative emphasis, and humor—all qualities that make it possible to convey ideas.

For this executive organizational sanctions against emotional expression reinforced a trend already at work in her personality, the rigid control of her feelings. Throughout her development she guarded against feelings and concentrated on intellect. As a result of this rejection of part of herself, her functioning lacked spontaneity and ultimately effectiveness.

One grave danger for authority figures is to extend isolation of thought from feeling to isolation from other people. Such a trend is disastrous in an executive power structure because it removes constructive exchange between the chief executive and the board and subordinates from the process of policy making.

A chief executive of a large corporation tendered his resignation, publicly giving the reason that he was in bad health. For a time before his resignation, he had been incapacitated by a stomach distress requiring surgery and then by an arthritic problem requiring bed rest. But the announced reason for the resignation hid a long and often bitter battle between him and his board of directors. The battle evolved because the company had suffered serious operating losses following a disastrous diversification program the chief executive officer had initiated. The executive was determined to hold on to his position; the board was equally determined to replace him.

A review of the history of the company under the chief executive officer's direction indicated that he had taken some important initiatives to overcome the company's loss of competitive position. But as he developed greater power and control over the organization, he isolated himself from subordinates as well as from board members. One board member was so opposed to the decision to diversify in areas far removed from the company's expertise and strength that he resigned, indicating that the chief executive officer refused to accept counsel from others. Leaks to the press reported the hostility subordinates felt toward the chief executive officer, with one person reporting that "he ruled by sheer terror."

Prior to his difficulties in this company, few facts about the chief executive officer's background suggested that he was vulnerable to self-isolation in a position of power. In fact, in the early days of his administration, to avoid upsetting many of the executives who were dedicated to the corporation's traditions, his moves appeared to be governed by caution and patience. But once he had his people in place, he seemed to change. He became overly ambitious in his estimates of what the company could do, detached himself from his board, and treated subordinates harshly.

Executives who detach themselves emotionally from subordinates and higher authority simultaneously probably overvalue themselves. Operating with an inflated ego and a sense of grandiosity, they show little regard for other people.

Grandiosity signifies a failure within the individual to control the aggression overflowing from the consolidation of power. Having acquired power and having consolidated dominance over real or imagined rivals, hidden identifications surface and take control over the personality. These hidden identifications reflect childhood fantasies about powerful parents, in themes of master and slave, of oppressor and oppressed. The aggression contained in these images arises out of a deep sense of loneliness and the constant fear that one can be abandoned by powerful people and left victim to a hostile world. In an effort to gain control over such fear, the person makes an unconscious identification with the aggressor, with the power figure who provides or withholds, gratifies or deprives, creates or annihilates life.

The appearance of grandiosity, particularly when an executive was deferential and compliant in his rise to power, would seem to indicate that power itself was the corrupting influence. But power can only corrupt when the grandiose fantasies already are in place because of early experience.

Grandiosity and loneliness: What part do they play in the lives of executives attracted to power? If they exist, they are suppressed to guard the executive's survival in the managerial culture. The ideal of this culture is to be low key in emotional involvement, to appear rational, to be totally in control of one's reactions, and to be predictable.

A middle-aged executive, soon after receiving a promotion, suffered an anxiety attack. He awoke abruptly with shortness of breath, sweating, and a sensation of constriction in his throat. In a state of panic (he thought he was having a heart attack), he called the police who rushed him to the hospital. After intensive observation and tests, his doctors assured him that he had not had a heart attack and that physically he was in good health. The anxiety attack recurred and subsequent physical examinations confirmed the earlier diagnosis, that he suffered from anxiety rather than heart disease. He was referred for psychotherapy.

During the course of therapy he described his current situation as lonely, without family, and centered mainly on work. Despite outward self-assurance, he held a rather low opinion of himself. Even the support of those who knew his work and the evidence of his recent promotion could not bolster his confidence in his ability to perform. Further exploration indicated a sense of disgust on his part over his isolated and promiscuous sexual life. He debased the type of partner he selected and noted the absence of any quality to these relationships other than the sexual activity.

His early life history indicated a pattern of emotional isolation from his parents. Although his father appeared to be the most important person in his life, the manager felt all through his childhood that he was a disappointment to his father. The manager, nevertheless, continued to seek approval. Unconsciously, however, he had identified with his mother. This identification proved to be a problem for him in working with men, in exercising authority, and in establishing good relations with women.

The anxiety attack following his promotion arose from the expectation that his subordinates would come to hate him just as he unconsciously hated his father. He reacted as a man under attack, and although the threat was self-generated, its effects were as damaging as a real threat from the outside world. Perhaps this self-generated threat was even more damaging in that he could neither identify the danger nor protect himself from it.

People compensate for their felt deficiencies. Some men who are short in stature try to overcome this self-defined inadequacy by behaving aggressively. To be called egotist and bully may seem light compared with the satisfaction of proving strength and adequacy. Literature is filled with plots about the person born at the bottom of the ladder who struggles to make it to the top of the ladder to enjoy a sense of victory that appears to go along with power, money, and social position. Cruelty and villainy may accompany this striving for power. In Shakespeare's *Richard III,* the protagonist is physically deformed and justifies his actions because nature cheated him.

> I, that am . . .
> Cheated of feature by dissembling Nature,
> Deform'd, unfinish'd, sent before my time
> Into this breathing world, scarce half made up,
> And that so lamely and unfashionable
> That dogs bark at me as I halt by them—
> Why, I . . .
> Have no delight to pass away the time, . . .
> And therefore, since I cannot prove a lover
> To entertain these fair well-spoken days,
> I am determined to prove a villain
> And hate the idle pleasures of these days.[14]

The need for power to overcome felt inadequacies goes deeper than real or imagined deficiencies to unconscious fears. Fear of failure is a familiar and even a plausible psychological condition. An individual afraid of failure will avoid the responsibilities that go along with power. The reasons for the fear of failure are found in the debilitating effects of unconscious fantasy. The most self-defeating fantasy is one in which power is acquired at someone else's expense. Frequently, the figure with whom this struggle for power persists in the unconscious is a parent of the same sex. Rather than risk the guilt and imagined retribution for succeeding in this oedipal conflict, inhibitions and the fear of failure become established in the mind. If success should come to them, their inhibitions interfere and they experience failure, the failure they initially feared.

The board of directors of a corporation in serious difficulty appointed a new chief executive officer. The directors were elated with the results of this new appointment. In short order, the new chief executive officer developed a turnaround plan. After he brought in new executives, he implemented an effective organizational structure. The changes seemed too good to be true and, indeed, about a year later unsettling information came to the attention of a few board members. Key subordinates reported alarm over changes in the chief's behavior and personality. These executives, not intent on making trouble, were devoted to their boss and loyal to the programs he had established to make the company successful. The subordinates observed that the chief executive officer suddenly withdrew from his work, seemed to show little enthusiasm for his job, and often displayed poor judgment. In addition, he drank excessively.

The board, after looking into the problem, decided to confront the chief executive. They hoped for an explanation that would relieve them of anxiety and would assure them that the chief executive would resume his familiar ways of running the corporation.

The chief executive officer denied vehemently that he had a drinking problem. He said that he had become depressed and had entered psychiatric treatment. He claimed that the drug prescribed for depression produced the symptoms that suggested he was drinking excessively. He was given a medical leave of absence. It turned out that although he was seriously depressed, he was also alcoholic, a condition that seemed to have surfaced in response to his success rather than in fear of impending failure. He ultimately had to resign.

Anxiety over success defies reason and common sense. Is it that success evokes hidden guilt feelings ("I am not deserving")? If so, then there would seem to be little difference between fear of failure and fear of success. There is, however, a substantial difference. In fear of success, the individual, rather than being guilt-ridden, is driven to gain power to fulfill unrealizable fantasies from the past.

Psychological explanations of why people corrupt power often evoke skepticism. People may react even more warily if the explanations depend on the theory of unconscious motivation. It all may appear unscientific and too pat. People often ask, by way of venturing their own opinion, if all neurotics were excluded from positions of power, who would be left? The answer is probably no one. It is true that power-oriented people have significant psychological conflicts. It is also true that power provides a stage on which individuals can act out their problems, reveal their dreams, and create a world that improves on the one they know and experience. Is all this unhealthy and the source of the corruption of power? Henry Kissinger is alleged to have said that power is a great aphrodisiac. It is a great therapy for some, while it is poison for others. The difficult task is to distinguish the one from the other.

The fundamental difference between those who corrupt power and those who seem to grow with it is the nature of their ideals and moral standards. Ideals and standards act as an inner parent to help form a character that is forward-looking and sensitive to the responsibilities that go along with power. To acquire power for selfish ends (consciously to accrue money for its own sake) or to dominate other people out of a need to control (unconsciously to compensate for felt deficiencies or to avenge past injuries) is fundamentally regressive.

The idea of the future takes shape and meaning from personal history. No one escapes totally from traumatic experiences in childhood. Although no one escapes the pains of development, some are fortunate to incorporate the ideals and standards presented to them by an adult who acts as a beneficent model. Much is made of mentorship in the preparation of leaders. But mentors appear usually long after maturation. Personality is established early in life. Those who set standards and foster positive ideals have an impact well before late childhood and adolescence. But once these constructive influences are established, individuals have the capacity to benefit from what models and mentors have to offer.

Standards and ideals incorporated through identification with good and giving parents continue their force as a result of character and unconscious mental activity. The individual finds from early influences means for taming power into a benign, but forceful, conscience and a forward-looking as well as humane ego ideal. The individual, thus, continually strives for achievement to build a vision of what might be, but is ever mindful of present human needs. Such leaders have no need to climb over other people's backs to achieve power, just as they will not inflict pain on others in the name of expediency. Those who find and accept the help that mentors offer internalize the image of models. They are unafraid of their own aggression because within their incorporated models is a standard that permits aggression in a measured and directed way toward human ends without the lust of self-aggrandizement. People who are ambivalent about aggression, framed as it may be in the structure of authority and power, have reason to mistrust their motives. They experience a vulnerability to their own power because their inner dialogue with early models contains a struggle between love and hate, acceptance and rejection, and the compelling need to rewrite their personal history.

There is ample evidence of the malevolent uses of power once the corrupting influences make their appearance. The history of this century is eloquent testimony to the suffering imposed by people who acquired power and then used it toward destructive ends. In political structures, including business organizations, the leader's irrationality will be the followers' suffering.

Even attempts to guard against the dangers of individual irrationality may result in the corruption of power. Organizational norms substituted for individual conscience make it nearly impossible for power holders to maintain commitments. As products of institutional standards, such managers give primacy to the organization, not the individual. They do not see themselves as harmful, but they do harm, because their individual consciences become subordinate to organizational norms. The good intentions of many managers recede in reaction to the anxiety of surviving in a large organization where power seems elusive. If managers believe that goals and purposes are derived from the organization's process and therefore lie strictly outside their personal convictions and the interests of constituents, then accountability disappears. If to escape the morbid effects of personality corrupting power, the heads of organizations are faceless individuals acutely attuned to the play of power, but without a deep understanding of the humane uses of power, then organizations will inevitably be politicized.

In an earlier day the corruption of power by the nature of organizations was identified as the "bureaucratic malaise." Bureaucracy fostered the separation of the individual from the role he or she was supposed to play. The virtues of bureaucracy are impartiality, the absence of prejudice, and objectivity. At its best, a bureaucratic organization counterbalances the impulsivity and destructiveness of troubled leaders. But, as Hitler's Germany indicated, bureaucracy has no human values. It can just as easily turn objective capacities and efficiency to killing as to working for humane purposes. This inability to judge ethically is a consequence of organizational politics, coupled with the narrow careerism of people deficient in substantive interests.

In theory, organizations are supposed to contain processes that prevent the corruption of power in the use of efficient means to serve bad ends. If striving for technical proficiency overwhelms humane purposes, the mechanisms for correction are supposed to intercede. But too often these mechanisms cause laxness in individual judgment and conscience. Mainly, organizational process involves interaction but heightens sensitivity to the acceptability of ideas and not necessarily their correctness as measured against economic and ethical yardsticks. After a time, the image of acceptance produces what the *Fortune* writer, William H. Whyte, called "the organization man," who substitutes corporate membership for individual identity in achieving self-esteem.[15]

The hold that organizations secure on the minds of their members arises out of some important needs. One of these needs is self-esteem, the assurance the individual seeks that he or she is a worthwhile person. In the past people derived self-esteem from successful performance and human relationships. In more recent times executives have tried to borrow self-worth from belonging to prestigious organizations, such as General Motors or IBM. Although these sources of self-esteem may be mutually enhancing, people tend to look in one direction or the other as their primary source of self-worth.

The corollary to self-esteem is self-knowledge, or what Norman Holland, the gifted literary scholar and critic, calls the "I."[16] Knowledge of the "I," or of identity, is elusive. It can be secure at times and then become blurred. Those moments (or years) when identity is diffuse are anxious times. What people do in these periods of self-doubt and confusion tells a great deal about the strength of their character as well as their ability to learn.

The professions or callings people pursue weigh greatly in their identities. In management the task of identity may pose more hazards than in other fields in which professional and personal knowledge grow hand-in-hand. In particular, the managerial mys-

tique may prove in the end to provide a faulty connection between the individual and the role. This faulty connection makes it
imperative that the individual dig more deeply for answers to the
question "Who am I?" Unfortunately, most managers are not introspective and are satisfied with their profession's answer. As a consequence, when they achieve power it may fail to enhance them
as individuals; instead it may reinforce tendencies already at work
for the corruption of power. For a powerholder, the diffusion of
identity sets in motion the need to defend against anxiety at the
expense of objectivity.

Chapter 11

Identity Diffused

*I*t is popular today to speak of organizations as having unique cultures. But it is not clear how the term *culture* can be used to describe modern organizations. If culture is simply any set of expectations that guides people in their behavior in organizations, then all organizations have and always will have a culture. But if the term has a richer meaning and intends to convey something about tradition, symbol, lore, and texture in human relationships, then culture is a fading phenomenon in business.

The absence of corporate culture is not necessarily considered a problem. It takes energy and care by a chief executive officer to support a culture, beginning with regard for the past and attention to ritual. For those chief executives who prize flexibility and the expansion of options, organization culture is a hindrance they would rather not have. To respect culture, it simply would not be possible to run a business objectively, as though it were a portfolio of assets that can be acquired, held, and divested depending upon how the numbers read.

Sanford Sigiloff was brought in to reorganize the Wickes Corporation under pressure from lenders when it became clear that the company had gotten into trouble over a program of acquisitions it could not manage and a debt load it could not support.[1] Sigiloff took the company into Chapter 11 of the bankruptcy code. He brought it out successfully after a series of hard moves and clever maneuvers that allowed him to control the various committees of creditors.

Sigiloff's story of his handling of the bankruptcy is especially interesting because he invited a reporter to follow his actions as they were unfolding. Evidently not unaware of the power of publicity, Sigiloff allowed a reporter into his inner circle. The result is a revealing account of a masterful tactician at work. Clearly, he would have had great difficulty in making his moves had he prized personal attachments and paid homage to corporate culture. The company was in deep trouble, in part because its former chief executive and board of directors ventured into acquisitions and debt load it was ill-equipped to handle. The net result was the transfer of power to Sigiloff, an executive who was so unencumbered by attachments and traditions that he could fire people and liquidate and sell businesses with ease in the interests of restoring liquidity and freeing the company from excessive debt.

All people have their own conceptions of human psychology. They assemble a set of rules from experience that may even lead them to believe they are fairly adept at influencing people to get what they want. When do you inform, request, argue, order, or threaten to get things done? When do you appeal to self-interest, seduce the other person through flattery, manipulate by creating a need and becoming the agent through whom that need can be satisfied, obfuscate to conceal your motives, or show muscle? Management as a profession has accumulated its own "book of rules" on how to use power and how to influence peoples' thoughts and actions.

Although Machiavelli had a fine appreciation of how these rules of manipulative psychology work, even he could not have envisioned the corporate state and its sophisticated, yet unwritten, rules on getting things done through people. Nor would he have anticipated the mentality of the modern manager who displays flexibility and adaptation found only in people who have little regard for history or tradition.

The question that needs to be answered is what manner of human beings are the ultimate flexible people? How do they think about themselves? Do they have an identity? Or is identity a limiting idea in understanding professional managers?

Are flexibility and adaptability virtues? Character traits describe human qualities, but they are also values. As such, flexibility and adaptability have become norms to which people aspire and to which they may be conditioned. These traits have become desirable and even necessary for people entering management.

In the minds of people who hold them, values represent good. They may seem so good that people aspire to them without limit; in other words, a person cannot be too flexible or too adaptable. But, according to Aristotle's golden mean, every virtue carried to its extreme becomes a vice. One of the hidden agendas of management as a profession is to foster flexibility and adaptability. As character traits that people adopt through their training and experience, flexibility and adaptability are common and functional in the real world. But as dominant character traits and, more significantly, as values of unlimited virtue, flexibility and adaptability become the source of many problems in personal and business relationships and in the effectiveness of organizations.

Organizations are not necessarily the best places to observe what happens to people and their work when they try to blend perfectly into their environment. The short-term effects tend to look good. The long-term effects tell a different story. Unfortunately, the place to observe long-term effects is the consulting rooms of the psychotherapists solicited to help undo the consequences of living like a chameleon.

The chief executive of a successful business, for example, became anxious and depressed following an injury in an automobile accident. Although the injury was not life threatening, the CEO was laid up for several weeks and was unable to follow his carefully drawn and fully organized routine. During this time his thoughts turned to his early family experience; he revived an old but seemingly forgotten feeling that he had been unloved by a restrictive and demanding mother and a detached, passive father. As a child and young man, the executive aggressively tackled whatever tasks life presented. In school he received top grades. Early in his business career he performed well, meeting his responsibilities first as a salesman and later as a sales manager and marketing executive. His unblemished record led to his selection as CEO, in which position the opportunity to create structure, where formerly he conformed to it, held little interest for him. He simply continued the routines and procedures of his predecessor and produced results that satisfied his board of directors.

After the accident he reexperienced the feeling of being unloved, to which he had adapted by working hard, as though his accomplishments by other people's standards would overcome his sense of being unworthy and would subdue unacceptable desires and feelings. He had become a chameleon, changing form and identity to match whatever standards life's tasks presented to him. In his forced passivity following the accident, he unwillingly encountered his hidden feelings of self-doubt and loathing, which he had incorporated as a child in response to a cold, ungiving, and highly controlling mother and a withdrawn, disinterested father.

When Sigmund Freud was well into his investigations of mental disturbances, the clinical pictures that captured his attention were the syndromes known as hysteria and obsessional neuroses. Hysteria symptoms include physical dysfunctions without a known or identifiable organic cause and emotional conditions in which individuals show trancelike states or, less flamboyantly, are oblivious to their own behavior, especially in relations with other people. Psychiatrists once thought that hysteria was a malady that affected only women. The term comes from the Greek *hystera,* which means "womb."

Besides demonstrating that hysteria afflicts men as well as women, Freud offered a convincing and pioneering explanation of the causes and dynamics of hysteria. His theory revolves around the complex of both conscious and unconscious motives that lead to the onset and course of hysteria. Hysteria is an illness of unrequited love and remorse. The sexual taboos of society force the individual to repress forbidden wishes. The net result is the formation of a bizarre and, to untrained eyes, mysterious illness that seems unrelated to any visible cause.

An obsessional neurosis consists of the presence of disturbing and isolated thoughts that appear repetitively. Closely related to these recurring thoughts is the compulsion to perform certain acts repetitively and ritualistically. The thoughts appear at odd times and are unrelated to anything the individual is involved in at the time. Often, the afflicted person must perform in response to the thought, some ritual to make the thought go away, or to prevent, the person believes, its transformation into reality. An obsessional thought, for example, is an idea that haunts a young woman that her father will die in an automobile accident. When she has this thought she might feel compelled to repeat a passage from some poem she had memorized a long time ago or she might feel that she has to promise to forgo a cigarette or dessert at her next meal.

Obsessional thinking and compulsive behavior resemble superstition. They resemble thoughts every child experiences and often acts out in games, such as avoiding cracks in pavement because "Step on a crack, break your mother's back." Superstition, magical thinking, and ritualistic behavior occur to some degree in every normal adult, and, therefore, everyone should be familiar with the nature of obsessive thinking.

Obsessional disturbances are illnesses of unresolved aggression and guilt. Obsessional thinking is conscious and overelaborate. In hysteria feeling is on the surface and exaggerated, at the expense of logical thinking. Hysteria appears to be the consequence of repression and inhibition of sexuality; obsessional neuroses arise as a result of feelings of both love and hate toward parents, an ambivalence that the individual cannot resolve. Frequently, love is exaggerated in the form of idealizing a parent or a parent substitute, while the aggression goes underground only to reappear as particular disturbances in thinking and acting. The symptoms often include a deep sense of guilt, which is displaced onto all types of activities, for example, compulsive hard work driven by the fear of pleasure. Hysteria and obsessive thinking were often considered the "classical" neuroses because of the frequency with which they appear and their impact on the early development of psychoanalysis.

Beginning with Freud, psychoanalysts were alert to the part that society and the family play in the origin of these illnesses. For example, sexual repression occurs when parents are excessively repelled by sexuality. Children then believe that sexuality is sinful and brutal.

Authoritarian families with unusually strict moral codes play a part in the formation of the classical neuroses. It could be argued that the obsessions are consequences of moral overkill, where the individual's conscience becomes so strict and punitive as to make a thought seem the equivalent of an act. Conscience becomes so tyrannical that the individual has little room for growth in personality or in moral judgment and therefore becomes a victim of guilt for which there is no objective justification.

As society's standards change, parallel changes occur in the family and in the individual. The sexual inhibitions that were part of the Victorian culture continued into the twentieth century. But the sexual revolution of the 1960s, after the discovery of the pill, illustrates how changing mores in society may follow quickly on the heels of technological discoveries that make possible what was once impossible. The so-called liberation of youth did reduce some of the societal pressures that contribute to the development of hysterical and obsessional illnesses, but did this increase in freedom in sexual activity result in freedom from neuroses? Evidence suggests that among the more highly educated, that is, among those likely to enter the managerial ranks, the incidence of disturbances has not diminished (indeed, it may have increased). But a shift has occurred in the forms these illnesses take.

The shift occurred in two stages. The first stage was the disappearance of the well-delineated symptoms found in hysterical and obsessional illnesses. In their place an illness of character appeared in which the symptoms were embedded in the individual's style of thinking and acting. When symptoms invade character, the person's modes of behaving take on exaggerated styles that dominate that individual's relationships. Obsessional illness, for example, may be manifest not in clearly defined obsessional ideas or compulsions, but in general demeanor with such traits as ambivalence, overthinking, and isolation of thought from feeling. After World War II psychoanalysts began to talk about hysterical and obsessional character neuroses as the most frequently observed complaints.

The second stage appeared during the 1960s and led to serious debate among specialists. Patients who were often well on their way toward success in their careers came for help complaining of a feeling of emptiness. The feeling of emptiness left them impaired in their ability to make commitments. Failures in intimacy, in or out of marriage, resulted from their inability to open themselves to another human being. Ending relationships was easily rationalized as discovering that the other person did not measure up to their expectations. They could move in and out of relationships and jobs with the greatest of ease, but at all costs seemed to avoid anything permanent. Emotionally these patients had learned to live out of a suitcase and preferred a temporary state of mind over a settled feeling. They often had difficulty settling on a career, but even when they had, the shape of the career had a temporary quality. For them this sense of temporariness appeared as a virtue and a talent. They appeared so gifted they could do whatever they wished in pursuit of their immediate desires. They could attract the attention of superiors, move adroitly in their work, and cross the lines of various disciplines with relative ease. They epitomized the flexible individual, which led the psychoanalyst Helen Tartakoff to characterize their plight as that of "the normal personality of our time."[2] They suffered the illness of adaptability which, while attractive on the outside, meant impoverishment on the inside.

Faced with too many choices and an excess of possibilities, these patients sought role experimentation as their way out of the commitment dilemma. They felt that by making a commitment they were running the danger of entering one door while closing many other doors. By not making a choice they ran the risk of prolonging their adolescence and "finding themselves" too late in adulthood. The solution to this dilemma was to take advantage of their ability to experiment with roles, to be flexible, and to practice the art of duping other people, including authority figures and potential lovers.

Seemingly, no better place exists for this flexible personality than large organizations. There are no demands for loyalty, but there are enormous rewards for people who are good role players, who know how to calculate, who can shift their stance, who adopt the coloration of their surroundings, and who understand how to play the game of control and compliance.

A gifted young woman, armed with an MBA, set out to confront the corporate world. Driven by a need to surpass her brother and solidify her position as her father's favored child, she learned to adapt. She read the magazines for career women and dressed the part, stereotypically in mannish gray skirts, white blouses, and muted silk scarfs. She concentrated on her style of living and style of working, learning to be the serious contributor in group meetings, to submit her reports on time, and to be "one of the boys" during after-hours drinks and dinner. Promotions and salary increases came her way, and she felt she had a secure grip on the corporate ladder, climbing rung by rung to the pinnacle of success.

Not long after she achieved a vice presidency, she began to have difficulty concentrating. Her mind would wander during meetings, she had difficulty focusing on her subordinates' problems, and the once easy task of completing assignments became struggles to meet deadlines.

Frightened by the accompanying loss of confidence, she sought psychiatric help. She discovered she was in the midst of a rebellion against her self-imposed compulsion to adapt, to play roles, and to blur any latent images that felt like "the real me." After an intensive period of psychotherapy, she changed careers, recognizing that her role playing, though successful, had separated her from genuine substantive interests that could not be satisfied in her present company. The more successful she had become in her company, the more she had to rely on role playing to assure her continued success, because the higher she moved in the hierarchy, the more detached she felt from the real work of her organization.

There are defenders of this adaptive type. Robert Jay Lifton, a psychiatrist and social scientist, made a name for himself with his studies of survivors of the atom bombing of Hiroshima and soldiers who had been brainwashed while they were prisoners of war in Korea. He wrote an essay about a "new kind of man," capable of change and living in a state of flux.

> I should like to examine a set of psychological patterns characteristic of contemporary life, which are creating a new kind of man—a "protean man."... We know from Greek mythology that Proteus was able to change his shape with relative ease—from wild boar to lion to dragon to fire to flood. But what he did find difficult, and would not do unless seized and chained, was to commit himself to a single form, a form most his own, and carry out his function of prophecy. We can say the same of protean man, but we must keep in mind his possibilities as well as his difficulties.... The protean style of self-process, then, is characterized by an interminable series of experiments and explorations ... each of which may be abandoned in favor of still new psychological quests. I would stress that the protean style is by no means pathological as such, and in fact may well be one of the functional patterns of our day. It extends to all areas of human experience—to political as well as sexual behavior, to the holding and promulgating of ideas, and to the general organization of lives.[3]

If Lifton had studied business as conducted in large organizations, he immediately would have recognized the broad frontier it provided for his protean man. What Lifton finds so attractive in this prototype is the capacity and willingness to take on and discard roles. This role flexibility is harmonious with what organizations under the influence of the managerial mystique need and what the individual requires for defensive security. Although Lifton indicates that the protean style does not necessarily provide happiness, he nevertheless concludes that the style should be seen less as pathological and more as adaptive to the requirement of the times.

Looking from the outside, Lifton made a point of asserting the positive side of the protean style. From the inside there is a dramatic shift to the negative side of the flexible man or woman as self-absorbed, narcissistic, absorbed in an idealized self-image, and usually incapable of loving another person. This view suggests impairment of character, the lack of a cohesive self or what some observers call identity diffusion. With little self-understanding and little feeling of self-worth, the individual adapts to the social milieu in which he or she happens to be. This personality type should not be confused with the survivor, who under conditions of crisis has to adapt to stay alive. The flexible personality appears successful, and nowhere more than in large corporations.

The chief financial officer of a fast-growing, medium-sized corporation became the center of an argument between the CEO and a division president who criticized the financial officer for failing to develop automated record keeping routines and to issue timely operating reports. The CEO responded to this criticism by pointing to the CFO's long hours of hard work, his earlier successes in developing a line of credit, and his ability to respond to the CEO's special project needs. Indeed, the chief financial officer was responsive to the CEO. His characteristic approach was to discover where his power lay, to seek approval from the dominant power figure, in this case the CEO, and to set priorities in direct correlation to the power of his "clients."

The adaptive types often escape the chief financial officer's plight of failing to outrun time and circumstance by leaving one organization to join another where the adaptive mode can continue to work. It is difficult to judge from a resumé if job changes come about as a ploy in the cover-up of identity diffused, but careful interviewing can reveal the real motivation. The executives bereft of a strong personal identity simply apply their adaptive capacities to the interviewing situation. They try to manage the interview instead of taking an interest in the content of the discussion.

In *The Temporary Society*, published in 1968, Warren G. Bennis and Philip E. Slater joined Lifton in seeing the adaptive individual in a positive light.[4] The basis for their appraisal is political.

Bennis and Slater argue that the flexible individual is a requirement of a democratic society. According to them, democracy is not a form of government that a society chooses, but rather one that evolves from a set of conditions rooted in industrialization, the ethos of science, and the growth of professionalism. In their terms, democracy is inevitable for all institutions, including government, business, and education.

Large organizations facing rapid technological change, competitive pressure, and the shift from a national to a global economic outlook must adopt democratic practices in order to survive. To Bennis and Slater, authoritarian structures retard the advance of democracy just as "great men" impede progress. Large corporations replace great men with the "solid management team." [5] At the same time, the "organization man" is disappearing and being replaced by the professional whose commitment is not to helping the organization, but to solving problems. Coming from democratic families and educated in egalitarian and pluralistic schools, the new breed is a product of the scientific revolution. They demand open organizations responsive to changing pressures from within and without the organization. According to Bennis and Slater, these new professionals are remarkably compatible with their conception of a democratic system that "seeks no new stability, no endpoint" and has no purpose but to "ensure perpetual transition, constant alteration, ceaseless instability." [6] They are, in a word, adaptive.

Lifton, Bennis, and Slater all believe that this new type, while successful through adaptability, will not necessarily be happy. The flexible personality will feel alienated, full of psychological strains, and plagued by feelings of ambiguity and meaninglessness. The solution for this unhappiness is to cultivate a society that values interchangeability of people, places, and jobs, other-directedness, and the development of more flexible moral patterns. Bennis and Slater accept homogenization of people as a satisfactory outcome, provided all individuals become more varied in their character traits: "Each [individual] must have the capacity to be introverted and extroverted, controlled and spontaneous, independent and dependent, gregarious and seclusive, loving and hostile, strong and weak and so on." [7] In their view, this complete individual represents the new norm for a democratic and organizational society.

Not too surprisingly, the model of this new personality—call it narcissistic or protean—originates from the study of adolescents. Faced with the monumental tasks of separating from their parents, making commitments to other human beings and to a career, and reacting to the shock that time stands still for no one, adolescents typically engage in a period of role experimentation. This role experimentation often appears bizarre and ominous because of the rapidity with which roles are embraced and then abandoned. Almost all individuals engage in role experimentation; it is a natural part of growth. Problems arise when the individual cannot find a sense of self and remains fixed in this adolescent pattern.

In *The Joke*, a novel about the "paradoxes of history and private life," the Czech author Milan Kundera describes events that occurred during the adolescence of his protagonist, Ludvik, after the Prague spring. Role playing is Ludvik's form of adaptation to the Communist party's attempts to defeat individuality and promote the dominance of the state. To demolish individuality, the party required students to attend "study groups" which criticized and evaluated each member, their dedication to Marxism, the state and the party. Ludvik later reflects about himself, the study groups, and his current girl friend:

> Sometimes (more in sport than from real concern) I defended myself against the charge of individualism. I demanded that my colleagues prove to me why I was an individualist. For want of concrete evidence they would say, "Because you act like one." "How do I act?" "You have a strange kind of smile." "And if I do? That's how I express my joy." "No, you smile as though you were thinking to yourself."
>
> When the Comrades branded my conduct and my smile as *intellectual* (another notorious pejorative of the times), I actually believed them. I couldn't imagine (I wasn't bold enough to imagine) that everyone else might be wrong, that the Revolution itself, the spirit of the times, might be wrong, and I, an individual, might be right. I began to keep tabs on my smiles, and soon I felt a tiny crack opening up between the person I'd been and the person I should be (according to the spirit of the times) and tried to be.
>
> But which was the real me? Let me be perfectly honest: I was a man of many faces.
>
> And the faces kept multiplying. About a month before

summer I began to get close to Marketa (she was finishing her first year, I my second) and like all twenty-year-olds I tried to impress her by donning a mask and pretending to be older (in spirit and experience) than I was: I assumed an air of detachment, of aloofness; I made believe I had an extra layer of skin, invisible and impenetrable. I thought (quite rightly) that by joking I would establish my detachment, and though I'd always been good at it, the line I used on Marketa always seemed forced, artificial, and tedious.

Who was the real me? I can only repeat: I was a man of many faces.

At meetings I was earnest, enthusiastic, and committed; among friends—a provocative busybody; with Marketa—cynical and fitfully witty; and alone (and thinking of Marketa)—unsure of myself and as excited as a schoolboy.

Was that last face the real one?

No. They were all real: I wasn't a hypocrite, with one real face and several false ones. I had several faces because I was young and didn't know who I was or wanted to be. (I was frightened by the differences between one face and the next; none of them seemed to fit me properly, and I groped my way clumsily among them.)[8]

Instead of navigating the hazards of adolescence and emerging with a confident sense of who they are, it appears that many adults maintain these selected modes of adolescent behavior. The end result is the dominance of what Christopher Lasch termed "the culture of narcissism." According to Lasch, modern pathology represents a heightened version of normality. Lasch believes that every age "develops its own peculiar forms of pathology, which expresses in exaggerated form its underlying character structure."[9] It pays, therefore, to study the pathological outcomes of the narcissistic personality to understand what is occurring in the American culture and society. According to Lasch, the narcissistic type is "facile at managing the impression he gives to others, ravenous providing it; unappeasably hungry for emotional experiences with which to fill an inner void; terrified of aging and death."[10]

The patients of psychoanalysts, who are less inclined to seek intensive psychoanalysis as their illnesses match the requirements of their work, suffer from vague dissatisfactions rather than delineated symptoms. They feel vaguely dissatisfied with life, have a sense of futility and purposelessness, of emptiness and depression, and go through violent oscillations of self-esteem, in reaction to the opinions of others.

As long as individuals meet with success through their capacity for adaptation, they may be able to disregard, temporarily, the feeling of emptiness by means of hard work and the admiration others accord them. To the extent that they can avoid the appearance of bizarre adolescent behavior while presenting themselves as quintessentially flexible, they will not progress from many of the conflicts of adolescence.

There are two explanations for this perpetuation of the normal pattern found in adolescence. First, it is what organizations encourage in response to rapidity and intensity of change. Organizations need people who are flexible, can take on many roles, and can abandon roles without becoming disabled by a sense of loss. This explanation supports the view held by many, although with opposing value judgments, that given the circumstances existing in society today, narcissism is not pathological but is normal.

The second explanation looks inside the individual in an attempt to understand the narcissistic armor that makes role flexibility and adaptability a necessity rather than a freely chosen style, as some observers claim it to be. Interpretations vary, but the most convincing is that fear of attachment arises from the inability to mourn the losses endured earlier in life. If one makes attachments and commitments, one becomes vulnerable to loss. The narcissist prefers to feel little or nothing rather than to endure the pain of the losses that are inevitable.

This fear of loss and the inability to mourn is pathological. But the fact that organizations and the managerial role create little tolerance for loss and mourning confounds the problem of individual pathology and social adaptation. The problem becomes clearer, however, when examining the debris these managers leave behind. The pathology is evident in their personal lives, particularly as their flexibility, combined with the inability to commit, leaves their children burdened with excessive rage.

This flexibility and adaptability will probably be harmful to organizations in the long run. With a leadership gap in business, creativity is becoming difficult to engender and sustain. Certainly adroitness and cleverness are plentiful, but these characteristics should not be confused with creativity.

Approaching the end of his life, a widely known corporate CEO toyed with the idea of writing his life story. He met with a psychoanalyst, who was also his friend, to consider how to write this autobiography. What began as a discussion between friends turned into a form of therapy in which the elderly businessperson reflected on his inability to get close to his business associates, siblings, wife, and children. On numerous occasions he heard from them that he was inscrutable. He presented many faces to the world, not unlike Milan Kundera's Ludvik, out of inner doubts about who he was as a man, a father, a community leader, and a powerful corporate head.

Unlike Ludvik, this elderly CEO took enormous satisfaction from his unfathomable character. He also found it useful in enhancing his power. By keeping subordinates uncertain about where he stood on significant corporate issues, he allowed contenders to imagine they had gained his support. In fact, he seldom had developed positions on substantive matters. His conceptual abilities were modest and his analytical talents average at best. Yet, he coveted power and early in his career discovered that keeping a safe distance from important policy debates never revealed his limitations, but instead accentuated other people's need of him to get done what they wanted. As a result, business successes became his, while the failures belonged to others. Occasionally he would belittle his abilities to associates and friends: "I'm not a business genius. There are a lot smarter people than I." His listeners would perceive this self-effacement as modesty, particularly when he made these remarks with his characteristic charm.

One day he tripped over his free associations, as he described to his psychoanalyst friend his relationship to his father. His father was inept when it came to business decisions. He couldn't handle stress, he relied more and more on his son, yet he was critical, reluctant to praise, and sulky when his dependence on his son became evident. The CEO wondered what his father really thought of him. Did his father appreciate all that he had done in running the business and in leading the family?

The CEO choked and then cried as he bitterly lamented that he wanted his father's praise and appreciation and never got it. It became clear that the CEO harbored the belief that his power had been an illicit prize in the never-ending rivalry with his father. He wanted power, but felt guilt over its acquisition. Consequently, he had to become unknowable to others just as he was unknown to himself. He felt he was acting on many stages in his varied experiences with power. Above all, he basically mistrusted his adroitness and felt unfulfilled despite the objective successes in his business career.

Leadership and creativity have a great deal in common. Lasting transformations in art, science, and business require that an individual accept a vision that originates from within. If the person feels empty, there will be no visions. But the creative person also has to understand the world as it exists and be willing to present a vision so that other people understand it. People who face their losses rather than bypass them may be able to release potential creativity and ability to lead. They are the opposite of those who, like human radars, send signals out to discover what the world expects from them in order for them to adapt. If business makes the totally adaptive personality its ideal, then there will be little room for creativity and leadership. In the end organizations will suffer because they will exclude the individuals who live by personal investment in work and in people.

Chapter 12

Stress and Power

To leave office, whether as a result of a lost election, a change of administration, a loss of a job, or a desire for another profession, is a stressful experience because with the loss of power may go the foundations of self-esteem. To say this should not be so is to be naive. Anyone who has had power and has lost it knows the painful depression and rage that accompanies the loss. To make matters worse, there is no socially accepted way to mourn, as there are mores and rituals to help us grieve the loss of a loved one.

People who lose power, in business and government, experience a loss of self. Who they are has become so intertwined with the role they played that they feel stripped of self and social recognition. The absence of the tangible manifestations and symbols of power hurts. To step outside a power structure is like entering a new world where no one knows you.

Symbols of power help executives maintain a sense of identity. Recognition from others reinforces the satisfaction derived from the power based in the office a person holds. Even though less obvious in America than in Europe and Asia, deference and respect are expected for a person who has considerable power. For example, most executives hate to fire someone and usually get a subordinate to do it. They do so not only to avoid emotional confrontations, but to avoid being exposed to a breach of the deference to which they have become accustomed. When relinquishing power, either willingly or unwillingly, the person soon realizes what living outside this atmosphere of deference is like: chilly, to say the least, and frightening, because it becomes difficult to hold on to one's sense of self in the absence of constant recognition from others.

Lee Iacocca tells in his autobiography of the pain he endured following his separation from the Ford Motor Company.[1] He freely vented his anger at the man who fired him, Henry Ford. According to Iacocca, before being fired, he was subjected to a deliberate campaign to destroy the respect that he had enjoyed as president of the company. Meetings were called, and he was not asked to attend. People close to him lost their jobs. The power structure at the Ford Motor Company was reorganized more than once during this period of purgatory to strip Iacocca of his rank in the company. According to Iacocca, Henry Ford hired McKinsey & Company, one of the leading management consulting firms, and paid them over a million dollars to create a new top structure called the Office of the Chairman and Chief Executive. This new office consisted of a troika of power holders at the top echelon where formerly there were only two, Ford and Iacocca. The purpose of this harassment was to force him to resign, which he refused to do. The harassment continued over a three-year period and finally ended only when Henry Ford, in the presence of his brother William, told Iacocca that he was no longer president of the Ford Motor Company.

Iacocca describes the experience: "After I was fired, it was as if I ceased to exist. Phrases such as 'father of the Mustang' could no longer be used. People who had worked for me, my colleagues and friends, were afraid to see me. Yesterday I had been a hero. Today I was sombody to be avoided at all costs."[2]

Iacocca was luckier than most people who have to endure the stresses of power loss. He fell into the top job at Chrysler shortly after he was fired, and this job not only restored him to a position of power, but also gave him the chance to get even with Henry Ford and the directors who failed to support him at a crucial time. The stresses of the Chrysler job—of finding a way for the company to survive, of negotiating with bankers, government officials, and union leaders—were not psychologically harmful when compared with the earlier stress of losing power. The symbols of office were his once again.

President Truman, contemplating the problems General Eisenhower would experience on becoming president, said, "He'll sit here and he'll say 'Do this! Do that!' *And nothing will happen.* Poor Ike—it won't be a bit like the Army."[3] Truman expected Eisenhower to experience deep frustration at how little gets done and how infrequently orders are followed, at least in the direct way they are issued. Of course, Truman did not consider that Eisenhower was a highly skilled politician who in his various jobs in the military had learned to negotiate, bargain, and persuade. He had had some good teachers and a great deal of on-the-job training, beginning with his stint under General MacArthur in the Philippines and ending as supreme commander of the allied forces, where he had to deal with the monumental egos of Field Marshal Montgomery and General Patton.

Veterans of the ways of power are not necessarily disturbed by the idea that they cannot expect instant results when they make decisions. In the general scheme within an organization, they are content to be the key players. Whatever the action, being a key player in power relations, not getting one's way, is what really counts. However, when they are removed as players, the action goes on without them. The loss of power damages self-esteem because the people "on the outs," away from the action, continue to imagine what it is like to be there.

Iacocca reflects in his book why he endured the painful humiliations over the three-year period that culminated in his loss of power. Why do executives in similar situations cling to office as long as possible? Iacocca is straightforward in his reflections. He loved his job, which provided deference and respect, not only from his subordinates, but also from a national dealer organization. He keenly enjoyed making close to a million dollars a year. He thought there were no alternatives in the automobile business and that was where his heart belonged.

The absence of an alternative increases the pain of losing power and the tendency to stay on and hope to survive. The urge was so strong in Iacocca's case that he even expected, or fantasized, that finally the board of directors would vote for him against the wishes of Henry Ford and that he would ultimately win this power struggle. Iacocca rationalized his fantasy in terms of his value to the company and his greater abilities as compared with those of his rival. He later recognized that he was being naive, even deluding himself, because he could not bear to be taken out as a player in the automobile arena that he loved and knew best.

A chief executive officer of a large company who was past

retirement age called in a consultant to discuss management succession. Among the first questions he posed was whether he would stop being invited to join boards and public commissions once he relinquished the title of chief executive officer to his successor, now president and chief operating officer. The consultant said frankly that his clout would diminish in the eyes of other people, particularly influential business and political figures. Over a number of meetings with the consultant, the chief executive officer began to face the psychological stresses resulting from the loss of power. He described what he would miss in terms of a game: the speed of moves, the action and the challenge of beating an opponent in circumscribed, and largely symbolic, conflict. As with many other executives who have difficulty "letting go," the problem was not so much that he believed only he could run the business, but that relinquishing power meant that he would be outside the action and that the play would proceed without him.

The stress that people experience within an organization has the same basis as the stress from losing a position. Power protects from stress by giving a sense of control over one's actions. The lack of power is associated with a sense of helplessness, which is the source of feelings of stress. A young executive well on her way toward becoming a chief executive of a business described what having power meant to her and how, in securing power, she felt protected from stress. Besides fulfilling her long-standing ambition, to have power in a business meant that she could set and enjoy a pace and timing that suited her temperament. When an individual feels out of harmony with the pace of activity, he is apt to show symptoms of stress. A pace that is too slow is boring; one that has irregular starts and stops or is too fast is apt to create anxiety. The more power one has in an organization, the more probable that the timing and pacing match personal preferences. Other people adjust to the power figure's inclination, and what may be stress reducing for the chief may become stress inducing for the subordinates.

Being subject to another person's preferences in scheduling can also induce stress. A chief executive may prefer early morning staff meetings. For those subordinates who commute, this preference means they have to meet the sunrise commuter train. Far from complaining, the subordinates recount all the reasons why an early start is exactly the schedule they prefer. In fact, they are rationalizing the truth that whoever is number one sets the pace to which others adjust.

Another aspect of how regulating time affects stress is in the needs people have for feedback. The need for gratification or the inability to tolerate the frustrations of delayed feedback places pressure on the individual. Some executives live on a short tether to their particular "report card." In some businesses, retailing being a good example, the interval between acting and knowing the results is brief. Executives in short-cycle businesses learn how they are doing in absolute terms, in comparison with past performance, and in comparison with their competitors. In long-cycle businesses with delivery of a product years away from the date a formal contract is signed (shipbuilding is a good example), there are no immediate results to provide esteem or by which performance can be evaluated. Why some people prefer long cycles and others short cycles in assessing their performance is not clear; there seem to be complicated psychological reasons behind this difference.

To avoid stress, a person has to feel some harmony between need for closure and the time cycle natural to the activities within the organization. No amount of power can allow an individual to create a cycle of work not intrinsic to the situation, which includes the kind of marketplace, technology, competition, and customs associated with the industry. But people with power have the means to select their favored environment. For example, chief executive officers will make acquisitions or divest businesses with their underlying preferences in mind.

In the United States executives in the for-profit sector rarely move to the not-for-profit sector, whether it be government, philanthropy and social service, or academia. Apart from questions of skill transferability, the basic reason movement is so rare is probably closely connected to predilections for pace and quality of time. Action moves more rapidly in the for-profit sector of the economy, and for people whose needs and temperament are satisfied by rapid action, the pace in not-for-profit organizations seems incredibly slow. Getting used to this slower pace requires a major adjustment, an adjustment that occurs only with stress. One of the reasons for the seemingly trivial activities that engage people in organizations with a relatively slow pace, including academia, is to help people avoid the stress connected with waiting.

A school committee that reviews grading standards and procedures will absorb much time and attention. Although the end result of such work is hardly important, the absorption of time in this collective activity seems to relieve anxiety for many.

The idea that businesspeople do not move to not-for-profit sectors because of economic disincentives is not compelling. If economic motives are most important, why do executives in not-for-profit sectors fail to move to the for-profit sectors, given the higher money rewards in business?

The fundamental element in temperament that seems to affect preferences for pace is the balance between active and passive modes. In a study of normal personality development conducted at Harvard University, one subject reported that he experienced stress when action stopped and he found himself in a passive state. Finding a challenge, a series of obstacles to overcome, was a necessary condition for a feeling of well-being. Here is how he expressed his reaction to the interviewers.

> It's always been much harder for me to be on top of the pile than to be down in the pile. Once I get on top of the pile I don't know what to do with myself, and I very soon don't do anything, and it very soon catches up with me again. And I feel more at home when I'm submerged and when things are closing in on me, when I feel myself cornered. Then I sort of gird my loins and look for ways out and there always seems to be one. It's a miserable way to live; I don't know why I do that, but I've always done it that way. . . .
>
> There's almost nothing that I've done that held any even sustained interest for me that I was not also afraid of. It's true even in my present position. It's true of horseback riding; I love to ride, but still being on horseback often sort of scares me. But the general sort of situation that I find myself propelling myself into, whether it's by obsession or desire I don't know, is one in which I'm in the middle of a situation which terrifies me—not necessarily terrifies me, but frightens me to a certain extent—but which I can ultimately set to rights and get out of. I don't know what force propels me into them, but I've always gotten in them and I seem to always get out of them.[4]

A conscious distaste for passivity is easy to observe in people. Courting passivity is more subtle. An executive found his fortunes turning from bad to worse. He had trouble holding a job and his marriage was in jeopardy. It did not take long to discover that this executive wanted to be in a passive position relative to his colleagues. He was more comfortable as an observer than as a participant and eventually would get into difficulty when he failed to perform in crucial situations, where other people had every reason to depend on him for completing important work. He was an intelligent and attractive individual, and it was not always clear to his bosses that he was on the verge of failing to perform, so that by the time they realized what had happened, it was too late to prevent serious problems.

This executive had two options. He had to overcome his passivity or to find work that would be more harmonious with his temperament. To change his temperament would be no small matter. The easier course for him to follow was to change his occupation.

Hard work and activity seldom cause psychological illnesses or stress reactions. The harmful agent for most executives is the feeling of helplessness that goes with a lack of action or a lack of power. An executive accustomed to power and a certain pace may be more at risk of sudden stress reactions, such as coronaries, when first starting a vacation than when fully occupied with his job. In place of the outer stimuli of work comes an inner world of feelings and fantasies that are not necessarily pleasant. In fact, one of the side functions of hard work and concentration on external events is to mute the insistence of these inner stimuli, which come alive during moments of passivity or inactivity.

Executives would be healthier and more creative if they learned to tolerate and even enjoy a cessation of activity. Most executives are so fearful of their fantasy world that they lose exposure to a potentially rich source of ideas as well as a deeper understanding of human nature.

The feeling of mastery can exist in all types of occupations and in solitary as well as organizational work. A master mechanic at home with his tools is no less secure than a high-powered executive in a position of command. They both operate with a sense of mastery, are fully absorbed in the tasks at hand, and are buffered from the unwelcome intrusion of disconcerting and painful fantasies. Not so fortunate are individuals who have neither a skill nor a position in an organization to assure well-being.

The conventional image of the work of an executive as highly stressful grew out of the assumption that executives would find it stressful to make decisions that involve risk and that affect countless lives. Instead, the source of stress needs to be restated. Power, or being in a position to make these kinds of decisions, can be therapeutic. Its opposite, the lack of power and the sense of helplessness, is often what causes stress illnesses.

In the early 1970s the Canadian Broadcasting Corporation conducted a study of stress reactions that provided a unique opportunity to examine the relationship between power and psychological stress.[5] CBC was the center of many political storms following World War II. In 1952 it was the agency authorized to construct and operate facilities that would bring television into Canadian homes in all sectors of the vast country. The technical and engineering groups emerged as the power centers of the organization during the construction period.

The construction period led to a deep conviction by top management that the way to run a successful radio and television operation was to centralize decisions. But as so often happens in large organizations, a successful concept became overextended and controlling beyond its fruitful applications. The headquarters office in Ottawa was oriented toward the government, parliament, and the secretary of state who was responsible for CBC. It was far —in miles and mentality—from the programming (or operations) centers in Toronto, for the English-speaking population, and Montreal, for the French-speaking population. Toronto and Montreal were concerned about programs, including the artistic and journalistic sides of broadcasting. Because of the changing consciousness of the French-speaking population of Canada and their new aspirations, the French network became a rallying point for what ultimately became the separatist movement in Quebec. The head of this movement, who was to become the premier of Quebec when the separatist party defeated the liberals in the provincial election, was a CBC journalist and producer named René Levesque. In 1958 Levesque led a strike in Montreal of French-speaking producers, which brought into public view not only the hostility between the programming centers and the policy and administrative center in Ottawa, but also between the French and English language groups in Canada.

The head of CBC at the time of the strike was an engineer named J. Alphonse Ouimet. Because of the succession of government commissions appointed to study CBC, along with the internal reports generated within CBC to respond to various commissions, there was much information and opinion available to the public concerning CBC's problems. Besides being informants to the various studies, the employees were part of the public interested in the results. The exposure of CBC to constant public criticism was now becoming a contributing factor to its morale problems. In response to the mounting criticism of CBC from the public and from its opposing internal factions, Ouimet decided to bring more key executives to Ottawa where they were to function under his scrutiny. For example, the two network vice presidents, from English-speaking Toronto and French-speaking Montreal, were moved to the Ottawa headquarters, which became known as "the Kremlin." This physical separation of the network heads from their people intensified the suspicion, hostility, and mistrust between administration and operations.

In 1944 CBC had established a personnel and administration department for relieving executives, particularly in programming, of onerous staff and administrative details. Soon dubbed the "pest and aggravation" department, the bureaucracy that emerged from it was cited repeatedly as a deterrent to creativity in programming, the main product of CBC. Writing to one of the government commissions investigating CBC, one executive called personnel and administration "that fungus growth that now covers the whole CBC like a green mildew."[6]

In response to the criticism, Ouimet drew an even tighter ring around himself and headquarters and, undoubtedly without conscious intent, created a fortress mentality. The enemy consisted not only of government bodies and the press, but also of CBC programming and operations staff. In addition, the bicultural split became a battleground. Headquarters harbored constant fear that Levesque and his groups would use the French network as a political tool to foster the separatist movement.

In 1968 Ouimet resigned under fire. He was replaced by George Davidson, a career civil servant. Davidson appointed as his executive vice president Laurent Picard, who had distinguished himself in his studies at the Harvard Business School in preparation for an academic career in business education in Montreal. The division of labor between Davidson, who was English, and

Picard, who was French Canadian, approximated the classic division between an "outside" and "inside" executive. Picard was to concentrate on budgeting, programming, and administration within CBC, while Davidson was to focus on governmental and public relations, although as president and chief executive officer Davidson was responsible for the whole organization.

Davidson and Picard decided to decentralize CBC. Under this plan the two network vice presidents moved their offices back to the operations centers of Toronto and Montreal. Davidson and Picard wanted to close the rift between programming and administration and saw the move of the network heads closer to operations as an important first step. But having made this move, the question remained of how to influence if not control operations. Even though two noncontroversial executives now headed CBC, neither had prior experience in broadcasting, public communications, the arts, or journalism. How could they gain the respect and support of the operations people when they were not identified actually or symbolically with the arts and crafts of radio and television broadcasting?

Davidson and Picard had become aware of some disturbing reports of stress illnesses among key people in CBC. The reports included cases of the general malaise called "burn-out," depression, alcoholism, and suicide. They chose 3,000 employees in the top management, operations, and technical staffs as subjects for a study on stress. The two executives were aware of the lines drawn between operations and administration. Their decision to undertake the study visibly conveyed their concern for the well-being of CBC employees and their conviction that at the heart of the corporation was the talent and creativity of the programming groups.

The personnel of CBC defined as key subjects greeted the study with enthusiasm. They believed that much needed to be done to improve the conditions of work and morale, which in their perception would lead to improvements in the quality of the product. The information provided by interviews, questionnaires, personality tests, attitude surveys, and personal histories made it possible to measure the incidence and prevalence of stress symptoms. Using the CBC as a self-contained universe (it was impossible to draw comparisons with other organizations), statistical analysis isolated the locus of stress illnesses and suggested lines of inquiry into probable causes. The study concluded with recommendations to reduce the prevalence of stress symptoms and otherwise improve the morale and productivity of the key people.

Measuring the incidence and prevalence of symptoms was a straightforward task. Five syndromes (groupings of stress symptoms) became the focus: (1) emotional distress with depressive reactions predominating, (2) use of medication without medical prescription or definitive diagnoses, suggestive of feelings of malaise, perhaps hypochondriasis, (3) coronary illnesses and hypertension, (4) gastrointestinal disturbances, and (5) allergy and respiratory problems.

The analytical portion of the study produced some surprises and also difficulties in explaining the problems discovered. The syndromes were not distributed at random throughout the organization, nor were they a simple function of the capacity of individuals to tolerate and deal with stressful events. People in management jobs were relatively free of stress symptoms. People in operations jobs showed higher than expected quantities of symptoms, particularly the emotional distress syndrome. The technical staff, which included engineers and accountants, also showed higher than expected symptoms, particularly syndromes that involve physical difficulties.

The management of CBC greeted the results with reserve and discomfort. The implication that the climate at CBC proved comfortable for management and debilitating for operations and staff people conceivably could have accentuated the rift between management and operations people. It tended to confirm the belief that had been expressed to the various investigatory commissions that what was good for those in charge of CBC was not necessarily good for those responsible for generating its product. Another interpretation of the results, one that placed management in a more favorable light, suggested that management people were stronger psychologically and could cope more readily with an atmosphere that was equally stressful to all occupational groups. In other words, assuming the ability to cope with stress is one of the conditions that lead to advancement in management, this fact could account for the lower frequency of reported symptoms among management as compared with operations and staff.

Careful analysis of the data indicated that the environment at CBC was different for management than for operations and staff. The staff were reacting to the loss of power that accompanied the decentralization moves of the new administration. The operations people were reacting to a sense of powerlessness that continued to prevail. The decentralization that brought the network leadership back to Toronto and Montreal was insufficient to provide them with the sense that "what I do makes a difference." And here is the crux of what provokes stress reactions in organizations, and in life in general.

A sense of efficacy, or the feeling that what a person does makes a difference, is the essence of the subjective experience of power. One response to the feeling of helplessness, the opposite of the sense of efficacy, is apathy. By reducing the intellectual and emotional energy invested in work, frustration diminishes and the situation becomes more tolerable than it is if the feeling of helplessness dominates the individual's consciousness. Whether stress reactions appear depends on the person's ability to divert energies into more fruitful activities. Interests cultivated outside of work prevent stress symptoms that arise from the lack of efficacy in work. If attention and interests cannot be easily diverted, apathy will mask anger, which emerges only in the appearance of stress symptoms.

There is meaning to psychological symptoms, but it is often presented in a code language. It is worthwhile to decode the language to interpret what the symptoms mean. Some of the code reflects cultural experience. In the CBC study, for example, members of the French ethnic group tended to have symptoms of emotional distress; when the level of frustration peaked, the French Canadians tended to become depressed and anxious. The English Canadians manifested their distress through the formation of physical symptoms, such as gastrointestinal disturbances. One of the French Canadian executives interpreted the English symptoms as a result of their eating Anglo-Canadian food; he asked, "Have you ever tried their cooking?" Behind his humor lay thinly veiled hostility toward the other culture. The study indicated that French-speaking subjects were accustomed to expressing their emotions, despite being unable to rectify the situation causing their frustration.

Early life experience also creates the pathways of frustration and the forms symptoms take. Some individuals learn early in life to repress their emotions. Such individuals are more likely than others to use the language of bodily distress to communicate to themselves and others their levels of frustration and inefficacy. Individuals who learn to recognize and express emotions may have stress reactions as severe as those of individuals who repress emotions. The fact that the reactions appear in emotional forms should not lead to the conclusion that the distress is dissipated or that it causes the individual no harm. To feel frustrated, helpless, and unable to change the situation is debilitating even if the emotions are recognized and expressed. To vent feelings is cathartic only if the person learns something and uses the new knowledge to make a difference in his or her life. Otherwise, catharsis is simply a momentary release, which will have to be repeated as the frustration level mounts once again.

It was suggested in the study that to improve conditions the top management of CBC take a bold path and promote decentralization well beyond the point reached with the return of the network vice presidents to Toronto and Montreal. The situation seemed ideal to foster leadership, participation, and performance by organizing operations into production units staffed with the range of talents and specializations necessary to produce programs. These autonomous production units would compete for funds, work under budgetary controls, and would be evaluated by their success in program development and performance. In a production unit, under the supervision of a highly visible producer, the sense of efficacy of every individual was more likely to grow than in their agglomeration in technical or craft categories.

The CBC study challenged the leadership to deal with the power variable. The people who held the power and were least affected by stress were asked to experiment with the structure of power to relieve stress in others even though that experimentation might lead to what they felt was a loss of power and a situation that would be stressful for them. A combination of circumstances and fear of the unknown led top management to abandon the recommendations of the study. George Davidson accepted the post of deputy secretary general for administration of the United Nations and so tendered his resignation. Picard succeeded Davidson as chief executive. As a newly appointed officer, he was not prepared to undertake the risks of bold experiments with power in CBC. The study was left to languish, although from a scientific point of view it was successful.

Any aggregation of people, including business organizations, who work together over a period of time develop a structure of beliefs. This structure, which the political scientist Nathan Leites called the "operational code" of the elite[7] and the anthropologist

Clifford Geertz called the "world view,"[8] helps provide both cognitive and emotional support for a particular way of looking at the universe. According to Geertz, "[the structure sums up], for those for whom it is resonant, what is known about the way the world is, the quality of the emotional life it supports, and the way one ought to behave while in it."[9]

There was a widespread and deep-seated belief at CBC, for example, that danger lurked ahead if irresponsible people gained access to air waves. This belief in impending danger led to an urgent feeling that behavior must be controlled. The obsession with control superseded the goals of producing high-quality programs for the Canadian audience. Eventually, this obsession also led to a fundamental mistrust between people responsible for the creative end of the business and the people entrusted with power to manage it.

Or, to take another example, it was an embedded belief at General Motors that creative technology can lead the organization astray, as seen in the story of the copper-cooled engine. The response to the specter of danger, as Alfred Sloan recounted in his memoir *My Years with General Motors,* is to weigh heavily toward maintaining the instruments of coordination. The end result is undervaluation of technical creativity and manufacturing innovation.

Identification with the power structure and belief in its sustaining myths have a number of functions, none of which are described in organizational manuals or statements of policies and procedures. Nevertheless, these functions perpetuate organizational cohesion and protect the power elite against stress until a crisis appears that calls into question the validity of corporate myths.

Chief among the functions of myths in a corporation is to make people who are believers feel good about themselves. Through myths they develop a self-image, identify with the power elite, and enjoy self-esteem. As long as the mythological structure is in place, the believers experience little stress as they go about their work in the organization. But, if the structure weakens or if an individual does not hold to the collective beliefs, life may become stressful, leading in many cases to the appearance of symptoms of stress illnesses.

What the managerial mystique has accomplished is to broaden the mythological structure beyond single corporations, to include those who are identified with the profession of management wherever they work. But as many executives have discovered in recent times, particularly in the mature industries overrun by foreign competition, and the banking industry with nonperforming debts, there is no free ride. Managers traded their ability to deal with reality for personal security and freedom from the stress experienced by those people who are not identified with the power elite.

One of the chief differences in the lives of those who plan and those who implement, between the powerholders and the performers, besides their vulnerability to stress is the speed with which reality conveys its messages. Top managers are often the last to know of impending problems, whereas a lowly production worker on the shop floor is among the first to know about quality problems and product integrity. People learn and change under the pressure of reality. But if one of the functions of collective beliefs and corporate myths is to preserve self-esteem for the elite, thereby relieving them of stress, the ability of the organization to survive is often threatened. Reality may not be able to penetrate the mythological structure until the corporation flounders and ultimately severs the bonds that unite those who follow with those who lead.

Part IV

The Cure: Leadership

Chapter 13

The Substance of Leadership

*I*t is surprising how we ignore the obvious in considering the art of leadership. The substance of business is business: making products and going to market with something of value to customers. Books on leadership consider personality traits, situation, and managerial styles, but they slide over or ignore the materials that engage executives' attention. Yet, these materials evoke talents that are particular, specialized, and essential to the success of a business. A marketer, for example, must understand customer needs and attitudes and apply technical knowledge to solve problems about how to price and promote products. All of the marketer's understanding and technical knowledge, however, is subordinate to the faculty that turns issues into opportunities and, when taken as a whole, describes leadership in business: imagination.

The difficulty in relating business substance to leadership arises, in part, from the conventional abstractions people use to understand leadership. Invariably, attention turns to leadership as interaction, relationship, and process, rather than the substance that occupies leaders' minds. Theories of leadership barely approach substance with concepts such as "initiating structure" and "task roles." For the social scientist, initiating structure implies that a leader issues directives, guiding people or telling them what to do. Acknowledging that there might be a directive side of leadership hardly does justice to the expectation that leaders should affect the content of policies and decisions. Similarly, the idea that leaders perform task roles grossly understates the contributions leaders make in the directions organizations take. Too much emphasis is given to the "social roles" leaders play to grease the wheels of human relationships to prevent friction. These typical concepts, that purport to describe the behavior of leaders, fail to reach the questions of what leaders do to help make a business successful and where leaders place their emotional investments and intellectual energies in running a business. The most cursory observation of business shows that leaders get excited about their work and, even if only by contagion, stimulate their subordinates. It is inconceivable that human relationships, at any level in a hierarchy, can be positive in the absence of good work that is involving and demands attention. To try to build relationships or morale without the excitement of work is vacuous and, in the end, demeaning.

The binding of leader and led in a cooperative relationship depends most on the respect the subordinate has for the leader's ability to originate ideas, suggest solutions to problems, and, above all, translate visions into far-reaching goals. The force a leader exerts has both direction and magnitude. Direction arises from the leader's command of the substance of the business, reflected in the decisions that move a company forward. Magnitude grows in direct proportion to the leader's emotional commitment to the ideas.

Leadership in business goes beyond encouraging and guiding other people to seek solutions to problems. Leaders must be able to contribute to the substantive thinking necessary to move a business beyond problems and into opportunities. There are many aspects of substantive thinking. The marketing imagination draws on acuities about people's needs and how to satisfy them with a product or service. This imagination is probably the most important in successful leadership because it is hardly possible to be right about many aspects of a business if the marketing side is wrong. Many chief executives who have financial imagination still lack a sense of products and markets. If, in addition, their financial acuity leads them to the point where they fail to acknowledge marketing and production realities, they sooner or later cause trouble. They mistake the possibility of synthesizing a deal for the economic soundness in back of the deal.

Attention to substance ensures a healthy enterprise. Likewise, people respect a talented individual who makes contributions to business success. And the basis of leadership, or the willingness of people to invest confidence in a human being, is the respect that flows from one person to another. When organizations disregard talent and, what is worse, prevent talented people from achieving positions of power, they are in the midst of decline.

One of the problems in business today is that this obvious fact about the foundation underlying respect for authority has been forgotten. In too many instances people are appointed chief executive because they are good controllers or have the ability to get along with people. Unfortunately, good controllers do not make the best chief executives because they lack substantive acuity about marketing and manufacturing and run the business by the numbers, misleading themselves by equating numbers with reality. The numbers are at best only a partial reflection of reality. As for getting along with people as a basis for leadership, rapport cannot overcome shortcomings in imagination. In addition, people who stress social skills in their style often fear the detachment that substantive assertion leads to, especially as people compete over ideas. To use imagination may for a time separate an individual from his or her associates and friends. But the ability to tolerate separation, a condition that may be essential for the play of imagination, without disrupting the significant bonds that maintain authority relations is essential in leadership.

Business needs talented people who apply their imagination to move an enterprise forward. To overcome a lack of imagination, authority figures may try to apply charm, seduction, and even deviousness—tactics that in the end diminish their authority. Leaders confident of their own imaginative capacity will recognize, respect, and draw on the talents of other people. Power holders who have little imagination are vulnerable to feelings of insecurity, may be threatened by other people's talents, and may withdraw when demands for substantive contributions are made on them. They often select as key subordinates people who are process- rather than substance-oriented. Instead of complementing managers' talents, the subordinates merely echo them. What is worse, these subordinates tend to be politicians, leading to a rut in which politics, self-absorption, and status-consciousness displace ideas in the daily interactions between managers and subordinates.

Imagination in business is the ability to perceive opportunity. Some business analysts rarely think beyond what exists or consider possibilities for new products or methods. The word *opportunism* as generally used has negative connotations of taking advantage of opportunity to others' disadvantage or in an unethical way. We use it simply as the ability to perceive and act on opportunity, with no negative implications. As such, it is the core of business thinking and the application of imagination. If imagination is the ability to visualize what might be from observation of what is, opportunism is the ability to give a vision practical shape. Opportunity in business, if not universally, can be approached in at least two ways. It can be sought aggressively or awaited passively. The aggressive way is to probe and act on the market, in effect, to change situations to create an opportunity. The passive way is to formulate an image of an advantageous situation containing several separate, well-defined elements, wait for the moment when the elements come together in reality, and upon recognition of that moment, move rapidly to accomplish a desired goal. The active and passive modes of opportunism differ in style, risk, and ultimately the personality of their practitioners, yet both are successful in business leadership.

Take the manufacturing imagination as an example. One of the most important visions in the history of manufacturing was the concept of interchangeable parts. It is difficult to attribute the invention or discovery of interchangeability to any one individual. Thomas Jefferson saw the significance of interchangeable parts in his attraction to Honoré Blanc's method of "making every part of a [musket] so exactly alike that what belongs to any one may be used for every other musket in the magazine."[1] Ironically, Jefferson, who most eloquently and passionately argued against introducing manufacturing to the agrarian economy of the new world, was the first to promote interchangeability, perhaps more out of necessity than desire. The opportunity existed in the need for armament to diminish dependency on other nations. The means existed in the concept that Jefferson first recognized while he was minister to France in 1785. Later, Eli Whitney, who like Blanc had a strong manufacturing imagination, took advantage of the opportunity afforded by the relatively large demand for military arms to promote interchangeability of parts.

The opportunity that a large market affords has stimulated other visions in manufacturing besides interchangeable parts. The idea of precision, the manufacture of parts to meet uniform exacting standards, also led the way to large-scale, economical production. In turn, precision stimulated the opportunity for designing and making machines that would meet tight tolerances.

Currently, the manufacturing imagination is incorporating information technology to produce machines, popularly known as robots, which simulate human motions. Up until the invention of robots, the displacement of human labor by machines had been largely restricted to the manufacture of parts; assembly of the parts into finished products was still accomplished by human effort. In the electronic industries the need for precision and the small size of the components propelled the development of automated manufacturing methods. Using printed circuits, for example, provided an entirely new approach to producing components in electronic instruments and products.

As with other types of business imaginations, the manufacturing imagination relies more on conceptualization than on crude experimentation. Trial and error, particularly in complex manufacturing programs, is useless and wasteful unless the activity is guided by underlying theory and conceptualization. Daniel E. Whitney, a section chief in the robotics and assembly systems division at the Draper Laboratory, provided a telling argument for conceptualization. He pointed out that in the absence of conceptualization, substituting a machine for a human is likely to create inefficiency much the way that a golfer who practices without a concept may develop bad style rather than an effective swing.[2] Many executives view robotics as a magical solution to restore our competitive edge, especially vis-à-vis the Japanese. However, they see robotics as a solution because of a mistake in conceptual thinking.

The conceptualization involved in most business imaginations begins with correct formulation of the problem. In the manufacturing imagination, for example, it is visualizing a totality in which parts and functions must interrelate. Even though the conceptualization is necessarily simple, it is never simplistic. In robotics, Whitney argues, the simple concept is to understand what people do (the functions they perform in relation to the total product and production process). The simplistic notion is to focus on how they do it and then to find a machine that will mimic this "how."[3] The mistake in conceptual thinking comes when executives focus on "how" rather than "what" and become convinced that what people do now, the robots will do. The move from focusing on a "how" to a "what" is a shift from the particular to the conceptual. And this shift is characteristic of business leadership, no matter what type of imagination is being applied.

While designing the car that became the Model T and planning its production, the elder Henry Ford used conceptual thinking, despite his later tendency to concretize. He had a vision of an automobile that would meet the needs of the farmer. The car had to be simply designed so that the owner could easily repair it; it had to be reliable; and it had to sell at a price the customer could afford. It was to be an automobile for the "little guy" in the United States, not for the "rich guy" for whom automobiles had been designed until Henry Ford came along.

A concept is alterable, and the concept of a product is therefore subject to infinite manipulations, a fact that can be dangerous. Because conceptual thinking is so flexible, it may never come to a conclusion and therefore never result in a salable product. Nevertheless, the extreme of concrete thinking—thinking, that is, focusing on a particular object as it currently exists and functions—leaves no room for contemplation and change. The failure to change associated with overly concrete thinking is a more widespread danger in business than the failure to close associated with conceptualization. Usually, people in business who do conceptualize are at the same time driven by the desire to see their vision become reality and the desire to profit from their efforts. Consequently, they are able to close and to bring their conceptualization into a form that will have economic value.

Imagination in business is not the same as creativity. Imagination may be relatively scarce, but creativity is even scarcer. If business leadership depended on genuine creativity, we would be in a predicament of great demand and little supply. Fortunately, business imagination and creativity are different. In all its forms—manufacturing, financial, marketing—business imagination is largely imitative and applied. It works on discerning and formulating problems based on need. It searches for solutions based on experience and analogy, without necessarily altering thinking in some major way as creativity does. While it may not be creative, strictly defined, it still is an exciting and important mental activity.

Soichiro Honda, founder of the Honda Motor Company, loved motors both as a concept and as a product. He did not invent the internal combustion engine, but he perfected it. Anyone visiting Tokyo in the late 1950s found the air foul and almost unbreathable. Recognizing the need for cleaner engines in congested cities,

Honda developed emission controls. By the 1980s emission controls in car engines had helped improve the air quality to the point where, even during the hot summer months, Tokyo is a pleasant city. With no formal education in engineering, Honda applied a technical and manufacturing imagination that was driven by a sense of esthetics in form, motion, efficiency, and design.

Hisashi Shinto restored the IHI Shipbuilding Company after World War II and later became chairman of the Nippon Telephone & Telegraph Company. The story of how he prepared IHI for the postwar surge in shipbuilding illustrates how conceptual thinking solved an immediate business problem while helping to solve broader problems such as unemployment and the threat of total destabilization of the Japanese postwar economy. Mr. Shinto had been elevated to head the IHI following General Douglas MacArthur's purge of wartime industrialists at the start of the military occupation of Japan. Mr. Shinto faced the grim situation of leading a company without work but with the need to maintain some semblance of order and continuity in a demoralized nation. Instead of acting out of panic, Mr. Shinto decided to think. His thinking began with the observation that Japanese shipbuilding practices were inefficient and lacked cost advantages other than labor rates. Although there were no existing orders for ships, Mr. Shinto believed that an opportunity awaited him and his company. Commercial shippers, sooner or later, would need new vessels to replace aging merchant fleets. He determined that his company would be ready with a cost-competitive product when the opportunity arrived. To develop an efficient method of shipbuilding that would make his yard highly competitive, he conducted a study of shipbuilding practices. He sought an analogy and found one in the experience of the United States aircraft industry during World War II.

Prior to the war aircraft had been custom-built one by one at a central site. When President Franklin D. Roosevelt set a production goal of 50,000 planes a year, aircraft manufacturers reconceptualized manufacturing and developed modular construction. The product is designed in such a way that it can be broken down into modules or major units, and the modules are built at separate sites specializing in a particular module. The modules are delivered to an assembly site, where, with good control of inventories and production schedules, the final product can be built speedily and without interruptions, avoiding problems bound to occur if there are large numbers of workers engaged in many assembly operations at the final site.

Mr. Shinto applied the concept of modular construction to shipbuilding. The application required the careful examination of product design to determine workable modules and the training of supervisors and workers to use the new approach. When Daniel Keith Ludwig, an American entrepreneur and shipper, came to Japan looking for inexpensive ships, Mr. Shinto and IHI Shipbuilding were ready to meet his needs and, of course, to provide employment in the use of production capacity.

The point could be made that IHI was fortunate in the appearance of Mr. Ludwig. The real point is that all the good fortune in the world would have been useless if the company had not been prepared to meet the needs of its customer as a result of the application of the manufacturing imagination. Mr. Shinto provided substantive direction, which is another way of saying leadership, by involving himself directly in the transformation of technical practices in his company. Obviously, he had the technical grasp to carry out his self-imposed task. Even though he used the resources other people provided, his attention, and that of the entire organization, never wavered from the vision he had established for the company.

There is a small, but interesting, postscript to this story. Avondale Shipyards, an American company, conducted a study on labor turnover and absenteeism. The study supported Avondale's intuitive realization that to compete successfully, the yard had to operate with fewer employees at varying levels of production. Inordinately high rates of labor turnover and absenteeism added considerably to the yard's productivity woes. Modular construction promised increased productivity and better wages and working conditions for a smaller but permanent cadre of employees. The Avondale management wisely turned to IHI for consultation even though, conceptually, the Japanese method of shipbuilding originally had come from the United States.

Opportunism, governed by conceptionalization, is also characteristic of another imagination important in business leadership. Indeed, the financial imagination is a study in opportunism. According to the theory of efficient markets, the exchange of information soon brings price and value into equilibrium. But for the financial imagination, the condition of disequilibrium, or the presence of an anomaly in the marketplace, provides the opportunity for advantage and gain. For example, when the price of a stock is well below the value inherent in assets or future stream of earnings, that anomaly leads people with the financial imagination to act. The epidemic of takeovers and mergers of the 1980s is a direct result of a major disequilibrium between stock market valuations and asset and earnings valuations. For companies in the business of making and selling products, as well as investment banks that profit from making deals, anomalies in valuations provide opportunities to acquire plants, customer bases, and new products by making acquisitions of undervalued companies.

Another type of anomaly in product types of businesses exists when a business unit has an unrealized potential as a result of management errors. Corporations with losing divisions will sell them to other companies to eliminate businesses that are a drain on their earnings record. A company confident in its ability to turn around someone else's loser will be able to acquire businesses at reasonable or even bargain prices. If successful, the acquirer will improve its earnings record and return on investment. The key in this type of transaction is for a firm to understand its own competence and to be able to discern opportunities below earnings potential because of problems inherent in running the business. To make such acquisitions requires, in addition, the ability to conceive methods of financing that take advantage of particular opportunities in the financial markets. "Structuring" deals is a talent in short supply and for which investment banks, and their clients, are willing to pay a hefty price. This ability is also found frequently among the top ranks of manufacturing and service corporations. The financial imagination requires an acuity in assessing and dealing with risk.

Dealing with anomalies in the financial market is not sheer gambling, even though risk is involved. Financiers usually have a plan that enables them to bring underlying values to the surface. The plan may include selling assets to other companies or spinning off business units from the main body of a corporation while retaining those units that the acquirer believes bolster the surviving company. In some cases the assets retained may cost little after taking into account the money realized from the various sales and spin-offs.

Perhaps the financial imagination is little more than a sophisticated version of everyone's search for a bargain. The aspect of the financial imagination that may go beyond bargain hunting is the ability to visualize in advance the various ways in which money can be made in a deal. Corporate raiders who have little inhibition in making hostile tender offers have honed this ability to a fine edge. They can make money if the tender offer is accepted, and they also make money when the target chooses to buy out the raider's holdings in the practice called "greenmail."

Financial imagination is an exercise in finding information and from that information discerning the existence of anomalies. Investment bankers spend huge sums uncovering and analyzing information in hopes of discovering disequilibria in markets. While they can gather much from reading company reports and SEC filings, people with financial imagination also mine relationships. And, to know and be known in the ranks of the high and mighty provides access not only to information, but also to participation in deals.

In his biography of André Meyer, Cary Reich described Meyer's obsession with keeping in touch.[4] He would chastise people for not coming to see him or calling him. From a psychological perspective, this obsession would appear to be a craving for affection and admiration from his important friends. However, the psychological motive (assuming there is some truth in this interpretation) reinforced a more obvious rational motive. To lose touch and drift away from the flow of information is disastrous to a financier. The reason people in high places associate with power holders and engage in blatant name dropping is less to bolster insecurity and to gain status than to show they are part of the information network and, therefore, should not be excluded.

Financial people thrive on partnerships. By entering into partnerships they not only gain access to deals, they also ensure they will maintain their position in the power and information networks. One cannot for long expect to be invited to participate in other people's deals without reciprocating the opportunity. Partnerships also have the advantage of spreading the risks of appraising information before making an investment. People with financial imagination, whether real or fancied, are often arrogant. They feel they know it all and therefore reject the advice and opinion of others. But getting and giving advice and opinions are skills. They require acuity and charm, tough-mindedness and tact, and the desire to make money without greed. Some claim that charm is the larger part, but charm soon becomes meaningless if the substance of the transaction fails to pay off. The ability to discover and recognize anomalies takes first rank in making up the financial imagination.

People with financial imagination use their acquisitiveness as a personal report card. To amass a fortune is testimonial to the person and directs others in reckoning with him or her. And the purpose of accumulating money is not necessarily to consume. Giving money away creates better standing than does conspicuous consumption, which can be taken as lack of discipline and a cause to doubt the person's reliability.

Financial acumen in business leadership has been historically a cause for controversy. Its excesses, apparent most often as speculation, have been implicated in social disasters such as economic depressions. In many cases the financial imagination overreaches and is impervious to restraint. The rise in corporate debt in the mid-1980s as a result of leveraged buy-outs and the merger mania deserves careful study as a possible result of the excesses of the financial imagination.

In the early 1980s an opportunity presented itself when the strength of the U.S. dollar made large sums of money available for investment. A new corporate finance vehicle appeared, popularly known as "junk bonds," and a spate of takeovers and conversions from public to private corporations absorbed much of this excess money in the American investment scene. Although junk bonds in corporate finance produced great activity on Wall Street and in corporation boardrooms and made large sums of money for investment bankers, serious questions have been raised about the economic value of this frenzy of financial maneuvering. Do the moves make corporations stronger? Do they enhance the competitive position of United States industry in the world markets against the aggression of Asian and European companies? Do they add jobs to the economy and promote the well-being of the population? Or, do they simply make the rich richer?

The politics and economics of the 1980s have tried to render these questions beyond debate. According to the principles of the free market, opportunity exclusively should govern behavior. Whatever excesses occur will lead to adjustments. Even though in the short term some people get hurt, in the longer term the market activity leads to the greatest good for the greatest number. Therefore, the ethical questions that arise concerning the kind of leadership offered through the financial imagination are, for the most part, resolved in economic terms. The exception, of course, occurs when people engage in fraudulent activity. But here, the redress is in the law and not in the revision of free market principles.

This free market argument, whether applied to the financial imagination specifically or to business leadership generally, is not entirely satisfactory. Government regulation or control on both pragmatic and philosophical grounds is not the solution either. The problem of excesses in the display of the financial imagination seems to lie in the character of people who seek power. Strikingly bad judgments in business decisions have often arisen from the financial imagination. Perhaps, in all fairness, it would be more accurate to criticize the misapplication of financial opportunism rather than the financial imagination itself. The best practitioners of the financial imagination are not oblivious to social and economic risk.

Heads of corporations tend toward bad judgment when they allow bankers, who are less than discerning when they have a great deal of money to lend, to feed their aggressiveness by urging companies to take out large loans. The incentive to put out money overcomes judgment on the part of both the banker and the businessperson. Also there surely is an element of greed at work. When a financial person sees the chance to make a killing, it is difficult to get him or her to exercise judgment and restraint. This deficiency is particularly the case in the type of opportunism that is compelled to probe for opportunity rather than wait for it to occur. The probers churn and make deals for their own sake; witness the activity of the promoters of conglomerates such as Harold Geneen, who seemed to dread the sense that he was not making things happen. Perhaps besides greed, there is an element of fear of passivity, of not being in control and even, ultimately, of being victimized by circumstances. The opportunists who know how to wait, as well as to deal, seem less vulnerable to greed and to the pressures exerted on them by the financial community.

The marketing imagination is the premier imagination in business leadership. A careful study of the manufacturing and the financial imaginations at work would show strong presence of a marketing sense in both. Like the other business imaginations, the marketing imagination involves opportunism and the analysis of information to discover anomalies. Like people with financial and manufacturing imaginations, people gifted with the marketing imagination do not shy away from imitating or adapting old lessons to new circumstances.

The feature that sets off the marketing imagination from other types of business acuities is empathy. The marketing imagination is intuitively attuned to consumer feelings, needs, and desires. This empathic capacity exists in industrial as well as consumer businesses. The marketer is concerned with customers' problems and solutions to those problems. This orientation toward other people's problems frees the mind of attachments to particular products and services. It focuses instead on what the customer needs to solve a problem in a more effective and economical way.

A business executive described how she uses the marketing imagination to explore the problems of customers she might like to serve. She makes it a practice to read many general newspapers and magazines as well as those more closely related to her type of business. When an article about a company or advertisement for a product catches her eye, either because it is in direct line with her company's work or because she senses a connection, she may call the head of the company that interests her. She asks questions related to how the company is now being served and often suggests lines of exploration of possible mutual advantage. This telephone conversation may lead to further exchanges of information and, in a reasonable number of cases, to new business.

Clearly, the person at the other end of the telephone call responds to this businessperson's knowledge and experience. But there is also a human quality that encourages responsiveness and further communication. Through her acuity, she easily conveys her understanding of the potential customer's situation and encourages a bond of interest and mutual consideration. Perhaps this appears as merely good salesmanship, but something more is at work here in the combination of keen observation, intellectual curiosity, technical knowledge, and the desire to communicate based on the sense of what the customer may need. The interchange results in both parties' learning something and leads to interest in further exploration.

Most chief executive officers feel too busy and distant to make "cold" calls. How do these executives keep their finger on the pulse of the marketplace and sense the concerns of the customer? Not from reports or operational review meetings in which written reports and the numbers contained in them are the center of attention, but from the empathy of the marketing imagination that permits flexibility in defining whose needs are at stake in a business relationship. It is not always obvious and should not be taken for granted. Mary Kay Ash built a cosmetics business presumably with products to serve the needs of women who were concerned about skin care. But there was another constituency with needs, and it played an important role in the success of her business. It consisted of women who, for a variety of reasons, needed flexible work hours, and could work out of their homes. Mary Kay Ash did not invent home parties as a medium for marketing and sales; Tupperware and Avon had used the approach successfully before her. But imitative or not, Mary Kay Ash made the method work for her company by providing large compensation and incentives for "beauty consultants" to recruit and train others. The consultants are not simply salespeople; they are trained to instruct women in skin care and to use the home parties for demonstrations. Of course, they sell products during these demonstrations, but the method of selling involves instruction and social stimulation. The consultants are offered high incentives to learn their job and to pay attention to their customers.

The Mary Kay Ash program was so carefully attuned to two constituencies, the women who bought the products and the women who wanted to work, that it expanded rapidly. At its peak over 130,000 beauty consultants were providing services and products to a significant multiple of their number.

The role of empathy in the marketing imagination differs from its role in the dynamic psychotherapies, where the critical feature in inducing change in the personality of patients is the ability of the therapist to, in effect, see through the eyes of the patient in order to understand, clarify, and interpret conflicts and defenses. This procedure occurs in an intensive one-to-one relationship. Empathy in the marketing imagination is seldom intensive and usually involves extrapolation from a single case to a large population. No one understands how this extrapolation proceeds nor the base from which it takes place. It seems apparent that there are a number of intricate steps from observing needs not currently satisfied to formulating a marketing concept. Empathy plays a critical role in this mental activity.

In 1983 J. C. Penney announced dramatic changes in its merchandising, customer orientation, and image. Donald V. Seibert, chairman and chief executive officer, interpreted the company's weakening profit performance as early indicators that mass merchandising and shopping malls were detrimental to J. C. Penney. Rather than await further indications, the company moved to differentiate itself from Sears and K Mart by abandoning hard lines and automotive centers to concentrate on becoming a fashion center. The imagination that drove this plan began with observations such as population shifts, heightened fashion consciousness, and the new affluence of the American middle classes. In the popular culture of the 1970s consuming became a way of expressing the pleasure principle, and no better expression existed than clothing and home furnishings. The company planned to spend more than $1 billion to support the new program. It intended to invest heavily in store modernization to project the new image of fashion. In 1984 it carried out a store promotion with the theme "A Salute to Italy," tying Italy's fashion reputation to the store and its aim of providing "something unique in fashion, styling, quality, and design sensitivity."[5] Other fashion promotions and an exclusive arrangement with the designer Halston sharpened the image of the company in soft goods merchandising. In November 1985 it scored a coup in arranging for Prince Charles and Princess "Di" to visit the Penney department store in Springfield, Virginia, in conjunction with the company's promotion of British goods.

Seibert's dramatic move was not without precedent in the history of J. C. Penney. In 1957 then Vice President William (Mel) Batten chaired a committee that recommended revamping the image of the company's stores. It specialized in soft goods and had, more or less, a rural image. Batten and his committee recommended that the company introduce hard goods, garden and lawn furniture, and automotive centers to emulate and compete with Sears. The change in the early 1980s reversed the course back to soft goods, but this time at a level of fashion and price that bore little resemblance to the J. C. Penney of its founder and his close associate, Earl Sams. Mel Batten had been a field personnel executive with Penney and had drafted a memorandum on the company's position in the market and its prospects in the light of population shifts and dispositions of the shoppers and their families. The headquarters' leadership was so impressed that they brought Batten to headquarters, backed his recommended moves, and ultimately appointed him chairman and chief executive officer. The change was highly successful, but did not become company dogma. Instead, dogma, if it existed, was in the idea of serving the consumer in a way that differentiated Penney from the pack.

The boldness of the moves and the integrated plan for achieving change are indicative of a marketing imagination at work in the highest levels of power in the corporation. Regardless of whether in the long run Penney's actions prove successful, they demonstrate a number of ideas about corporate leadership. First, corporate leadership is substantive. It involves ideas about what to do rather than about how to do things. Second, it involves vision, or what can be termed substantive imagination, that projects a company's future. Third, if a vision is worth risking energies and resources, leadership has the staying power to see the vision to its conclusion.

Chapter 14

Personal Influence

*I*n its pure form management mystique is a denial of personal influence. At every level of the hierarchy power is impersonal. Thought and action are directed by some structure, system, or procedure, not an individual. The choice of which actions are taken, which behavior is sanctioned, and which relationships are encouraged is derived from a process. Policies and decisions are justified by the legitimacy of the process, not the personal investment of an authority figure. It is striking that the ultimate test of a decision, its efficacy in the market, is beside the point and that no individual is accountable for decisions' success or failure because it is the process that produces them. If they turn out well, then the process is reinforced; if they turn out poorly, then no one is directly responsible. The fault is in the process, which must then be corrected. Accountability is by necessity diffuse and commitment low key, if not absent.

Along with substance, imagination, and talent, personal influence in leadership deserves careful attention. To form a leadership compact in business, with superior and subordinate personally committed to the actions taken, requires complete understanding of the forms of personal influence. The forms are not all alike in motivation and, consequently, have different effects on subordinates and organizations.

Social psychology generally defines influence as a result of a relationship between individuals with unequal power.[1] What does the power figure do or say that results in altering the behavior of the other? Actually, the power figure need not even be present for influence to occur. Psychologists have long studied a mechanism called identification in which the ideas, beliefs, and values of one person are incorporated into the mental attitudes of another. Through these attitudes the influence one person has over another persists.

Relationships between two people are often asymmetrical: One individual (the adored) exerts exceptional influence over the other (the adoring). That influence directs change in the adoring in anything from opinion to interests to tastes. Similarly, a parent exerts enormous influence over a child, not only because of the real dependency of the child, but also because of the child's need to maintain an image of the parent in a superior position for a sense of protection. Children attribute power to their parents and in doing so borrow strength for their fragile and newly forming egos.

Friendships are built and maintained on common interests, but once established offer opportunity for influence. Before it became popular to seek professional counseling for personal problems, friends would seek one another out, sometimes to ventilate pent up feelings and other times to get advice. Thus the bonds of friendship strengthened in the mutuality of aid and comfort and increased the possibility of influence.

Personal influence also occurs in alliances, which may contain elements of friendship, but are based on obligation. Alliances exist in politics where there are purposes beyond the spontaneous satisfactions of friendships. As the British journalist Henry Fairlie observed, alliances are built upon the tradition of *amicitia* in political relations.[2] *Amicitia* is a relationship built on mutual obligations in which power figures agree explicitly or implicitly to protect each other's interests. To maintain alliances through *amicitia*, all members of the alliance must demonstrate that they are capable of recognizing and fulfilling their obligations to act in one another's interests.

Unlike the bond of trust, *amicitia* is not open-ended or unconditional. Implicit in *amicitia* are the conditions that people accept obligations and are committed to their fulfillment, but never to the degree that one person in the relationship will expect the other to endure harm and neglect self-interest. Obligations are mutual, and therefore one member does not ask for conduct that will create an imbalance.

According to Fairlie, *amicitia* as applied to politics derives from the character of the official, particularly,

> in the connection which he makes between the ideals and the realities of political life; in the nature of his relationships with political friends and of his dealings with political rivals; in the manner in which he returns to the people the trust which he invites them to bestow on him; in the sense of the dignity of his office, and reinforcement of it from day-to-day with his own dignity; above all, in his awareness that he is the focus, not only of power but of affections, not only of interests but of loyalties, not only of anxieties, but aspirations, not only of functions, but of ideals.[3]

Amicitia is neither pure calculation nor pure emotion, but combines the two so that personal and mutual interests broaden as they coincide. Obligations are fulfilled and aims expand as individuals change. The relationship is both personal and utilitarian.

One of the factors underlying the success of real estate development firms such as Trammell Crow is the practical application of *amicitia*. Liberal compensation plans, which include equity participations in proportion to contributions to the firm, are usually sufficient motivators to keep developers working hard and creatively. But beyond the accumulation of equity, gifted developers stay on because of obligations incurred as they learn their craft and ascend the hierarchy. Recruited directly from graduate business programs, apprentice developers learn from experienced developers who, like themselves, began with little background in the field. Obligation is strengthened by the money incentives to remain with the firm to vest their equity interests. Early departures result usually in severe financial penalties. This combination of money and obligation is the basis for the modern version of *amicitia*.

While it can work well in enterprises based on explicit or implicit partnerships, the durability of the arrangement depends on leadership. Trammell Crow is a charismatic figure who elicits loyalty and commitment at the same time he offers the promise of accumulating wealth. But for the arrangement to endure requires generating new leadership. *Amicitia* falters when the hold of the charismatic leader weakens. Without the transfer of power to other strong leaders, the sentiments supporting *amicitia* disappear and turn into envy, rivalry, and outright conflict. Substituting committees for leadership often sets in motion the forces of decay, which become evident as key people feel released from their bonds of obligation and depart. For example, First Boston, the investment banking firm, lost Bruce Wasserstein and Joseph Perella, two of its most prominent merger and acquisition partners, who formed their own partnership with the expectation of controlling their own fate and increasing their personal wealth.

To suggest that *amicitia* can work only in entrepreneurial partnerships and not in corporations is short-sighted. The H. J. Heinz Company experienced remarkable success under the leadership of Anthony O'Reilly, its chairman, president, and CEO.[4] Return on equity in Heinz increased from 14.6 percent in 1978 to 24.6 percent in 1987, well above the average in the food industry. Top executives at Heinz have little hesitation in attributing the company's outstanding performance to O'Reilly's leadership, which created *amicitia* through strong personal commitment and highly lucrative compensation. Executives earn large cash bonuses through performance and equity participation in a generous stock option program. Speaking to a *New York Times* reporter, Paul I. Corddry, senior vice president and twenty-four-year Heinz veteran said, "Tony [O'Reilly] sets tough goals, but they are consistent, unambiguous, and fair. You couple that with ownership, and what you've got is a turned on, motivated, and congenial crowd of managers." David W. Sculley, president of Heinz USA, who has been with the company for fourteen years, added, "Tony is very competitive, and his scoreboard is the bottom line. But he is also motivated by friendship. He'll go that extra mile for people, so we'll go that extra mile for him."

Personal relations, ranging from love to alliance, can be differentiated according to the presence or absence of authority. Psychiatrist Jacob Moreno, a pioneer in sociometry and psychodrama, demonstrated the fundamental rift between relationships built on authority (work) and those built on intimacy (play). In his experiments he asked his subjects, young girls in a residential home, with whom they preferred to work and play. One of the rules Moreno followed to give weight to his experiments was that choices were not to be hypothetical, that is, work and play groups were to be formed based on the results of the test. Moreno found that his subjects chose different people for work and for play.[5]

Studies of kinship in preliterate societies reveal the same separation of authority and intimacy. In patrilineal societies, where authority flows from the father, the relationship between father and son is distant and respectful. The need for intimacy between a young male child and an older man is fulfilled in the special position of the mother's brother, who is friend, counselor, and helper. Both father and mother's brother influence the male child, but their influence is based on different relationships that satisfy different needs. The influence of the father is that of a model; the influence of the mother's brother is that of an older friend.

The presence of authority arouses a mixture of feelings, ranging from respect to fear, but not necessarily including warmth and liking. Often, the task subordinates face in working with authority is to establish a tolerable distance in the relationship. To be too distant is to lose the benefits of learning; to be too close is to arouse the feelings that affect the relationship. The relationship between authority and subordinate stirs strong, ambivalent feelings in both. It is difficult to hide strong feelings, whether hostile or friendly, and their presence may endanger the relationship. For example, many authority figures have difficulty accepting negative feelings such as the envy that may accompany a subordinate's competitive strivings with authority. In the extreme, young people with strong ambivalences to authority will keep distant, even to the extent of "dropping out" of society. It is not that they cannot benefit from the knowledge and experience that authority figures may have to offer, but that they cannot cope with the strong conflicting emotions aroused in the presence of authority.

A leader who arouses strong positive emotions and can influence belief and behavior is said to have charisma. Much has been made of charisma in the popular literature and the press since John F. Kennedy's presidency. The fact that certain types of leaders evoke adoration and reverence is incontestable. The idea that a leader must be adored has now become so popular that it is almost a requirement that politicians take lessons in how to be charismatic before they seek public office.

The term *charisma* originated in theology and means "a divinely inspired gift or power, such as the ability to perform miracles."[6] Sociologist Max Weber adopted the term to distinguish legal authority from the authority attributable to the special powers of an individual to inspire others.[7] In psychological terms the charismatic effect results from the incorporation of the revered figure into the psyche of followers. For Freud, this incorporation followed patterns laid down in early childhood. He suggested that the basis of group cohesion exists in the identification with the leader; the stronger the identification, the more cohesive the group.[8] Although it is common to make an analogy between the charismatic leader and the father, studies of charisma suggest that a more powerful charismatic effect occurs when the leader appears to symbolize mother as well as father. The mystery associated with the early maternal figure is transferred to the leader who evokes the same adoration the infant bestows upon the good and giving mother.[9]

The degree of influence leaders wield depends on their personal qualities, how followers respond, and circumstances. Subordinates amplify the characteristics they find necessary and appealing in a leader. Followers not only act in accordance with the directives of the charismatic figure, they also adopt values and beliefs to support their conviction that the leader is endowed with special gifts.

Studies of followers of charismatic figures in cult groups have shown them to be emotionally disturbed and alienated; they feel helpless to change their lives.[10] Their dependency makes them exceptionally vulnerable to distorted beliefs. Occasionally, followers lose the capacity to judge right from wrong and are willing to kill or take their own lives—witness the Manson gang and the cult of the Reverend Jones. The experience with some charismatic leaders, such as Adolf Hitler, seems more than enough to warrant the greatest mistrust of the emotionalism such figures may engender.

Most of the knowledge available about charisma comes from the study of political figures. These studies suggest that the charismatic effect is most likely to occur during crises. The charismatic figure promises a solution to the crisis. If the charismatic's program realizes early successes, such as the Ayatollah Khomeini's success in fostering the revolutionary Islamic movement, followers become convinced of his divine powers, more devoted, and more willing to follow directives.

The charismatic effect appears to be the result of the coincidence of a gifted individual, a crisis situation, and followers with heightened dependency. But its occurrence in one form or another is not exceptional. Every child at some point early in development endows parents with special powers. Teachers frequently inspire students to learn beyond all expectation. The adoration accorded athletes, actors, and others indicates that the charismatic effect is always present in everyday life. Professor Bernard M. Bass, a leadership researcher, states that

> charisma is to be found to a considerable degree in industrial, educational, governmental, and military leaders.... many followers described their organizational superiors as someone who made everyone enthusiastic about assignments, who inspired loyalty to the organization, who commanded respect from everyone, who had a special gift of seeing what was really important, and who had a sense of mission. The enhanced subordinate had complete faith in leaders with charisma and felt good to be near them. Subordinates said they were proud to be associated with charismatic leaders and trusted such leaders' capacity to overcome any obstacle. Charismatic leaders served as symbols of success and accomplishment for their followers.[11]

Obviously, a vast difference exists in the possible consequences of the charismatic effect in situations where leader and follower are neurotically bound and alienated from their society and in situations with a constructive purpose. Yet because charisma involves such intense emotion and commitment, it appears risky, a kind of leadership many would prefer to ignore. The psychological foundation of management is, in part, a substitute for, if not a defense against, the personal involvement contained in charismatic leadership.

There is a remarkable irony in this avoidance of charisma and personal influence in the management of large organizations. Modern management represents a sharp divergence from the early forms of corporate leadership in which a patriarchal figure, such as Andrew Carnegie or John D. Rockefeller, constructed large enterprises. These patriarchs were charismatic to their immediate subordinates, the masses of their employees, and the public at large. They were charismatic because of their boldness, their cleverness in constructing deals, and, of course, their wealth. The first Henry Ford electrified the American people with his Model T, the assembly line, and the unprecedented five-dollar-a-day wage rate. He gave voice to some of their old beliefs, prejudices, and fears as he preached the simple virtues of farming and the land, made a scapegoat of the Jews, and railed against bankers and capitalism. It did not take long for the public (and Ford himself) to believe that his powers went beyond the requirements of the automobile industry—he could be senator, president, or miraculous restorer of peace at the beginning of World War I.

But charisma also creates backlashes. In 1892 Carnegie's steel company used Pinkerton police to break a strike in Homestead, Pennsylvania, and ten men were killed. The general public as well as the employees blamed Carnegie for the deaths, even though he denied that he had ordered the use of Pinkerton's. The hostility that workers and the public directed against Carnegie was in direct proportion to his charisma. People and the press could ask how is it possible that so powerful a man cannot control his subordinates? The conclusion reached was that Carnegie's lieutenants must have been carrying out his orders. Carnegie's later generosity in building libraries and endowing foundations dedicated to public welfare barely compensated for this loss of respect. Similarly, the Colorado Fuel and Iron riots near Trinidad, Colorado, in the fall of 1913 led John D. Rockefeller and his associates to undertake a public relations campaign directed by the public relations consultant Ivy Lee.

The fall from grace of these charismatic patriarchs was partially a result of the difference between actions they took (or that were taken in their name) and the exceptional standards by which they were judged. But another way of interpreting their behavior offers more of an explanation of why the personal influence of patriarchal charisma has fallen into disrepute. Richard Sennett, university professor of humanities at New York University, interprets the demise of patriarchal leadership in business as a consequence of the type of authority it represented. Sennett calls it an "authority of false love," in contrast to the managerial ethos of "authority without love."[12]

According to Sennett, paternalism in the corporation is a metaphor that links the family and work by linking father and boss. The metaphor in this case does more than combine dissimilar images. It produces a new image that is more powerful than the original images combined, while creating expectations that are bound to fail. A boss in a corporation cannot deliver the promise of nurturance embedded in the image of father. Furthermore, the goals of the paternalism in a corporation are different from those of the family paternalism. The father not only cares for his children, he also promotes their growth and, ultimately, their independence. The father figure in the corporation may earnestly desire to nurture subordinates, but he does not promote their independence. He seeks personal domination over their lives as a form of control and as a means of assuring their conscientious effort.

Andrew Carnegie was the father figure for his immediate subordinates, as well as a charismatic figure for the enterprise as a whole. He assured the control of his lieutenants by instituting "the iron-clad agreement," stating the terms of participation in the equity of the corporations. In theory, Carnegie's lieutenants were his partners. They had reason to be grateful to him for sharing in the equity, but the terms for withdrawal were so onerous that in fact their paper riches really measured the degree of control Carnegie exercised over them. The richer they were on paper, the more difficult it would have been to accept the lesser sum they could in fact receive in withdrawing their equity. Carnegie illustrates how paternalistic control can in the end diminish rather than strengthen subordinates' independence. The promise of large rewards in the future with an indeterminate payout date seriously reduces the subordinate's autonomy while enhancing the chief's ego. This combination led Sennett to call the personal influence of the paternalistic leader an authority of false love. The authority of real love that a father displays toward his children seeks to enhance their growth and independence, even to the point where the father must endure the experience of rebellion on the part of his children. Fatherhood based on real love is gratified with ego growth on the part of the children.

That industrial paternalism more often than not is false love cannot be disputed. And, the tendency for this paternalism to seep into the structure and to permeate all levels of authority also cannot be disputed. The famous "bull of the woods" supervisor was authoritarian just as his boss and his boss's boss were. The idea of management was, in part, an antidote to this authority of false love. But, according to Sennett, it led to an authority "without love," that is, without personal regard for subordinates. However, understanding the psychological tyranny of earlier forms of authority should not be cause to consider all paternal displays as inappropriate. For that matter, to discard personal influence from modern organizations is outmoded, detrimental to the organizations, and ineffective. Personal influence is leadership, but not when it serves the purpose of enhancing the ego of the leader while diminishing the self-esteem of the subordinate. Charismatic leaders, who are perceived as father figures, can in this emotion-laden relationship promote the growth of their subordinates and the prosperity of their corporations.

A good example is the leadership of William Hesketh Lever (1851–1925), the first Viscount Leverhulme, who founded and built Lever Brothers. After his death the great marketing enterprise joined the Dutch and British margarine and soup companies to form the Unilever companies. Lever Brothers was the first company to manufacture individually wrapped bar soap made from vegetable oils instead of tallow. The company, under William Lever, was an innovator in marketing and advertising consumer products and in building a worldwide network of subsidiary companies for the manufacture and distribution of soap products. Lever Brothers also pioneered in benefits programs for employees, including pensions, unemployment compensation, medical payments, profit sharing, and insurance.

William Lever was a father figure for his executives and employees, but without the negative implications associated with paternalism in industry. It is true he tried to build a model community for his employees (named Port Sunlight after his famous bar soap), but he recognized limitations and later acknowledged that employees prefer to keep separate their work and private lives.

William Lever described his ideals of leadership for himself and successors as "natural business instincts." Following these instincts, a leader

hears what people have to say but has the prudence to keep his own mouth shut . . . never meddles or interferes with what does not concern him. I have never known him to be "talked over" from any object he had in view, he forms his own opinions and threats or persuasions are alike useless to turn him from his purpose. He shows great perseverance in attaining his object and is never quiet until he has realized his wishes. Of an unassuming nature he attaches more importance to the solid comforts of this life than to any more outward show. He insists on the strictest attention to their duties in all those who are in a position of trust with him but their duties performed he gives them the fullest liberty to follow their own affairs. He makes no promises and tells no lies and I may add enjoys the most robust health.[13]

Andrew M. Knox, a director of Unilever, described the effect of Lever's personality on people. Called the "Old Man" by his immediate directors and subordinates who had worked closely with him over the years, William Lever was "almost demonic [in the] energy which drove [him] on, ever restless to tackle something new, looking always to the future for opportunities to grasp. He was never satisfied with what he had."[14] Knox described Lever's attentiveness to detail. Lever displayed substantive acumen in understanding the needs of his customer, in product innovation, and in advertising and sales promotion, fields in which he was far ahead of his time.

Lever introduced long-range planning in which he asked for projections from the managers of the operating businesses. But he personally defined what the objective should be, called "the datum" for each unit, and expected managers to work hard to realize these goals. While the long-range planning was a control device, its end point had his personal commitment, which led in turn to the commitments of general managers. It was not simply a procedure that became depersonalized as it became routinized.

Lever, described as a builder and not a destroyer of men, displayed great sympathy for lower level employees. But he was not reluctant to be harsh with executives. On a visit to one of his subsidiaries, the chairman greeted Lord Leverhulme excitedly with a large sales sheet. "You will be glad to hear, your Lordship, that the sales of our company last month were an all-time record." "I've no doubt about that," Lord Leverhulme replied, "but what about the staff lavatories I complained about when I was here a year ago?"[15] To his nephew, who was a senior director and chairman of the control board, he wrote, "What steps [are] the Control Board taking with associated companies that are either making losses or below datum profits? If merely 'noting' same, then where does control come in? If you are not taking action then tell me and I shall take hold myself. I feel very hurt at the 'placid calmness' of nerve shown under circumstances that mean ruin."[16] While perhaps exaggerating his concern over "circumstances that mean ruin," Lever personalized the event which, besides emphasizing his displeasure, also gave meaning to supervision. If an executive is responsible, he must dig in and actively solve problems.

In concluding his recollection of William Hesketh Lever as a leader, Andrew Knox declared that Lever's death marked the end of an era. The era in which Lever built his enterprise was that of paternalism, but not of the sort that is self-aggrandizement at the expense of others. In Knox's mind, and undoubtedly in the minds of all those close to Lever, "it was a great era, and he was a great man of his era. He was also a good man. He could, and did, lift up people's hearts." [17]

The capacity of a leader to influence subordinates arises from a mixture of motives. As Max Weber pointed out, there are various bases of authority: authority born of tradition, of the legal framework, and of the charismatic effect. In modern corporations traditional authority carries little weight, particularly in an era of massive corporate takeovers and restructurings. Legal authority is, of course, present in the definitions of job responsibilities that appear on organization charts. The authority that derives from expertise, unlike positional authority, is proportional to the ability of the expert to apply his or her knowledge to solve problems. In theory, there is, or should be, no fear of the expert as a source of influence.

The charismatic effect is more complicated than the authority of position or expertise. There are cases of charismatic leadership in which neither position nor expertise are claimed. Gandhi, Schweitzer, and Mother Theresa appear saintlike in their self-denial and concern for a cause and the immediate well-being of the unfortunate. The charisma of these leaders approximates charisma as it was originally defined, meaning a special divine or spiritual gift. The influence of such charismatics is clearly personal. It also spreads beyond their immediate physical presence. Once they are gone, other, more bureaucratic forms of influence appear, although attempts are made to continue the unifying effects of the charismatic through "routinization," or maintaining the leader's ideals at the core of organizational process. This is a difficult task and usually does not succeed. Once the charismatic figure is gone, infighting and bargaining arise and whatever legacy remains of the earlier cohesion soon disappears, especially when organizations encounter setbacks.

Business provides ample opportunity for personal influence and the charismatic effect. Lee Iacocca is one among numerous individuals who by dint of substantive imagination and innovative ability become charismatic to subordinates and a wider audience.

The charismatic effect is not limited to chief executive officers and founders of corporations. Supervisors throughout an organization also become charismatic, but only when they exhibit different dimensions of personality and behavior than those of highly visible corporate leaders.

The foundation of personal influence and charisma that runs through many different levels of status and prestige is a common human response called awe. Superior talent, physical prowess, human sensitivity, self-discipline, and otherworldliness that includes self-denial and abnegation of the most basic needs evoke awe in the spectator. The emotion of awe is so common as to cause wonder that its association to charisma is not more widely understood. Every child experiences awe in relationship to parents. As with other prototypical events, the capacity for the awesome response remains latent, ready to be evoked in the presence of someone who exhibits rich talents and traits.

At least part of the charismatic effect depends on the expectations of the subordinate. A leader who has a reputation of charisma will evoke awe because of what the legends promise about his or her presence. The charismatic individual creates a narrative. He or she is continually telling a story that combines some vision of the enterprise with personal history. Or, subordinates infatuated with the leader create narratives. Stories told about charismatic leaders may be true, but in the amplification, the telling and retelling, people anticipate the feeling of awe and so feel it.

The gifted political scientist and veteran student of leadership James MacGregor Burns called attention to the capacity of leaders to transform people's values rather than simply to accept and act from them.[18] However, before a leader can change how other people think and feel, he must go through a personal transformation in which he is tested and changed. This psychological transformation produces objectivity and clear-sightedness that enable such leaders to remember and use the past. It is for this reason that teaching leadership is especially difficult. Although it may be easy to generalize the qualities leaders should have, it is more difficult to stimulate in the student the transforming experience that makes leadership in practice transcend the ordinary.

Konosuke Matsushita wrote a memoir on his experience as founder and leader of the Matsushita Electric Industrial Company. He called his memoir *Not for Bread Alone: A Business Ethos, a Management Ethic*.[19] True, he gives a scant account of experiences that might have contributed to a personal transformation: "I lost my parents and older brothers while I was still young and have suffered from a chronic lung condition. My condition often forced me to rest in bed for extended periods, and even in the early days I often had to direct my staff and associates from bed." But he conveys a capacity for reflection that is unusual for business executives but characteristic of charismatic leaders. Undoubtedly, the business was always for him, as the founder, a personal matter, unlike what the corporation is to a typical business executive.

Katsuhiko Eguchi, the head of the PHP Institute, wrote an introduction to *Not for Bread Alone*, in which he tells a little more about the possible causes of Matsushita's deep personalization of his work. Matsushita's father suffered economic catastrophe that resulted in the loss of the family's ancestral home and lands. Shortly afterward, the two older brothers died and the father, "unable to lead his family out of destitution himself, pinned his hopes on Konosuke, who became the Matsushita heir at the age of four. At nine, Konosuke left primary school and went to live in Osaka, where he became an apprentice in a charcoal brazier shop." [20]

Transformations that leaders undergo occur most frequently as a result of trauma. Consequently, they often feel as though they are being tested. Their ability to tolerate the stress and to meet the test successfully strengthen a unique combination of introspection, courage, determination, and optimism. People who are introspective tend to be somewhat pessimistic, if not depressed. The depressive side is seen frequently among gifted artists and writers. For business leaders, a depressive personality interferes with their ability to take command and to act decisively. Executives who are decisive and introspective are a rarity, but for that matter so are leaders. The ability to look within one's self and the ability to be enduringly optimistic are essential qualities in leaders.

The introspective capacity encourages deep thought about problems and methods for their solution. Both the problems and the search for solutions involve a leader in a test, perhaps reminiscent of an earlier test such as accepting responsibility for the legacy of hope transmitted from parent to child.

The life of Matsushita provides many illustrations of being tested with business problems. One occurred in 1952 when he sought to arrange a technical cooperation agreement with the Dutch company, N. V. Philips. The negotiations appeared to be foundering on the issue of royalty payments. In Matsushita's view, Philips wanted an excessively large royalty payment for its technical contribution. If he had begun overt negotiation for a lower fee by questioning the price, he would soon have found himself in the position of denigrating the value his would-be partner had placed on its technical capacities, which would hardly have contributed to a climate of cooperation. Yet he felt a lower rate was necessary for competitive reasons.

Matsushita recognized that the Philips people were confident that their expertise would contribute greatly toward the success of the joint venture. He admired their confidence and self-esteem. As he reflected on the situation, he realized that he, too, was confident of his company's management ability, which was a crucial ingredient to assure the success of the venture. Just as Philips deserved a better-than-average royalty for its expertise and the confidence invested in it, so, too, did his company deserve compensation for its unique management ability in which he had considerable confidence. He proposed to the Philips people that they pay a fee for the Matsushita management abilities while his company pay a fee for the Philips technical expertise. In this way both sides would give recognition to the other's unique contribution and at the same time they would establish a foundation of mutual respect.

At another time in his career, key executives informed him that his warehouses were full because the plants were producing beyond the company's capacity to sell household appliances. The remedy was to shut down and lay off people until demand caught up with supply. This solution troubled Matsushita. What justified injuring people who were not responsible for the problem at hand? And, once they had been injured, why should they trust him later and act in the best interests of the company? He sought for and found another solution: Put workers on a reduced work week with no reduction in pay. In return, the workers would take samples and go door-to-door to sell products. The idea worked and normal arrangements were soon reestablished.

The stories leaders such as Konosuke Matsushita tell have a point beyond merely recording interesting events in their careers. The purpose in telling the stories is to transmit values. Subordinates look to their leaders for indications of the beliefs and values that are intended to direct an enterprise. Embedded in these values are the guides to human conduct, the rules that should determine the quality of human relationships in the business.

All businesspeople need models and guides who show the way to interact, the tacit and explicit rules for social behavior in a particular system. Managers collect a set of rules from experience that eventually leads them to believe that they are adept at influencing people in order to get what they want in their daily exchanges.

Managers' ideas on how to influence people ignore traditional rules that leaders convey in the telling of their stories. These traditional rules grew from the tutelage authority figures used to give their subordinates and from everyday experience at a time when that experience involved both direct and intimate human relations. Unencumbered by the management structures, leaders followed some simple guidelines on how to deal with people.

Traditionalists in the art of using power, leaders give short shrift to broad philosophical questions concerning human nature. Whether humanity is inherently good or bad, virtuous or sinful, has little bearing on the problem of getting other people to work cooperatively in organizations. Instead, the rules of human relations follow from a practical psychology. For example, people want to be successful at what they do. Show them how to be successful and they will feel indebted to you; set up roadblocks to their success and they will retaliate with hate if not revenge.

If people have followed a successful course of action, they will continue to pursue this course. Asking them to do something different generates resistance. Simply explaining why a new course is better gets nowhere. In introducing change, protect incumbents by compensating them for their losses.

People are governed by strict rules of equity. Those who live by these rules earn respect. Violating the rules garners hostility. In introducing change, split the risk and share the reward.

A leader avoids issuing directives that cannot be carried out. Such directives are meaningless and, moreover, place the subordinate in a potentially humiliating position. The counter to this threat is evasiveness and untruthfulness, which in the end is destructive. Often, the best way to determine if directives can be carried out is to listen. But the art of listening is a challenge to the inclinations of executives to act and avoid passivity. Listening depends on the constructive use of passivity. The impulse to act is a barrier to understanding.

Listening is a skill that can be learned once a leader first recognizes its importance in authority relations. Some guidelines include:

1. Take an interest in the other person.

2. Avoid argument by suspending judgment on what the other person is saying. Avoid giving advice and directives until the other person has fully expressed his or her views. When the time comes to respond, make certain that you understand what the other person has said.

3. Listen with a "third ear." Following the advice of Elton Mayo, listen to what the other person wants to say, listen to what he does not want to say, and listen to what he cannot say without help.[21]

Although in the physical world every action brings a reaction, in the social world every initiative, especially from an authority figure, brings multiple reactions, some expressed but others hidden. To judge the effects of these reactions requires understanding the context in which a subordinate must respond to an initiative.

People operate in groups as well as individually, and they usually care greatly about their standing in the eyes of members of their group. When a subordinate's relations with those in authority enhance his or her standing with associates, the subordinate will tend to meet authority's expectations. On the other hand, if authority figures cause rifts between the individual and his or her associates, they should expect hostility not only from the individual but also from the associates. The force of empathy in groups is powerful. A group that sees fellow members harmed will close ranks in support, because the harm done to one, particularly if it appears unjust or arbitrary, will be experienced as harm done to all.

Ordinarily, leaders should not socialize with subordinates. Relations with authority usually involve tensions that interfere with easy social interchange. For authority to seek this interchange as a way of reducing the tensions will be perceived as seeking to ingratiate itself with subordinates, which will result in no friendship and loss of respect.

Leaders are expected to support their subordinates in the task of getting the job done while maintaining integrity as individuals and as group members. There is no ground for expecting to be loved while in a position of authority over other people. The authority can rightfully look for respect, particularly in asserting and maintaining integrity through behavior. Leaders avoid flattery and do not use it, or other forms of ingratiation, to gain subordinates' support. Even though actions speak louder than words, especially in moral and ethical concerns, the degree to which actions and words correspond measures leaders' sincerity and trustworthiness.

Leaders should not expect people to value them more highly than they value themselves, but they should limit their self-regard to what is realistic and continually demonstrable. Self-regard differs greatly from puffery, which will diminish respect from others, and from false modesty, which will elicit contempt.

At all times leaders should behave so that there is consistency between what they intend to have happen and what they are asking people to make happen. If a leader asks for a subordinate's opinion, with the intention of making the subordinate feel involved but without real regard for the substance of his or her views, the subordinate will feel neither involved nor particularly grateful for the so-called participation. The subordinate will only feel mistrust of the leader and the leader will find it difficult to engage the subordinate's interest when it really becomes necessary.

Leaders should not make promises they cannot fulfill. A leader's reputation rests in part on delivering benefits to subordinates that they have a right to expect. If subordinates believe something more is coming their way, the leader is obliged to deliver on the promise.

When leaders issue a directive or ask people to do something, they should be sure that people understand what is expected of them and how the proposed action fits into the purposes of the organization. When they present an initiative, leaders should be convinced that it is correct. If leaders do not believe in an initiative that comes from higher authority, they should dispute the problem with their boss. Leaders should not ask people to carry out an initiative simply because of a superior's wishes.

These rules of personal influence in organizations and the many others that should guide the behavior of authority figures are traditional and bound to the wisdom of experience, but they are eroding because they are no longer considered necessary in the ethos of the managerial mystique. Therefore, the lessons of time and experience are no longer being handed down from one generation to the next, from superior to subordinate. Modern business disdains the personal aspects of authority in which influence occurs both in the regard people have for one another and the substance contained in initiative.

The tendency is to value institutional process over personal influence as though the former represents continuity in leadership while the latter is a transitory experience. Personal influence often suggests manipulation. A dominant personality gains control of another's mind and suggests courses of action not in the best interests of followers. As Burns suggested, the problem of manipulation goes to the heart of the relationship of leader and led.

> When a leader or a teacher seeks to influence a person by appealing to the person's motive base, the implicit question is: to *what* specific motives is one appealing? Who is the true "I" that is appealing to the true "me" that is being appealed to? With what resources, or power base, is one appealing? For what end and for *whose* end? In what social environment—that is, in relation to the motives and resources of what wider groups and publics and leader-follower relationship? And over what time span?[22]

Burns's questions can neither be asked nor answered without examining the moral dimension of leadership. The moral dimension is more easily evaded by making influence impersonal. It is only through personal influence that responsibility can be both felt and accepted. This internalization of responsibility is the foundation for morality in leadership.

Chapter 15

The Moral Dimension

*I*n March 1987, John Shad, former head of the Securities and Exchange Commission and then ambassador to the Netherlands, gave $20 million to the Harvard Business School to support research and teaching in business ethics. Other donors intended to give an additional $10 million to augment Shad's gift. Significantly, John McArthur, the dean of the Harvard Business School, avoided soliciting funds from investment banking houses and corporations to complete the Shad program.

Shad decided to fund the ethics program because he was disturbed over the epidemic of insider trading on Wall Street. In commenting on his gift, Shad wrote:

> A very disturbing area is the recent rash of insider-trading cases against young men in their 20's and early 30's who are graduates of leading business and law schools—the cream of the crop. Ten recent graduates of Harvard, Stanford, Columbia, Wharton, and other leading business and law schools are convicted felons. Most will serve prison terms. They may be the tip of the iceberg—symptomatic of more serious problems in America today.[1]

Shad then asked some pertinent questions.

> Why were they willing to risk their brilliant futures and self-respect? While it may have been because of deep-seated psy-

chological reasons, other questions remain. Have the temptations become too great? Was it the challenge or the excitement of seeing if they could get away with it—if they could beat the system? Were they driven by peer pressures or rivalries to win the game in which the score has a dollar sign in front of it? Or has there been a change in moral attitudes in America since World War II as a result of the dispersion of families, rising divorces, the permissiveness of the 60's and the 70's, the Vietnam War and the drugs? The answer probably lies in a combination of these factors, but the question now is: What can be done about it?[2]

Shad expressed one answer to the question of what can be done with his $20 million gift to support education in ethics so that leaders of the future will be thoroughly sensitized to all of the ethical nuances with which they must deal in business. Professor David Vogel of the University of California Business School expressed the viewpoint of many educators when he wrote:

While schools cannot make people ethical, they can strengthen the commitment of those who have a well-developed sense of personal morality to begin with. They can help sensitize them to the kinds of ethical quandaries that will confront them in the business world and give them the analytical tools to enable them to think more clearly about the kinds of responsibilities and obligations individuals owe to one another in a market economy. Most important, schools can teach the nation's future business leaders how to manage their companies, divisions or units in such a way as to minimize the likelihood that those who work for them will violate either company policies or the law.[3]

Business and other professional schools are addressing ethical issues through programs that not only raise a student's awareness of the problem, but provide criteria for determining ethical business behavior in situations with conflicting values. Business schools, in particular, are now teaching students professional attitudes to guard against future unethical and illegal activities. One of the tenets of professionalism is objectivity, which overcomes (or should overcome) racial, religious, and sexual biases. Another tenet is to promote an "open system," which offers wide access to process and therefore allows many people to influence decision making. In the closed system of authoritarianism and personality cults standards of behavior vary with the leader and barriers to participation preclude widespread influence from associates and constituencies.

These tenets of professionalism are not isolated in academia. They exist as well in corporations. Boards of publicly owned corporations are required to appoint audit committees that issue written standards of ethical conduct in which positive statements as well as strictures appear. Companies avow that they will use open hiring practices, will deliver quality products, and will not tolerate sexual harassment, bribery, or other illegal practices. The audit committees of boards of directors generally review the ethics statements and approve them for circulation. These committees also provide procedures for communicating infractions, offering some protection to "whistle blowers." Once approved, management and staff receive and sign the statements to indicate that they are aware of the company's standards and that they intend to comply with and enforce them.

The problem with professionalism as an antidote to unethical conduct is that it takes too long before its effect takes hold. Moreover, even with some of our most respected businesses, it scarcely overcomes the incentives to act unethically and illegally. There was no question, for example, of E. F. Hutton's respectability on Wall Street or, for that matter, its professionalism in the investment banking industry. It came as a surprise, therefore, to many that Hutton had been kiting or "chaining" checks and bilking commercial banks out of millions of dollars in unearned interest.

The far-reaching Pentagon procurement scandal of 1988 showed that professionalism meant little to those trading information to circumvent the military's procurement procedures in awarding contracts. Besides officials in the Pentagon and former officials who became "consultants" on military contracts, the list of corporations implicated in these questionable and possibly illegal actions included Unisys, Litton Industries, McDonnell Douglas, United Technologies, and other defense contractors. Despite the acceptance of professionalism, the record of the 1980s demonstrates that the greater the play of market forces (that is, with the trend toward deregulation and a purer form of free competition), the looser the moral conduct of businesspeople, including professional managers with graduate degrees in business. The greater the opportunity to make money, therefore, the looser the moral standards of people in situations where they stand to gain a great deal by illegal and unethical behavior.

It is little wonder, therefore, that the Shad gift met with considerable cynicism in the press and little open approbation by leading business executives. Mr. Shad may have brought this cynicism on himself when he tried to cast his gift as a means of promoting successful business practice through high ethical practice. He commented: "I believe ethics pays, that it's smart to be ethical. I think those who go for the edges, like high rollers in Las Vegas are ultimately wiped out."[4] It is far from axiomatic that ethical practice pays, although many business educators and executives would like to believe this hopeful pronouncement. A stronger case could be made that so much unethical and illegal behavior exists precisely because it is the type of behavior that pays. Why else would intelligent people jeopardize their careers and livelihood?

The desire for money and all that it symbolizes too often quiets the voice of conscience that ordinarily restrains the impulses to cheat. It would seem that the mighty and the weak face similar temptations, although the stakes differ. For example, Robert B. Anderson, secretary of the Treasury in the second Eisenhower administration, was convicted of swindling and sentenced to a jail term. Paul Thayer, deputy secretary of defense in the first Reagan administration, was convicted of passing information to a stockbroker. He and his coconspirators paid the government $1,000,000 and Thayer, former chairman and CEO of LTV Corporation, was sentenced to four years in jail and fined $5,000. The Watergate scandal of the 1970s and the Iran-contra scandal of the 1980s, along with the questionable actions of Edwin Meese, former attorney general of the United States, suggest how far the mighty will go in pursuing their aims of gaining money and power.

Individual unethical activities by less well-known figures also affect major institutions. Indeed, stories of the lowly add pointed reminders that too little contemplation goes into action that is knowingly unethical and even illegal. R. Foster Winans, for example, who wrote the prestigious column "Heard on the Street" for the *Wall Street Journal*, entered into an agreement with Peter Brant, a stockbroker for Kidder Peabody, to reveal in advance the stocks that he intended to promote in his column. Brant paid Winans about $20,000 for the tips that made a lot more money for Brant. The amount seems so paltry against the consequences —Winans lost his job and after torturous legal action, including a negative decision by the U.S. Supreme Court, served a jail sentence. What could have motivated Winans to violate the codes of his profession, bring dishonor on his name, and bring considerable discredit to the *Wall Street Journal?*

Although Winans carefully avoids frank discussion of his inner thoughts and motives in *Trading Secrets*, his account of his misadventures in trading information for money, he provides enough information to suggest a number of conclusions about individual ethical misconduct.[5] The collusion did not involve other *Wall Street Journal* employees, a condition which leads to the conclusion that Winans's aim was a windfall. Indeed, Winans wanted the money so he could place a down payment on a weekend house he and his lover badly wanted. He would never have been able to accumulate $20,000 from his earnings, and the temptation was more than he could tolerate. Futhermore, the *Wall Street Journal* provided little community feeling among its employees, so Winans was unconcerned about letting down colleagues and friends. Winans suggests that his supervisors cared little about him or other employees, so loyalty to authority or to the institution counted little in his calculation of costs and benefits. The act itself, while concrete enough, was in Winans's eyes abstract so far as inflicting harm was concerned. Who was harmed? As with so many white-collar crimes, the victims are depersonalized, abstract, and therefore more easily overlooked. Undoubtedly, the idea that a crime without victims cannot be a crime will be presented as a defense in the insider trading cases.

The ethical problem becomes even more abstract when the individuals recognize they are violating the law, but rationalize their behavior by claiming they are serving a higher purpose. The rationalization makes it appear not just that the actions are harmless, but that, after calculating costs and benefits, they are actually beneficial to the institution or to others (aside from being personally beneficial).

In unethical conduct of a broader scope, some major corporations have engaged in what might be called a monopoly of speculative deceit. On April 18, 1961, for instance, forty-five corporate executives from twenty-nine companies in the electrical equipment industry, including General Electric, Westinghouse, and Allis-Chalmers, were convicted of conspiring to fix prices, rig bids, and divide contracts on equipment valued at \$1.75 billion annually. The conspiracy was so pervasive that it included insulators valued at a couple of dollars to turbine generators valued at millions.[6]

General Electric's ethics policy was required reading for executives. Instruction 2.35 stated: "It has been and is the policy of this Company to conform strictly to the antitrust laws." General Electric's sales manager for the transformer department believed, and presumably communicated to his subordinates, that GE's antitrust policy did not apply to his group's activities. He said, "[The antitrust directive] didn't mean the kind of thing we were doing, that Antitrust would have to say that we had gouged the public to say we were doing anything illegal."[7] This sales manager also reported that he and his associates understood that "this was what the company wanted us to do."[8] Another defendant in this case, who had been an executive at GE's switch gear department and later transferred into the circuit breaker division ostensibly to promote communication with competitors, corroborated the view that executives in product divisions were acting on word "from higher up." He said, "I think the competitive situation was forcing [the company leaders] to do something, and there were a lot of old-timers who thought that collusion was the best way to solve the problems. That is when the hotel-room meetings got started. We were cautioned at this time to not tell the lawyers what we were doing and to cover our trails in our expense-account reports."[9] This executive believed that his boss followed the tenet of "live and let live" and the practice of advising employees "to contact the competitors."

Despite the many convictions and ruined careers of men valued in the community and loved in their families, cynicism prevailed. For example, one executive stated, "One thing I have learned out of all this is to talk to only one other person, not to go to meetings where there are lots of other people." Many defendants maintained that they were simply "fall guys" and that conspiracy was a "way of life in American business."

Because of this cynicism, many people do not believe that education and the tenets of professionalism will elevate ethical standards. They believe that the answer to the question of what can be done about the situation is law and regulation. With teeth to enforce them, laws will alter the calculations that place self-defined standards ("I can do this because no one gets hurt while I get rich" or "It's okay because it's for the benefit of the company") above legal and communal standards. Laws evolve in an attempt to support what the community wants and expects, and corporate attorneys inform executives about new standards that are expressed through judiciary and legislative processes. A General Electric attorney pointed out how the law is evolving: "[A] business corporation will be held criminally liable for the acts of an employee so long as these acts are reasonably related to the area of general responsibility entrusted to him notwithstanding the fact that such acts are committed in violation of instructions issued by the company in good faith." [10] This interpretation means that merely having a written ethics policy does not absolve the corporation of responsibility when its employees and other agents violate the law while conducting the corporation's normal business. A stricter legal standard increases vigilance and does not wait for education and professionalism to achieve what society expects from its citizens.

Some industries appear repeatedly in the annals of corporate fraud and new industries continually join them. In the Pentagon procurement scandal, defense industry executives hired former government officials as consultants to provide inside information and act as liaisons with government agencies while bidding for military contracts. Their argument against conviction for fraud will be that the corporate executives, government officials, and consultants acted to facilitate rather than harm government procurement and the defense effort. The defendants will claim that they overcame bureaucratic red tape and assured that contracts fell into the hands of the corporations most able to perform, thus helping rather than hindering the objectives of military procurement. Not only will they claim that there was no "crime," because their actions were "victimless," but also they will assert that their actions served a higher purpose in circumventing narrowly drawn and unintelligible competitive bidding regulations. Predictably, as with President Reagan in the Iran-contra scandal, higher level officials will be able to claim they had no information about such practices and that if they had known, they would have stopped them.

What we are observing in the current scene of legal and ethical violations is the ubiquity of deniability. Top management regularly denies knowledge of anything dishonest going on and blames any such actions that are uncovered on bad characters farther down in the hierarchy. The only hint remotely suggesting responsibility at the top of the hierarchy is in the cliché a "failure of communication." The claim is that top management holds fast to ethical principles and obedience to the law, but its intentions are not understood at lower levels in the organization. The chief corporate officers invariably are presented as honest, ethical, and scrupulously law-abiding. Their only error, if it can be called an error, is in not making a great enough effort to communicate the corporation's ethical standards or in not succeeding in making them clear. Top management offers the faint-hearted self-incrimination that fault lies neither in intent nor in personal honesty, but simply in failing to communicate. This is the essence of deniability, and if anything vitiates the idea of leadership, it is deniability.

On May 2, 1985, E. F. Hutton pleaded guilty in federal court to 2,000 counts of mail and wire fraud. The court fined Hutton $2 million and ordered it to return money to over 400 banks. When charges against the company became public knowledge, Hutton repeatedly maintained that its financial practices were not criminal, but merely reflected "aggressive cash management."

A number of government agencies conducted probes, including two congressional investigations, a Securities and Exchange Commission study, a justice department study, and various state inquiries. The Justice Department charged that Hutton officials increased interest income and defrauded banks by using deliberate overdrafts without the banks' knowledge. The department's three-year investigation showed that, in a practice called "chaining," Hutton managers shuffled more than $10 billion from one account to another, with nearly $1 billion in uncollected funds obtained interest-free from July 1980 through February 1982, when interest rates ranged from 18 to 20 percent.[11] The Justice Department further discovered that Hutton had arranged sequential deposits and withdrawals in an array of regional banks. By exploiting delays in check clearing, Hutton was able to reinvest as much as $250 million a day and earn interest it would not otherwise have made. Hutton responded to these charges by claiming that low-level employees instigated these chaining practices in isolated actions that deviated from company policy, but that did not violate the law.[12]

Business has taken a leaf from government in embracing deniability, which protects the chief executive and other senior officers at the expense of lower level executives and staff. A new industry has arisen in special investigations offered by law firms. These investigations are comparable to President Reagan's appointment of the Tower Commission to investigate the Iran-contra scandal. They are quite different from the work of special counsel appointed under the aegis of the judicial branch of the government following congressional legislation designed to ensure independence of a special counsel's study and judgment. As might seem predictable, the Tower Commission found that President Reagan did not know of the sale of arms to Iran or the diversion of funds from these sales to the contras in Nicaragua. According to the Tower Commission, the fault lay with an over-zealous staff and not with the chief executive. At no time did President Reagan call in his subordinates to get the facts directly from them, an omission that defies common sense but that supports the principle of maintaining the posture of deniability.

Sometime during the investigation into Hutton's practices, its senior executives decided to hire former Attorney General Griffin Bell and his law firm as independent investigators. They paid his firm $2.5 million of which more than $800,000 went to Bell himself. Bell and his assistants were given this charge: Determine whether Hutton's practices were illegal, and if so, ferret out the individuals responsible.

After investigation, Bell exonerated Hutton's senior management, including its chairman and chief executive officer, Robert Fomon, and its former president, George Ball. According to his findings, any direct management responsibility did not go higher than a senior vice president in charge of the company's cash management. Bell stated that this vice president failed in his duties by not detecting the illegal overdrafting. As for Fomon, Bell concluded that although "all this happened on Fomon's watch," Fomon could not be held responsible for the actions of the lower level managers.[13]

Bell further concluded that no member of top management was criminally liable for participating in or encouraging improper overdrafts. Bell said that "there is no question" that Hutton's former president and other senior officials received memoranda and data on interest income showing the results of improper conduct, but that the evidence was insufficient "to charge these officials with a crime."[14]

Bell named several branch managers who were actively engaged in wrongdoing. He stated that their overdrafting activities were so excessive "that no reasonable person could have believed that this conduct was proper." The federal investigation named six managers who were fined between $25,000 and $50,000, placed on one year's probation, and received a letter of reprimand. Bell also cited several regional managers "whose conduct was such that no reasonable person could have believed that this was proper conduct." Three of these regional managers received thirty-day suspensions without pay.[15]

In conducting the investigations and presumably in reaching conclusions, Bell and his staff uncovered eighteen documents detailing the drawdown and transfer activities. The documents show that top management actively encouraged Hutton branch managers and cashiers to boost interest income by aggressive drawdowns. Memoranda indicate that top management further encouraged raising branch profitability by depicting how such profitability could boost a branch manager's personal earnings. Finally, the documents showed that Hutton took great pains to establish and monitor the interest income of each branch and even reported the relative rankings of branches, presumably as a goad to the laggards to increase their interest income. Several memoranda stress that Hutton branches should strive to earn interest income at least at the level of the average of interest as a percentage of gross revenue.[16]

There is an interesting footnote to the Hutton story of who knew and who was culpable. John M. Pearce, a former branch manager at Hutton, brought suit against Bell and his law firm, seeking $10 million in damages. Pearce claimed that Bell had defamed him in the 1985 investigation. Pearce claimed that he was following Hutton's policy of overdrafting bank accounts and that Bell had unfairly placed the blame on him, as a branch manager, while holding blameless senior management, the real perpetrators who had created the policy that Pearce merely carried out. Griffin Bell was exonerated on June 20, 1988. The moral of this story seems to be that in taking on special investigations on behalf of companies that are both the target of legal proceedings and the agency that hires and pays the investigators, law firms should receive indemnification before the investigation begins. So far, no concern seems to have been expressed, either in the legal profession or in business, about the potential for securing deniability in having distinguished personages and prestigious law firms support the presumption that top managers do not know what goes on down the line where ethical and legal infractions are most likely to occur.

Of course, if special counsel finds a smoking gun—evidence of a directive from a chief executive to subordinates to do something illegal such as collude with competitors to fix prices, kite checks, or falsely bill the defense department—the special counsel will report the findings and lay the blame at the feet of the executive. But special counsel or law enforcement agencies will seldom, if ever, find such smoking guns. The legal process follows its own rules. Above all, it will not inquire into what goes on in the minds of people. It will not stretch its procedures or lend special energy to questions of whether a wink and a nod or a passing hint provided the directive from on high that set in motion a series of grossly illegal and unethical actions. Suppose a chief executive comments to subordinates how stupid this predatory pricing is and how much better life would be if people followed the principle of live and let live. Is the CEO responsible if the subordinates initiate a chain of action that results in collusion to fix prices? In legal or quasi-legal proceedings, the finding will be lack of evidence of culpability. In human terms he or she is responsible, but the chances are good that another principle of protecting authority will hold sway. No one will report on having heard the chief executive's musings and how they were absorbed and acted upon. The penalties for violating this principle are too severe. Therefore deniability will be maintained. Oliver North and John Poindexter will sacrifice themselves before they will tell what encouraged them to act as they perpetrated the Iran-contra activities.

The argument could be made that deniability is a sign of weakness in the consciences of subordinates, that even though they receive "signals" about what they are expected to do, they do not have to act on these signals. They could ignore them if their ethical standards tell them they would be embarking on a misadventure to accept this communication and follow its consequences down the path of collusion and deception. This argument, while literally true, is made basically to diffuse the issue of accountability and, in the end, to support deniability.

The clearest example of deniability is where a chief executive officer issues verbal directives to engage in unethical or illegal acts, but forms a collusion with other executives to suppress any evidence that the directive has been issued. President Nixon supposedly did not know that his agents were going to break into the Democratic headquarters in the Watergate, yet he expressed a desire for information that might link party leaders to some scandal involving union heads or mobsters. President Nixon also may have been worried that the Democrats had some information that would incriminate him, such as illegal contributions from industrialist Howard Hughes.

How deep deniability has penetrated the mentality of management is illustrated by the often stated belief that the only mistake President Nixon made during Watergate was to keep the tapes. Had he destroyed them, say supporters of deniability, his presidency would have been preserved. No direct evidence would have linked him to the crime or the cover-up and, consequently, there would have been no impeachment proceeding or need to resign from office.

There need be no overt or explicit collusion to suppress directives for the game of deniability to be played. In government some degree of deniability is legitimate on the grounds of national security. Society accepts the idea that some duplicity and deniability are necessary to protect the national interests, especially in matters of war and peace. When Soviet Chairman Nikita Khrushchev announced that the Russians had shot down a U2 reconnaissance plane on May 1, 1960, President Eisenhower denied that the United States government had authorized a spying mission over Soviet territory. When it became evident that the Russians had captured Francis Gary Powers, the pilot of this ill-fated effort in high altitude espionage, President Eisenhower admitted that the United States had authorized this flight.

The episode embarrassed President Eisenhower and led to the cancellation of the summit meeting in Paris scheduled for May 17, 1960. If it had not been a standard practice before then, it soon became practice that the president was not to know of specific secret missions and intelligence activities, although he and his agents would control the policies that would spawn these actions.

But even in the affairs of state, there are limits to the acceptance of expedience, deniability, and lack of accountability, at the expense of moral standards. When former Attorney General Edwin Meese claimed exoneration in Special Prosecutor McKay's finding of no indictable crime, he attempted to ignore ethical standards. As hard as he tried through press conferences, speeches, and public relations devices (he even fired his press chief for not doing enough to paper over the ethical questions raised about his conduct in office), Meese could not overcome the judgment of the community that his actions were below the threshold of acceptable behavior by an officeholder, let alone the chief law enforcement officer of the United States.

The American community accepts competition as a way of life. It also accepts the principle of pursuit of advantage in competition. The tough fighter is not only accepted, but admired. The sports coach who drives his players hard becomes a hero and lionized for his aggressive competitive spirit, if the team wins. But while valuing competition, the community also expects fair play. Men and women are supposed to compete hard to protect their interests and to win, but they are not supposed to take advantage of their power to harm others. In business the law forbids monopolies and practices such as predatory pricing to squeeze out competition. The community supports taking every advantage allowed in the tax laws, such as shifting business from one state to another to benefit from lower tax rates, but it will not accept pushing such advantage to the point that a powerful and wealthy corporation pays little if any taxes.

To avoid reporting taxable income, General Electric and other corporations in the defense industry took advantage of a provision in the tax code that allowed the spread of profits. But when this advantage became public knowledge, even conservative politicians such as President Reagan and former Secretary of the Treasury and Chief of Staff Donald Regan supported legislation to remedy this defect in the tax code that allowed a profitable corporation to pay little or no taxes.

Cultures vary in their tolerance of deviations from moral standards. In the United States the standards are stricter than in many European countries concerning moral rectitude among public officials and corporate executives. Many well-educated and sophisticated Europeans were genuinely perplexed over the impeachment proceedings against President Richard Nixon and his resignation from office. To them, Watergate and the cover-up were acceptable transgressions. These same Europeans describe as common many tax-evading practices and express astonishment at the degree of compliance with the tax laws (still) in the United States. Despite its frontier heritage, where law followed sometimes belatedly in the tracks of the pioneers, Americans abide by the law and expect others to do the same, including the rich and the powerful. And, the standards for judging business executives are somewhat stricter than the standards for public officials.

A good example is Harold Geneen's role in ITT's attempts to influence officials in Nixon's administration (including possibly Nixon himself, albeit indirectly) and his involvement with the CIA in attempts to influence the presidential election in Chile and, subsequently, to prevent Salvador Allende Gossens from becoming president in that country's 1970 election.

Harold Geneen displayed an inordinate need (as well as capacity) to control the actions of his subordinates and the fate of the various enterprises that operated under ITT's conglomerate tent. But as all human beings eventually discover, the gap between desire and actuality in controlling others often becomes unbearable and may lead to unwise actions. The desire to control may become so intense as to create a situation in which the executive and his or her corporation are out of control. Whether the situation reached this extreme in Geneen's case is a matter of interpretation, but it is clear that Geneen became involved in near scandals and the possibility of perjury indictment, ultimately resulting in loss of confidence among members of his board of directors and a strengthening of their resolve to force Geneen to retire.

During 1968 ITT acquired twenty domestic companies, including Continental Baking, Pennsylvania Glass Sand, Levitt and Sons, Rayonier, and Sheraton Corporation of America. At the end of the year, as the political climate seemed to shift with the election of Richard Nixon, a man from whom big business presumably had little to fear, ITT moved to merge with Hartford Fire Insurance Company.

But on June 6, 1969, Nixon's attorney general, John Mitchell, made a speech that seemed to indicate an antitrust, anticonglomerate policy on the part of the administration. By that time ITT had announced its pending merger with Hartford, and it had been approved by the stockholders. The acquisition of Hartford was important to Geneen and ITT, for Hartford promised to give an extraordinary cash flow to ITT. As the head of ITT-Avis, Winston ("Bud") Morrow put it, "What intrigued Geneen was that it would be the ultimate money tree. He could take a seventy-five-million-dollar loss and not even think about it. . . . This would give him the final flexibility, the linchpin to go for what he wanted—becoming the number-one-sized corporation in the world." [17]

But Richard Nixon's new assistant attorney general for antitrust, Richard W. McLaren, a Chicago lawyer who had given much of his energies to defending clients in government antitrust actions, was equally determined to attack ITT for antitrust violations. In the spring of 1969 he instituted a series of suits against ITT under Section 7 of the Sherman Act, adding Hartford in August. Incensed, Geneen tried to see Nixon, and when this was seen as inappropriate, he talked with a host of people close to Nixon, including John Connally, John Ehrlichman, John Mitchell, and Charles Colson. A Senate investigating committee report later said, "It is probably a status symbol in official circles to have been lobbied by Harold Geneen personally. . . . "[18]

With a sense of backing a righteous cause, Geneen apparently enjoyed fighting this battle with McLaren, whose position on antitrust was probably untenable since even the opponents of big business doubted that Section 7 could be applied to conglomerates. It may have been McLaren's plan to push the suit up to the Supreme Court to get a ruling that would extend the application of the Sherman Act, but the case was settled by compromise before that happened.

By the summer of 1971, with Hartford secure and a climate of lessening hostility to conglomerates, Geneen was ready to get on with his goal of making ITT the largest corporation in the world. Unfortunately, the out-of-court settlement of the antitrust suit, although arranged in June, was not announced until the last day of July. Five days later the media carried news of ITT-Sheraton's contribution of $100,000 and a challenge pledge of a further equal contribution to the San Diego Convention and Tourist Bureau as part of an effort to lure the 1972 Republican convention to that city. In spite of considerable local opposition, Nixon had been exerting pressure on key people to have San Diego as the convention site. Ralph Nader, an adamant opponent of conglomerates, noted the coincidental timing of the settlement and the ITT contribution. He asked Richard Kleindienst, deputy attorney general in charge of ITT's case, whether the two events were connected. Kleindienst firmly denied any connection.

Then, in February of 1972 Jack Anderson's column in the *Washington Post* contained a memorandum allegedly written by Dita Beard, the flamboyant Washington lobbyist Geneen had hired in 1961. Beard's memo, titled "Subject: San Diego Convention" and dated June 25, 1971, was addressed to William Merriam, head

of the Washington office. Among other statements linking the convention pledge with the antitrust settlement, Beard wrote: "I am
convinced . . . that our noble commitment has gone a long way
toward our negotiations on the mergers eventually coming out as
Hal wants them." [19]

The bizarre circumstances surrounding Dita Beard's disappearance when Anderson published his column and reappearance,
sequestered in a Denver hospital, and the hint of scandal in high
places attracted intensive media coverage. Both Kleindienst and
ITT were harmed by the inconsistencies and confusions that came
out during questioning. But while Kleindienst's testimony during
confirmation hearings was garbled, Geneen's appeared to be a
model of candidness. He answered almost all questions with a
combination of openness, humor, and disavowal of any wrongdoing. But then he was asked about the frenzied shredding of documents that took place in the ITT office in Washington in the wake
of Anderson's accusations. Geneen answered:

> I really don't know any of the details of it other than the fact,
> as it was reported in the press, and I talked to our counsel. I
> know that some, or at least I am told that there were some,
> kind of documents that were shredded. I am satisfied . . . that
> this was probably more a reaction to the feeling that our
> files were suddenly opened to the public or something, and
> certainly not any kind of an action to, you might say, prevent
> a review of our files by any legitimate agency. [20]

Geneen and the ITT office had broken no laws by lobbying
nor were they on trial. Although many people questioned the
morality of such backstairs efforts, lobbying high officials was commonplace. But the behavior of many of the ITT witnesses and their
lawyers had provoked considerable criticism of their almost flip-
pant approach to the ethical issues being raised.

During a recess of the Kleindienst hearings in March 1972,
Jack Anderson published another series of memos reportedly
taken from the ITT files. They strongly suggested that ITT had
helped the CIA try to prevent Salvador Allende Gossens from
becoming president of Chile in that country's 1970 election. Once
again Anderson's accusations precipitated congressional hearings.
Senator William Fulbright of Arkansas called for a subcommittee
investigation of the role played by American multinational corpo-

rations in United States foreign policy. Because of the politically sensitive nature of the issues, the hearings were postponed until after the 1972 presidential election. When they finally began on March 20, 1973, the Watergate disclosures had begun to uncover a wasp's nest of lies and intrigue.

The subpoenaed documents and the barrage of questions uncovered the fact that ITT had clearly engaged in discussions with the CIA about how best to interfere in the Chilean election. The testimony of ITT witnesses was contradictory and evasive. Senator Frank Church, who chaired the subcommittee, commented, "It just doesn't hang together. It's just unbelievable."

When Geneen took the witness stand, Church pressed him on the question of ITT's suggestion to the CIA to contribute to a fund to fight Allende. Geneen replied:

> I think I previously testified to the committee that I did not have any independent recollection of this subject. I said that I felt that I may well have . . . from shock of recognizing that, you might say, our Chilean investment was going down the drain, I might well have come back and said, "Can we?" in effect.
>
> . . . Mr. Broe [CIA's chief of clandestine services, Western Hemisphere] . . . said it was not the government policy and it died right there and I might add if I had given it more serious consideration I might have rejected it myself, but I thought of it, if I would place myself in the probability of saying can I help, and it died right there as not being government policy.[21]

Geneen later swore that ITT had not made a political contribution to any political party in Chile. Church commented, "It is obvious . . . somebody is lying. We must take a very serious view of perjury under oath."[22] Later evidence showed that ITT had indeed given at least $350,000 to Jorge Alessandri Rodriguez's right-wing National Party.

Both Geneen and ITT were badly hurt by the Chile hearings and the revelations of Watergate. The justice department filed perjury charges against two ITT witnesses. Although Geneen finally escaped prosecution, he was under the shadow of a possible indictment for perjury for denying, in his testimony at the Kleindienst and Chile hearings, that ITT had given money to prevent

Allende's election. It hung over him until 1978 when the statute of limitations ran out.

Harold Geneen disregarded the proposition that a chief executive must protect his position and use deniability to avoid being directly implicated in unethical or illegal practices. That he and his company should never have gotten involved in the Chilean affair is the main lesson to be drawn from this sordid experience. But too often the ethical substance is obfuscated in the process of maintaining the CEO's deniability. Professionals focus on the question of what is best for the corporation in areas where the law (and not necessarily the ethics) is unclear. Individual dishonesty is an uninteresting question both as a practical and academic matter. Some people will steal if the stakes are high enough and if they think they can get away with it. The more interesting questions arise when people act, easily overcoming a guilty conscience, because they think they are working for the best interests of the group and the corporation. Here, "ethicists" in business and in business schools have little to say compared with the humanists for whom truth about the human condition is an absolute value.

In a vitriolic commentary, Irving Kristol cast doubt on the ability of the academic community to teach morals and ethics and, indeed, its moral standing. Kristol, who is a leader in the neoconservative intellectual community, dismissed John Shad's gift to the Harvard Business School as "nice but naive."[23] According to Kristol, when the academic community abandoned moral turpitude as a cause for dismissal of tenured faculty, it lost its claim to teach ethics or moral philosophy. But beyond whatever bitterness lay behind Kristol's criticism, there is a serious question about the intellectual, as well as moral, foundation for study and teaching in ethics. Many inside and outside the academic community feel it is worthless. As Kristol states,

> In this process of character formation, what we call "education in ethics" has no positive role to play. On the contrary, its influence is bound to be negative. If graduate students in ethics pursue their studies seriously, it can certainly sharpen their wits, which is no bad thing in itself. But as we have had occasion to learn—and John Shad knows this better than anyone—being sharp-witted is perfectly consistent with being immoral.[24]

There is a deeper challenge for academics in researching and teaching business ethics. How strong is the commitment to truth? How will researchers establish the truth that presumably will become the basis for courses on business ethics? The need for answers to these questions makes irrelevant the banalities and good intentions that seem to dominate the attitudes found in business schools as they approach business ethics.

Jeffrey Sonnenfeld and Paul R. Lawrence, when they were, respectively, a doctoral candidate in organizational behavior and the Wallace Brett Donham professor of organizational behavior, interviewed forty executives in large companies in the paper industry with divisions active in the corrugated box business.[25] The companies in which the interviews took place derived 4 to 5 percent of their revenues from sales of folding cartons. Sonnenfeld and Lawrence did not disclose the identity of the companies or the executives interviewed. They also did not reveal the number of companies studied and the distribution of the executives by status or by company. The purpose of the interviews was to throw some light on price fixing that resulted in criminal convictions of forty-seven executives in this industry. Federal investigation revealed price fixing in consumer paper, fine paper and stationery, multiwall bags, labels, and corrugated and other folding boxes. By 1978 over 100 suits had been filed against the paper industry.

With this background of extensive collusion in many parts of the paper industry, rivaling in scope and significance the electrical generating equipment cases of 1960, it seems that it would have been potentially productive for the authors to have examined the relation between top management and the actual participants in the collusion. Instead, they chose to accept at face value the claim of top management that they were unaware, indeed stunned and chagrined, that their ethics policies had been violated. The authors say,

> Executives tremble over what may be going on in the field—despite their internal directives and public declarations. One CEO well expressed the frustration common to executives in convicted companies:
> "We've tried hard to stress that collusion is illegal. We point out that anticompetitive practices hurt the company's ethical standards, public image, internal morale, and earnings. Yet we wind up in trouble continually. When we try to

find out why employees got involved, they have the gall to say that they were 'only looking out for the best interest of the company.' They seem to think that the company message is for everyone else but them. You begin to wonder about the intelligence of these people. Either they don't listen or they're plain stupid." [26]

The authors approached their study beforehand with a belief that the problem was neither deafness nor stupidity on the part of the lower level executives and staff who colluded to fix prices, but instead, "that many well-meaning, ethical top managers simply are not getting their message down the line." [27] In other words, top management is ethical, and lower level employees are either unethical or ill-informed about the company's moral standards. It is the familiar "failure in communication." To confirm their preconceptions, and undoubtedly to give some recognition to the obvious, the authors offered this reassurance:

> The shock for those companies with strong, well-publicized ethical positions, is perhaps most severe. In case the reader is skeptical, our interviews with the senior people in these companies left us without a shred of doubt about the sincerity and completeness of their personal commitment to legal compliance. In fact the top people we spoke to in the major forest product companies desperately want to know how and why they got on the wrong side of the law so that they can be sure it never happens again. [28]

As this article illustrates, researchers based in business schools face difficult personal and professional dilemmas in investigating sensitive issues such as price fixing and other illegal behavior. The psychology of deniability can easily dominate the research. One might conclude from this example that business school professors are unworldly and uncommonly lacking in everyday "street smarts." But this conclusion itself may be naive. A deeper problem exists in the co-option of business schools by its constituency. Business schools inadvertently may be supporting deniability and thereby vitiating the moral foundation of research and teaching, which is the search for the truth.

What in fact is going on in corporations? The August 5, 1988, front page of the *New York Times* reported five stories on business fraud, including Hertz Corporation's guilty plea to charges of defrauding customers and insurance companies by inflating and inventing collision repair costs and the conviction of Mario Biaggi and five other defendants in the Wedtech case. The epidemic of fraud is symptomatic of the near collapse of the moral foundation of management. There is no amount of professionalism and proficiency in "doing things right" that will take the place of responsibility and accountability at the top of the hierarchy. If chief executive officers do not know what is going on in their corporations, it is either because they consciously avoid knowing or have no talent and taste for directing people in their work.

The main character in Arthur Miller's play *All My Sons* is Joe Keller, a simple man who has worked most of his life in order to provide for his family and leave a substantial legacy to his sons. His individual efforts have been rewarded by a prosperous business in which he takes pride. He is not callous, ruthless, or greedy, and he is not overcome with a lust for power and great wealth. His life is guided by two values: the worth of individual effort and the sanctity of family loyalty. He has a strong sense of practicality which has in effect defined his sense of morality; his family represents an absolute right for his actions, and his family loyalty is the moral end.

Keller decides to allow a shipment of cracked cylinder heads for airplane motors to be sent to the Air Force. He takes this risk for the sake of his business and family. The business is to provide a prosperous life for his two sons. Twenty-one pilots crash and die as a result of the defective parts. Joe escapes a prison sentence by allowing his partner to take the blame. As the play proceeds, Joe Keller's guilt is disclosed, not only to his family, but to himself. Joe's older son Larry, an army pilot, commits suicide on a combat mission in atonement for his father's crime.

Chris, his younger son, desperately pushes his father to understand that nothing can mitigate his guilt: A man must be responsible not *only* to his family, but, ultimately, to all men. There can be no evasion of the burdens of individual human responsibility. In the final moments of the play, Chris says to his mother, "It's not enough . . . to be sorry. You can be better! Once and for all you can know there's a universe of people outside and you're responsible for it." Chris insists that his mother understand the moral nature of the crime his father has committed: the failure to acknowledge his connection to a larger world and society.

The constant memory of his son's suicide and the revelation that it may have been the result of defective cylinder heads which he himself provided force Joe to reflect on the rationalizations he had for his actions. He begins to understand the nature of moral and familial obligation and he hints at the realization that private acts are never really private since the consequences of his act (to ship defective parts) extended far beyond what he anticipated. Joe finally commits suicide.

This stark and relentlessly tragic play contains a truth few in business will question, although they may not accept its full implications. Moral questions are concerned with the interrelatedness of people and of organizations to individuals and a world society. These questions will be answered too narrowly if the principle of deniability continues to hold sway in corporate life. And, the dilemmas of the business schools intensify as they take on the task of education for leadership, in which the moral dimension looms large.

Part V

Conclusion

Chapter 16

Restoring Leadership in Business

*M*achiavelli, the first modern practitioner of the case method, observed that for a leader to gain the esteem of followers, he had to display unusual talents in the form of great works. "Nothing makes a prince more esteemed than great enterprises and evidence of unusual abilities. . . . Furthermore, a prince should show that he is an admirer of talent by giving recognition to talented men, and honoring those who excel in a particular art."[1]

Talent and its appreciation by others will carry a leader far. Yet, apart from activities such as sports or the arts in which, to use Tom Wolfe's apt metaphor, the single combat warrior dominates, today social esteem flows toward the skillful and not the talented. This idealization of skill reflects the naive belief that a good organization with ordinary people will outperform an ordinary organization structure liberally sprinkled with stars.

The American society values the team and is suspicious of the individualist who stands out in comparison with other members of the team. There are many kinds of talent, but this much is certain: Individual creativity always exceeds expectation, a phenomenon that led the leadership researcher Professor Bernard M. Bass to call his most recent book *Leadership and Performance Beyond Expectations.*[2] Management is geared to establishing goals that it can be reasonably sure it will meet. To go beyond that level of expectation requires vision and inspiration that can come only from individual talent.

The one big idea of the managerial mystique revolves around

the dichotomy of order and chaos. If left to their own devices, managers believe, people will descend into chaos because of irrational motives, conflicting interests, and unrestrained emotions. The imposition of structure and process will establish control and prevent a descent into chaos. Order will reign provided there is constant vigilance to guard against people's perverse tendencies.

Managers seldom issue directives and, for that matter, seldom reach decisions in the classic sense of considering alternatives and arriving at a point of personal commitment. Action flows from process, and power is employing process in organizations. If process is flawed, it can be corrected, unlike substantive decisions, which are not easily reversed.

Leaders are bold in identifying themselves with substance but also are vulnerable to being trapped by their own enthusiasm for substantive ideas. They reject the one big truth in favor of the many small truths about human nature and the world around them. They accept imperfection and the notion of progress through conflict rather than an ideal of perfect harmony and balance. In the words of Isaiah Berlin,

> No more rigorous moralist than Immanuel Kant has ever lived, but even he said in a moment of illumination, "Out of the crooked timber of humanity, no straight thing was ever made." To force people into the neat uniforms demanded by dogmatically believed-in schemes is almost always the road to inhumanity. We can only do what we can: but that we must do against difficulties.[3]

It may appear strange at first glance to view the modern manager as an ideologue, holding to a single truth. After all, isn't it the manager who practices "the art of the possible," and considers the "best as the enemy of the good." Managers may have started running organizations as pragmatists, but along the way toward forming the managerial mystique, they began to think like ideologists. They came to believe in their one big truth: there is an ideal condition of order and that through process one can control large numbers of people to assure this order and avoid chaos.

The members of the managerial elite of today, and conceivably the future power holders graduating from America's business schools, prefer the security of devoting themselves to the idea of order, especially with its implicit promise of success and money. The notion of talent, with its erratic expression and results and its stimulation of change, is too risky to provide the comfort modern managers seem to need. Talent is a cause of insecurity because it appears to be a gift (and cannot be acquired by following a course of study) and because it is difficult, if not impossible, to control. Managers prefer to think about structure, order, and predictability of people and events. They prefer skills they can practice, rather than the chance discovery of talent that, once revealed, makes a demand upon them to live up to the standards talent imposes.

The hidden danger for managers, a danger they only dimly perceive against the background of their structured life, is boredom. Managers evade the messages boredom communicates that goals are too narrowly drawn, that relationships are without depth, and that the self-imposed routines cannot sustain the illusion that compulsive work is the equivalent of productive work. After all, how long does it take before all the tricks of the trade have been used to get through the demands of the budget cycle? How many budget cycles can one go through before such activity becomes an empty formality?

A difficult experience for managers is to recognize the shallowness of the human relations surrounding their work life. An astonishing lack of camaraderie exists in large corporations. Managers seem incapable of generating affection. Without affection toward the chief, there can be little warmth among the peers directly below the chief. And, as one descends this hierarchy of icy detachment, the joy of work is singularly absent.

This kind of analysis applies in the world of politics as well as business. What will historians say about Reagan's presidency as a reflection of his character? He is often compared to Franklin Delano Roosevelt, who he admired and ostensibly adopted as a role model, despite their very different political parties and beliefs. Both men were called "great communicators," and, whether by intention or accident, both led the nation through a major change. In Roosevelt's case, the nation was in crisis, first with the monumental economic depression, and then with the international madness that resulted from Hitler's poisoned mind. Reagan faced no such manifest crises, yet, for a time at least, he altered the conception of government's relation to its citizens and, hence, the obligation of citizen to one another.

Whatever other differences historians find in comparing these two men as leaders, they will take notice of the difference in their relations to their subordinates. Roosevelt had subordinates who were loyal, admired him, and felt genuine affection for him. He operated with a strong cabinet and a lean staff. He sought ideas as well as personal renewal from them. He often invited key cabinet officials to join him on holidays for relaxation as well as conversation, for good-natured bantering as well as serious discussion of issues of great substance in affairs of state.

Strikingly, Reagan seemed beset by subordinates who worked in his administration and then wrote "kiss and tell" books that on the whole painted unflattering portraits of him. David Stockman, Donald Regan, Larry Speakes, his surrogate son Michael Deaver, and his real son Michael Reagan all felt at liberty to promote their personal interests at the expense of the president's interests. It is true that some subordinates were loyal even to a fault, for example, Edwin Meese, Oliver North, and John Poindexter. But this loyalty was so myopic as to be no loyalty at all, since in a number of ways, these subordinates caused trouble for their chief in how they decided to advance his policies and programs.

There is not just one type of personality that inspires loyalty, and styles of chief executives vary widely, but the absence of loyalty and camaraderie, both in government and business, between a chief executive and his or her subordinates indicates a fatal weakness in America's leadership. At the top of the power structure, when there is an absence of personal concern and regard, the worst faces of power are bound to appear.

Unlike Europeans, Americans have trouble dealing with a Machiavellian character. Consciously, we still yearn for boldness and the open use of power and prefer not to think about the craftiness and cunning of the leader as manipulator. Most people react to this aspect of personality as the dowager who upon learning of Darwin's discovery that humans are related to the apes exclaimed first that she hoped the idea is false and second that if it is true, she hoped it does not get around. While in some idealized versions of leadership there is no place for cunning, in reality no leader can be without some elements of the tactical imagination that instructs how to get from here to there.

As James MacGregor Burns points out in his biography, Roosevelt could act deviously and was able to switch roles and positions as circumstances suggested. Yet beneath the surface of affability, flexibility, and smoothness existed a core of steel that defined the man and his leadership. This core was constructed of a moral sense of responsibility to do what was right, to teach, and to transform a society bent on destroying itself.[4]

In another era this sense of responsibility evolved from the aristocratic concept of *noblesse oblige*. In modern times it develops not from position, but from an awareness and respect for talent and the need to express this talent in recognizable good work. The effect of good work is to spread the enthusiasm that drives it, and thereby to stimulate productive effort at all levels of an organization. That this effect may be limited to the higher levels of the organization is a challenge to modern leadership in business, a condition to be overcome and transformed rather than accepted as the natural order to which people must adapt.

One of the reasons the industrial revolution diminished the appreciation for work was a limitation in the thought processes of the industrial leaders of the nineteenth and twentieth centuries. They were anything but teachers, with knowledge to share and power to spare in their dramatic construction of giant enterprises. The failure of earlier leadership in business resulted from the inability to think conceptually and abstractly about their work. For Henry Ford, the most extreme example of a rigid thinker, the product was fixed in his mind as a whole, definitive object, rather than, as marketers like to emphasize, a combination of functions with changeable value to the customer. Andrew Carnegie separated his thinking into compartments. In one compartment of his mind was what he did in his role as an industrialist and financier, unrelated to his thoughts about the purposes of the corporation and its relation to its employees and to the society at large. In another compartment he could express his desire to improve the human condition through libraries, educational foundations, and the support of the arts. In still another compartment he could direct his energies to restoring castles in Scotland. All three of these compartments, and the many others that undoubtedly existed, appeared to have impermeable boundaries that prevented the images and ideas contained in one compartment from invading and influencing any other.

The great paternal leaders of the past gave way to modern managers. Equipped with their bag of tools and their attachment to the managerial mystique, modern managers could indeed coordinate and control, but in due course lost sight of the substance of work in business. Where their predecessors in business leadership had limited views of reality, the modern manager distorted reality by displacing substance with process.

The business schools, which in recent times have spewed MBAs from their halls at ever increasing rates, support this distortion of reality. They have followed rather than led business in blind acceptance of the managerial mystique. They have served as socialization plants to fit managers for the life of process found in modern organizations. The business schools have taken an uncritical stance to their main constituency, and, as a result, have discouraged searching examination of business practice.

Change for both business schools and corporations depends on the ability and willingness of authority to deal with a dilemma. Managers believe in organizational cohesion. To achieve this cohesion, they believe their associates have to feel good about themselves. As a management consultant turned educator put the problem, "Suppose Lee Iacocca had taken a leaf from President Reagan's book and publicly criticized Chrysler's employees as Reagan had criticized Washington's civil service? Would it have improved morale and stimulated employees to work hard and join in the effort to save Chrysler?" While Reagan and Iacocca were in different situations (Reagan evidently wanted a scapegoat in the "Washington establishment" to solidify his position with his conservative constituency), leaders risk their future with open criticism of employees as a group. To keep people feeling good about themselves may require that the status quo be maintained. However, maintaining the status quo may leave problems unsolved, prevent growth, and lead to crisis.

This dilemma is easily solved in times of crisis, when it is clear that survival depends on action and change, particularly where the leadership is new to the situation and not identified with the causes of the crisis. But, unfortunately, by the time a corporation's symptoms are evident, the illness is so far gone that a cure may be difficult if not impossible to achieve. Leaders must be critics rather than cheerleaders, yet their critical stance must avoid negativism. To be critical and positive is to be substantive. Therefore, leaders have to lead in the content and direction of change. To be a critic and merely the convener of process will depress subordinates and make them anxious.

In a political system in which there is a division between the symbolic and operating heads of government, one aspect of this dilemma is resolved. A monarch reigns and represents cohesion and continuity, while a prime minister governs and expresses criticism and need for action and change. Increasingly, the presidency in the United States is moving toward the split between symbolic and operating leadership, with certain unfortunate consequences in accountability and responsibility. But as a legacy of the managerial mystique, this same tendency to divide symbolic and operating leadership in business will lead to disastrous consequences, especially in the total politicization of work and human relationships.

Leadership in business is the fusion of work and human relations. Good ideas and exciting directions for an enterprise generate enthusiasm, support, and cohesion. Self-esteem follows not from submerging oneself in the team and following process, but from facing problems, assuming responsibility, and doing good work.

Notes

Introduction: *The Managerial Mystique, pages 1–7*

1. *The Tower Commission Report* (New York: Bantam Books, 1987).

2. David Reisman, *The Lonely Crowd* (New Haven: Yale University Press, 1951); William H. Whyte, *The Organization Man* (New York: Simon & Schuster, 1956).

3. *Time,* July 15, 1974.

4. Ibid.

5. Ibid.

6. *Time,* November 8, 1976, 38.

7. Abraham Zaleznik, "Managers and Leaders: Are They Different?" *Harvard Business Review,* May–June 1977.

8. William James, *The Varieties of Religious Experience* (Cambridge, Mass.: Harvard University Press, 1985).

9. *Time,* November 8, 1976, 38.

10. Ibid.

11. Christopher Lasch, *The Culture of Narcissism* (New York: Norton, 1979).

12. Lee A. Iacocca, with William Novak, *Iacocca: An Autobiography* (New York: Bantam Books, 1984).

Chapter 1: *The Leadership Gap, pages 11–20*

1. Unpublished manuscript.

2. Harold Geneen, with Alvin Moscow, *Managing* (Garden City, N.Y.: Doubleday, 1984), 182–96. See also Robert J. Schoenberg, *Geneen* (New York: Norton, 1985), 90.

3. Edward C. Meyer, "Executive Forum: Leadership—A Soldier's View," *The Washington Quarterly* 6, no. 3 (Summer 1983).

4. For corroboration of General Meyer's views, see Richard A. Gabriel and Paul L. Savage, *Crisis in Command: Mismanagement in the Army* (New York: Hill & Wang, 1978).

5. Chester E. Finn, Jr., "Education That Works: Make the Schools Compete," *Harvard Business Review,* September-October 1987, 63.

6. Garry Wills, *Reagan's America: Innocents at Home* (Garden City, N.Y.: Doubleday, 1987).

7. *The Tower Commission Report* (New York: Bantam Books, 1987).

8. For a detailed description of the lecture on success, see Frank B. Copley, *Frederick W. Taylor: Father of Scientific Management,* vols. 1 and 2 (New York: Harper & Brothers, 1923).

9. Cary Reich, *Financier: The Biography of André Meyer* (New York: Morrow, 1983), 355–56.

10. An Wang, with Eugene Linden, *Lessons: An Autobiography* (Reading, Mass.: Addison-Wesley, 1986), 220.

Chapter 2: Management and Leadership, pages 21–39

1. Letters to the Editor, *Harvard Business Review,* July-August 1977.

2. Ibid., 148–49.

3. Alfred North Whitehead, *Process and Reality* (New York: Macmillan, 1930), 11.

4. Cary Reich, *Financier: The Biography of André Meyer* (New York: Morrow, 1983).

5. Chester Barnard, *The Functions of the Executive* (Cambridge, Mass.: Harvard University Press, 1938), 168–69.

6. Michael B. McCaskey, *The Executive Challenge: Managing Change and Ambiguity* (Cambridge, Mass.: Ballinger, 1982).

7. Henry Murray, *Explorations in Personality* (London: Oxford University Press, 1938).

8. Abraham Zaleznik, Gene W. Dalton, and Louis B. Barnes, *Orientation and Conflict in Career* (Division of Research, Harvard Business School, 1970), 316.

9. Ibid., 294.

10. Abraham Zaleznik, "Managers and Leaders: Are They Different?" *Harvard Business Review,* May-June 1977, 73.

11. H. Edward Wrapp, "Good Managers Don't Make Policy Decisions," *Harvard Business Review,* September-October 1967, 93.

12. Alfred P. Sloan, Jr., *My Years with General Motors* (Garden City, N.Y.: Doubleday, 1964), 93.

13. Michel Crozier, *The Bureaucratic Phenomenon* (Chicago: University of Chicago Press, 1964).

14. Richard E. Neustadt, *Presidential Power: The Politics of Leadership* (New York: Wiley, 1960), 6.

15. Morton Halperin, *Bureaucratic Politics and Foreign Policy* (Washington, D.C.: Brookings Institution, 1974).

16. David Stockman, *The Triumph of Politics: Why the Reagan Revolution Failed* (New York: Harper & Row, 1986), 278.

Chapter 3: How Managers Think, pages 43–61

1. Alfred P. Sloan, Jr., *My Years with General Motors* (Garden City, N.Y.: Doubleday, 1964), 22.

2. Ibid., 23.

3. Ibid., 3.

4. Thomas J. Peters and Robert H. Waterman, Jr., *In Search of Excellence: Lessons from America's Best-Run Companies* (New York: Harper & Row, 1982).

5. Richard T. Pascale and Anthony G. Athos, *The Art of Japanese Management: Applications for American Executives* (New York: Simon & Schuster, 1981).

6. Sloan, *My Years with General Motors,* 23–24.

7. David Moment and Abraham Zaleznik, *Role Development and Interpersonal Competence* (Boston: Division of Research, Harvard Business School, 1963), 145–51.

8. Michael C. Jensen and William H. Meckling, "Theory of the Firm: Managerial Behavior, Agency Costs and Ownership Structure," *Journal of Financial Economics* 3 (1976): 305–60.

9. Robert Lacey, *Ford: The Men and the Machine* (Boston: Little, Brown, 1986), 124–25.

10. Abraham Maslow, *Motivation and Personality* (New York: Harper & Row, 1970).

11. Abraham Zaleznik, C. Roland Christensen, Fritz J. Roethlisberger, and George Homans, *The Motivation, Productivity, and Satisfaction of Workers: A Prediction Study* (Boston: Division of Research, Harvard Business School, 1958), 3–16.

12. S. A. Stauffer et al., *The American Soldier,* vol. 1, *Adjustment During Army Life* (Princeton, N.J.: Princeton University Press, 1949).

13. Niccolò Machiavelli, *The Prince,* trans. and ed. Mark Musa (New York: St. Martin's Press, 1946).

14. Machiavelli, *The Prince,* 213, 215.

Chapter 4: Rationality and Efficiency, pages 62–76

1. Taylor's testimony before the Industrial Relations Commission, cited in Frank B. Copley, *Frederick W. Taylor: Father of Scientific Management* (New York: Harper & Row, 1923), 1: 216. Also cited in Sudhir Kakar, *Frederick Taylor: A Study in Personality and Innovation* (Cambridge, Mass.: MIT Press, 1970), 67.

2. Frederick W. Taylor, "Workmen and Their Management," Unpublished lecture manuscript (Cambridge, Mass.: Harvard Graduate School of Business Administration, 1909), 6. Also cited in Kakar, *Frederick Winslow Taylor,* 65–66.

3. Thomas J. Peters and Robert H. Waterman, Jr., *In Search of Excellence: Lessons from America's Best-Run Companies* (New York: Harper & Row, 1982), 42.

4. *The New York Times,* April 20, 1987.

5. Theodore Levitt, "Management and the 'Post-Industrial' Society," *The Public Interest,* Summer 1976, 69–103.

6. *Ibid.,* 87–88.

7. Abraham Zaleznik, *Worker Satisfaction and Development* (Boston: Division of Research, Harvard Business School, 1956).

8. U.S. Congress, House Special Committee, *Hearings to Investigate the Taylor and Other Systems of Shop Management* (Washington, D.C.: Government Printing Office, 1912), 3: 1414. Also cited in Kakar, *Frederick Taylor,* 62.

9. David Halberstam, *The Reckoning* (New York: Morrow, 1986).

10. Alfred P. Sloan, Jr., *My Years with General Motors* (Garden City, N.Y.: Doubleday, 1964), 390.

11. Cecelia Tichi, *Shifting Gears: Technology, Literature, Culture in Modern America* (Chapel Hill, N.C.: University of North Carolina Press, 1987).

Chapter 5: Cooperation, pages 77–90

1. David Halberstam, *The Reckoning* (New York: Morrow, 1986).

2. Erik Erikson, *Gandhi's Truth* (New York: Norton, 1969), 229–392.

3. Richard C. S. Trahair, *The Humanist Temper: The Life and Works of Elton Mayo* (New Brunswick, N.J.: Transaction Books, 1984).

4. Fritz J. Roethlisberger and William Dickson, *Management and the Worker* (Cambridge, Mass.: Harvard University Press, 1947), 189–252.

5. William Dickson and Fritz J. Roethlisberger, *Counseling in an Organization: A Sequel to the Hawthorne Researches* (Boston: Division of Research, Harvard Business School, 1966).

6. Abraham Zaleznik and David Moment, "The Lightner Company (A-G)," *Casebook on Interpersonal Behavior in Organizations* (New York: Wiley, 1964), 456–500.

7. Elton Mayo, *Some Notes on the Psychology of Pierre Janet* (Cambridge, Mass.: Harvard University Press, 1948).

8. Ralph White and Ronald Lippitt, "Leader Behavior and Member Reaction in Three 'Social Climates,'" in Darwin Cartwright and Alvin Zander, *Group Dynamics, Research and Theory* (New York: Harper & Row, 1951), 585–611. See also Kurt Lewin, *Resolving Social Conflicts,* ed. Gertrude Nussbaum (New York: Harper & Row, 1948), 71–83.

9. Douglas M. McGregor, *The Human Side of Enterprise* (New York: McGraw-Hill, 1954).

10. Abraham H. Maslow, *Motivation and Personality* (New York: Harper & Row, 1954).

11. Peter F. Drucker, *Concept of the Corporation* (New York: New American Library, 1983).

12. Ibid., 134.

13. Ibid., 135.

14. Chester Barnard, *The Functions of the Executive* (Cambridge, Mass.: Harvard University Press, 1938), 45.

15. P. Drucker, *Concept of the Corporation,* 173.

16. Barnard, *Functions of the Executive,* 46–61.

17. Chester Barnard, *Organization and Management* (Cambridge, Mass.: Harvard University Press, 1949), 112.

18. T. Boone Pickens, Jr., *Boone* (Boston: Houghton Mifflin, 1987).

Chapter 6: Control, pages 91–108

1. Douglas M. McGregor, *The Human Side of Enterprise* (New York: McGraw-Hill, 1960).

2. Richard Sennett, *Authority* (New York: Knopf, 1980), 84–121.

3. H. Thomas Johnson and Robert S. Kaplan, *Relevance Lost: The Rise and Fall of Management Accounting* (Boston: Harvard Business School, 1987), 16.

4. Ibid., 19–46.

5. Ibid., 209–24. See also Robert H. Hayes and William A. Abernathy, "Managing Our Way to Economic Decline," *Harvard Business Review,* July-August 1980, 67–77.

6. Robert N. Anthony, *Management Accounting, Text and Cases* (Homewood, Ill.: Irwin, 1960), 321.

7. Ibid.

8. Johnson and Kaplan, *Relevance Lost,* 10–13, 191–223.

9. David Halberstam, *The Reckoning* (New York: Morrow, 1986), 204–6.

10. This account of the formation of the Air Force management control system and the Harvard Business School's Army Air Force Statistical School during World World II relies upon the archives of Baker Library, at the Harvard Business School. Professors Edmund P. Learned, Myles L. Mace, and Kenneth R. Andrews provided other information from their personal experiences.

11. John Von Neumann and Oskar Morgenstern, *Theory of Games and Economic Behavior* (Princeton, N.J.: Princeton University Press, 1947).

12. John F. Heplin, "Army Air Force Statistical School" (typescript, 311), included in U.S. Army Air Force Statistical School materials, 1942–1945 (Archives E4.4). Archives of Baker Library, Harvard Business School.

13. Halberstam, *The Reckoning,* 205.

14. Robert Lacey, *Ford: The Men and the Machine* (Boston: Little Brown, 1986), 358–63, 401–19. See also Anne Jardim, *The First Henry Ford: A Study in Personality and Business Leadership* (Cambridge, Mass.: MIT Press, 1970).

15. Halberstam, *The Reckoning,* 212.

16. Harold Geneen, *Managing* (Garden City, N.Y.: Doubleday, 1984), 118.

17. Ibid.

18. Robert J. Schoenberg, *Geneen* (New York: Norton, 1985), 314–16.

Chapter 7: Professionalism, pages 109–123

1. Erving Goffman, *The Presentation of Self in Everyday Life* (Garden City, N.Y.: Doubleday [Anchor Books], 1959).

2. Max Weber, *The Protestant Ethic* (New York: Scribner's, 1952), 181.

3. Max Weber, *The Theory of Social and Economic Organization,* trans. A. M. Henderson and Talcott Parsons (New York: Oxford University Press, 1947).

4. Thorstein Veblen, *The Theory of the Leisure Class* (Boston: Houghton Mifflin, 1973), 133.

5. Robert Merton, *Social Theory and Social Structure* (Glencoe, Ill.: Free Press, 1968), 51.

6. Niccolò Machiavelli, *The Prince,* trans. and ed. Mark Musa (New York, St. Martin's Press), 127.

7. Chester Barnard, *The Functions of the Executive* (Cambridge, Mass.: Harvard University Press, 1935).

Chapter 8: Molding Managers, pages 124–141

1. Michael Spence, *Market Signaling: Information Transfer in Hiring and Related Screening* (Cambridge, Mass.: Harvard University Press, 1974).

2. Arlene Glotzer and Bruce S. Sheiman, *Lovejoy's Guide to Graduate Business Schools* (Newark: Monarch, 1983).

3. Joel M. Stern, "In Defense of MBAs," *Fortune,* August 10, 1985, 223–37.

4. Ibid., 233.

5. Frank C. Pierson et al., *The Education of American Businessmen* (New York: McGraw-Hill, 1959); Robert A. Gorden and James E. Howell, *Higher Education for Business* (New York: Columbia University Press, 1959).

6. Abraham Flexner, *Medical Education in the United States and Canada* (New York: Carnegie Foundation for the Advancement of Teaching, 1910).

7. "Business Fads: What's In and What's Out," *Business Week,* January 20, 1986.

Chapter 9: Politics Prevails, pages 145–160

1. *New York Times,* June 21, 1987.

2. Leo Tolstoy, *War and Peace* (New York: Penguin Books, 1978), 1339–1400.

3. George Breuer, *Sociology of the Human Dimension* (Cambridge: Cambridge University Press, 1982), 31–33.

4. George C. Homans, *Social Behavior: Its Elementary Forms* (New York: Harcourt Brace Jovanovich, 1974), 185.

5. Abraham Zaleznik, C. Roland Christensen, Fritz J. Roethlisberger, and George C. Homans, *The Motivation, Productivity and Satisfaction of Workers: The Prediction Study* (Boston: Division of Research, Harvard Business School, 1958).

6. W. L. Bion, *Experiences in Groups* (New York: Basic Books, 1961).

7. *Fortune,* February 9, 1980.

8. *New York Times,* June 29, 1987, D2.

Chapter 10: The Corruption of Power, pages 161–179

1. Lord John E. E. Dalberg-Acton, *Essays on Freedom and Power* (1861–1910), selected and with an introduction by Gertrude Himmelfarb (Boston: Beacon Press, 1948), 25, 28.

2. Ibid., 364.

3. *Fortune,* July 1, 1966, 117.

4. Harold Geneen, with Alvin Moscow, *Managing* (Garden City, N.Y.: Doubleday, 1984), 97.

5. *Business Week,* May 15, 1978.

6. *Forbes,* May 1, 1968.

7. Robert J. Schoenberg, *Geneen* (New York: Norton, 1985), 200.

8. Ibid., 86.

9. Geneen, *Managing,* 100–101.

10. Ibid., 101.

11. *Dun's Review,* November 1965, p. 41.

12. Geneen, *Managing,* 54.

13. Schoenberg, *Geneen,* 239.

14. *Richard III,* act 1, sc. 1, lines 18–31.

15. William H. Whyte, *The Organization Man* (New York: Simon & Schuster, 1956).

16. Norman H. Holland, *The I* (New Haven, Conn.: Yale University Press, 1985).

Chapter 11: Identity Diffused, pages 180–194

1. "Wickes Company, Inc.," *Wall Street Journal,* August 2, 1985, 1.

2. Helen Tartakoff, "The Normal Personality in Our Culture and the Nobel Prize Complex," in *Psychoanalysis: A General Psychology: Essays in Honor of Heinz Hartmann,* ed. Rudolph M. Lowenstein, Lottie M. Newman, Max Schur, and Albert J. Solnit (New York: International Universities Press, 1966), 222–52.

3. Robert Jay Lifton, "Protean Man," *History and Human Survival* (New York: Random House, 1961), 316, 319.

4. Warren G. Bennis and Philip E. Slater, *The Temporary Society* (New York: Harper & Row, 1968).

5. Ibid., 11.

6. Ibid., 12.

7. Ibid., 82.

8. Milan Kundera, *The Joke* (New York: Penguin Books, 1983), 24–25.

9. Christopher Lasch, *The Culture of Narcissism* (New York: Norton, 1978), 41.

10. Ibid., 38.

Chapter 12: Stress and Power, pages 195–209

1. Lee Iacocca, with William Novak, *Iacocca: An Autobiography* (New York: Bantam Books, 1984).

2. Ibid., 129–30.

3. Richard Neustadt, *Presidential Power: The Politics of Leadership* (New York: Wiley, 1960), 9.

4. Robert W. White, *Lives in Progress* (New York: Holt, Rinehart & Winston, 1975), 79–80. This was part of a study of normal individuals undertaken through the Center for the Study of Personality, Harvard University, founded by Dr. Henry A. Murray in 1938.

5. Abraham Zaleznik, M. Kets de Vries, and J. Howard, "Stress Reactions in Organizations: Syndromes, Causes and Consequences," *Behavioral Science,* May 1977.

6. Austin E. Weir, *The Struggle for National Broadcasting in Canada* (Toronto: McClelland and Steward, 1965), 410.

7. Alexander L. George, *The "Operational Code": A Neglected Approach to the Study of Political Leaders and Decision-Making* (Santa Monica, Calif.: Rand Corporation, 1967). See also Nathan Leites, *Kremlin Moods* (Santa Monica, Calif.: Rand Corporation, 1964).

8. Clifford Geertz, *The Interpretation of Cultures* (New York: Basic Books, 1973).

9. Ibid., 127.

Chapter 13: The Substance of Leadership, pages 213–228

1. Letter from Thomas Jefferson to John Hay in David Hounshell, *From the American System to Mass Production: 1800–1923* (Baltimore: Johns Hopkins University Press, 1984).

2. Daniel E. Whitney, "Real Robots Do Need Jigs," *Harvard Business Review,* May-June 1986, 110–16.

3. Ibid., 111.

4. Cary Reich, *Financier, The Biography of André Meyer* (New York: Morrow, 1983).

5. J. C. Penney, *Annual Report,* 1983.

Chapter 14: Personal Influence, pages 229–247

1. Julius Gould and William L. Kolb, ed., *Dictionary of the Social Sciences,* compiled under the auspices of UNESCO (New York: Free Press, 1964), 332.

2. Henry Fairlie, "The Lessons of Watergate: On the Possibility of Morality in Politics," *Encounter* 43, no. 4, 1974.

3. Ibid., 13–14.

4. *New York Times,* Sunday, May 8, 1988, sec. 3, 1.

5. Jacob L. Moreno, *Who Shall Survive? A New Approach to the Problem of Human Interrelations* (Washington, D.C.: Nervous and Mental Disease Publishing Company, 1934).

6. *The American Heritage Dictionary,* ed. William S. Morris (Boston: American Heritage and Houghton Mifflin, 1969), 227.

7. *From Max Weber: Essays in Sociology,* ed. and trans. H. H. Gerth and C. W. Mills (London: Kegan Paul, Trench, Trubner, 1947), 245–52.

8. Sigmund Freud, "Group Psychology and the Analysis of the Ego," *The Standard Edition of the Complete Psychological Works of Sigmund Freud* (London: Hogarth Press, 1955), 18: 67–110.

9. Erik H. Erikson, *Gandhi's Truth* (New York: Norton, 1969), 402–6.

10. Harrison M. Trice and Janice M. Beyer, "Charisma and Its Routinization in Two Social Movement Organizations," *Research in Organizational Behavior* 8 (1986): 129.

11. Bernard M. Bass, *Leadership and Performance Beyond Expectations* (New York: Free Press, 1985), 43.

12. Richard Sennett, *Authority* (New York: Knopf, 1980), 50–83.

13. From a letter dated April 5, 1988, to Lever Brothers' agents announcing

the birth of his son William Hulme. Quoted in Andrew M. Knox, *Coming Clean* (London: Heinemann, 1976), 76.

14. Ibid., 42.

15. Ibid., 42.

16. Ibid., 59–60.

17. Ibid., 79.

18. James MacGregor Burns, *Leadership* (New York: Harper & Row, 1978).

19. Konosuke Matsushita, *Not for Bread Alone: A Business Ethos, a Management Ethic* (Tokyo: PHP Institute, 1984).

20. Ibid., 17–18.

21. Elton Mayo, *The Social Problems of an Industrial Civilization* (Boston: Division of Research, Harvard Business School, 1945), 73–74.

22. Burns, *Leadership,* 457.

Chapter 15: The Moral Dimension, pages 248–269

1. *Wall Street Journal,* February 7, 1987.

2. Ibid.

3. *Wall Street Journal,* April 27, 1987.

4. Paul Desruisseaux, "Harvard Will Seek $30-Million for Program on Business Ethics," *Chronicle of Higher Education,* April 8, 1987, 1.

5. R. Foster Winans, *Trading Secrets* (New York: St. Martin's Press, 1986).

6. Richard Austin Smith, "The Incredible Electrical Conspiracy," 1, *Fortune,* April 1961, 133.

7. Ibid., 136.

8. Ibid.

9. Ibid., 137.

10. Richard Austin Smith, "The Incredible Electrical Conspiracy," pt. 2, *Fortune,* May 1961, 225.

11. *Business Week,* February 24, 1986, 98.

12. Ibid.

13. *Wall Street Journal,* August 29, 1985, 3.

14. *Wall Street Journal,* September 13, 1985, 5.

15. *New York Times,* September 6, 1985, D6.

16. *Cashflow,* September 1985, 32.

17. Robert J. Schoenberg, *Geneen* (New York: Norton, 1985), 239.

18. Ibid.

19. Ibid., 271–72.

20. Senate Committee on the Judiciary, *Hearings on Nomination of Richard G. Kleindienst of Arizona to Be Attorney General,* 92d Cong., 2d sess., 1972, 666.

21. House Antitrust Subcommittee of the Committee on the Judiciary, *Investigations of Conglomerate Corporations,* 91st Cong. 1970, pt. 3.

22. Senate Subcommittee on Multinational Corporations of the Committee on

Foreign Relations, *Multinational Corporations and United States Foreign Policy;* Schoenberg, *Geneen,* 288; 93rd Cong., 1970–1971, 427.

23. Irving Kristol, "Ethics Anyone? Or Morals?" *Wall Street Journal,* September 15, 1987.

24. Ibid.

25. Jeffrey Sonnenfeld and Paul R. Lawrence, "Why Do Companies Succumb to Price Fixing?" *Harvard Business Review,* July-August 1978, 146.

26. Ibid., 146.

27. Ibid.

28. Ibid.

Chapter 16: Restoring Leadership in Business, pages 273–279

1. Niccolò Machiavelli, *The Prince,* trans. and ed. Mark Musa (New York: St. Martin's Press, 1946), 185, 191.

2. Bernard M. Bass, *Leadership and Performance Beyond Expectations* (New York: Free Press, 1985).

3. Isaiah Berlin, "On the Pursuit of the Ideal," *The New York Review of Books,* March 17, 1988, 18.

4. James MacGregor Burns, *Roosevelt: The Lion and the Fox* (New York: Harcourt Brace Jovanovich, 1956), 474–75.

Index